CROSS BORDER TALES

MAINE, NEW BRUNSWICK, AND *MORE*

To Rosalie & Joe Killian,
Our circle of friendship
covers more years than most!
Love & All the Best,

Laurie & Charlie McGowan
August 11, 2015

CHARLES E. McGOWAN

Cross-Border Tales
© 2015 by Charles E. McGowan
ISBN 978-1-940244-32-7

Printed in the United States of America

Distributed by www.indieauthorwarehouse.com

To Laurie,
who has crossed the border with me
for fifty-nine years.

Deserted St. Dominic Catholic Church,
Allandale, New Brunswick, 1955

CONTENTS

FOREWORD

In the summer of 2012, my husband answered our land line just as we were about to walk out the door. Soon, he was embroiled in what I could tell was going to be a lengthy conversation. I busied myself in my office while he took this engrossing call. When I came back downstairs, I found written on the back of an envelope sitting on the dining room table a telephone number and a name: Charlie McGowan.

It seemed this McGowan character was working on a book and was looking for an editor. Now, as a Maine native who has been writing about her home state for many years and who does editing and writing coaching on the side, I have to say I get a number of these calls. Usually, they're from people who don't really have an interest in writing. Most of them think that since they're from Maine and I'm from Maine, *I* should write their story for them—for fun! "Poor old kook," I said regarding the number. "I'll give him a call on Monday and scare him off."

Except Charlie wasn't a kook, and he did want to write. I asked him about his writing background and experience. Well, none really. He was a retired oral surgeon. Had he done any training—workshops, writing groups, seminars? No. Did he have a formal plan for the book? Nope, just mountains of research and a tale to tell. I told him he probably wasn't ready for me, that I usually worked with more advanced writers. This remark was met with polite resistance. He had read my most recent book, *Glorious Slow Going*, and my essays and articles in *Down East* magazine. I had a Maine woods-related last name. He was sure I was the editor for him. He was very persistent.

Finally, I relented and told him to send me some pages.

What arrived was a mess of scraps of genealogical research, scattershot childhood recollections and pages and pages of nineteenth-century posy about river drives and woods life. But there were also glimpses of vivid and evocative prose. A description of his family's New Brunswick ancestral home was rendered so clearly I could actually taste the molasses cookies and frigid, hand-pumped well water.

He had a witty and lively narrative voice—a natural storyteller. Within this morass of pages, I also found a section in which he talked about gazing down at the Maine coast and New Brunswick, Canada, during cross-Atlantic flights and how the terrain below represented his life's story. It was both elegant and elegiac. The image stayed with me for days. I told him if he was willing to get rid of some of his research and borrowed material, if he would hammer out a solid structure and if we could move this flight scene to the opening as an overview that we could probably work together.

And work we did.

For the next two-plus years, Charlie and his book—and consequently, Charlie and his lovely wife, Laurie, along with cameos by some of their offspring—became a mainstay of my life. Charlie and I met for work sessions whenever he and Laurie came through Portland or, if the time of day was right, a pop or two. He dropped off or sent me pages (sometimes overnight, an extravagance this Yankee found unnecessary), and I went at them. I was not gentle. I wrote "Yikes, adjective avalanche!" when he got on one of his alliterative sprees. Pages became riddled with the proofreader's delete marks. I told him when he was boring me ("I skipped all the business about George's land grant") and when he was including too much family information that would not be of interest to a general reader. He accepted my edits and admonishments with grace and humor (and perhaps a finger or two of Irish whiskey). After countless and fearless revisions, a miracle happened. A book emerged.

And not just a book for his family, either. This memoir will enchant any reader with an appreciation of the outdoors, the Maine and Canadian woods, and the pleasures of friends and family. You're unlikely to find a more amiable narrator or a life story more joyfully told. At so many junctures working on these pages, I said to myself, "I wish I had been there. I wish I was a part of this story." I challenge you to feel any different.

I suppose I could've ignored that phone call, "lost" Charlie's number these two-plus years ago, but what adventures both on the page and in person I would've missed. It was my good fortune that I returned that call and, subsequently, became party to this large life so well lived and equally well told. We are all richer for the telling.

I'm already looking forward to working on the sequel.

Elizabeth Peavey, Portland, Maine, August, 2014

PROLOGUE

I experience an innermost sense of place on night flights from Europe above the province of New Brunswick, Canada and coastal Maine. Pitch-black gaps of forest or sea blend with sparse to sparkly groups of land lights reviving a silent, slow-motion sequence of my family history. Unknown in the darkness below are the Maritime Canada ports of entry where, in the middle 1800s, my maternal great grandparents Annie Munro arrived from the Scottish Highlands and George Baylis from England.

Sitting beside my wife, Laurie, in a starboard window seat behind the wing, I can observe whatever might emerge out of the darkness below. Cabin lights are dim with passengers quietly anticipating arrival in Boston within the hour. Outside, all appears still except for the strobe reflections on which the aircraft seems to float. Beneath is a hypnotic here-and-now conjoining with the mystery of what once happened. The British Airways flight monitor screen reads 525 mph at 38,000 ft. The next screen flashes our current position and highlights *Saint John*, New Brunswick on the Bay of Fundy, *Fredericton*, the provincial capital on the St. John River, and northern Maine "Shire Town," *Houlton*, on the Canadian border. That northwest trajectory is the path of my Canadian family migration and settlement in the St. John River Valley of New Brunswick.

When I'm on overnight eastbound flights approaching Ireland, the rising sun casts subtle rays on snowfields of clouds and eye-catching reflections off the sea. From the coastline inland, landscapes depict quilted assortments of United Kingdom soil from whence my ancestors came.

Those in-flight flashbacks encourage me to chronicle my ancestral northeast history, starting with what I've lived through, sifting through extensive memorabilia, and digging deeper into whatever bit of history I encounter. Told in the same way that Laurie and I have confronted life, memorable happenings will evolve out of the unexpected. Reliving my past and recording the unforeseen have been a thrilling double-dip!

When driving in Maine, overhead chalky jet trails suggest routes and roots in my story. Most of my tales take place within an egg-shaped area of the northeast where the focal points are Massachusetts to the south and the St. John River Valley in eastern New Brunswick, as much as 500 miles to the north. Coastal Maine and Moosehead Lake mark the east and west bowed perimeters of my "Egg." Keep in mind, Maine square mileage is equal to that of the other five New England states. This entire region is also a time capsule of family events preceding and within my 82 years.

This territorial egg and I have been fried (mostly sunny-side up), scrambled, boiled (hard and soft), deviled, pickled, baked, and coddled. Among Newfoundland/Labrador, Prince Edward Island, and Nova Scotia, New Brunswick is the only Atlantic province that borders the U.S. at Maine. Tourism brochures of the 1930s called New Brunswick, "The Portal to the Maritimes." In *The Northeastern Borderlands* 1987 conference papers, participant Professor Graeme Wynn referred to this northeast as an international sphere and a "Greater New England." I learned to walk and talk in cross-border time, and it's been the same ever since. We all cross the border for a reason, and I need to talk about it by telling you the inside story through the people who lived it.

You're going to encounter a lot of historical detail from settlement and city. You will also be invited into the lives and backyards of people that I hold dear. Although you may never have seen the spectrum of the northeast, I'll try to make the territory as tasty and truthful as I have found it. I can only say, "Hang in there if a country road gets rough or muddy, and the going slows down to a crawl. Have faith that every fork will lead to a place that you'd like to visit."

My Scottish and English kin found lands of hope along the St. John River at the top of my northeast nesting egg. The river was discovered by Samuel de Champlain and Pierre de Monts on the feast day of St. John the Baptist in 1604. First Nation Maliseets called it "Oo-las-tuk," the goodly or beautiful river. I hark back to it as a biographer did in 1845, "Silver-rolling."

The St. John headwaters arise in Quebec, and in northern Maine above Moosehead Lake. Jointly, they flow through wilderness for 124 miles. For the next 75 miles through forest and farmland, the river becomes the Maine—New Brunswick international boundary. Its final 217 miles to the sea are totally within the province. Navigable from the capital of Fredericton to the City of Saint John on the Bay of Fundy, it's historically been known as the "Rhine of North America." In the 1800s, the port of Saint John, "North America's Liverpool," was the stepping-stone for upriver migration.

At a conspicuous bend in the river course where Nackawic Stream enters the St. John, my Munro and Baylis ancestors settled in Southampton Parish, York County. The forested ridges, fertile slopes, clear creeks, and rippling brooks were ideal for farming and lumbering, and the lay of the land had a flavor of the Scottish Highlands.

Combining that background with my own encounters, I promise to share worthy and high-spirited particulars. Relax, and look out the cabin window with me. We'll gaze into the dense darkness or rising-sun vistas below that inspire the tales I'm about to tell.

NEW ENGLAND AND EASTERN CANADA

RILEY BROOK

QUEBEC

NEW BRUNSWICK

HOULTON WOODSTOCK
NACKAWIC

MT. KATAHDIN
MOOSEHEAD LAKE
FREDERICTON

MAINE
VANCEBORO MCADAM

BANGOR

VERMONT

ASHLAND

FREEPORT
PORTLAND
HARPSWELL

NOVA
SCOTIA

NEW
HAMPSHIRE

PORTSMOUTH

EAST

DOWN

CHELMSFORD, LOWELL,
WINCHESTER, WOBURN

MASSACHUSETTS
BOSTON

CONN

R.I.

FALMOUTH CAPE COD

NEWPORT

MYSTIC
SEAPORT
MARTHA'S VINEYARD NANTUCKET

donahuedesign

BOOK I

FAMILY

*No man has ever lived that had enough
of children's gratitude or woman's love.*
William Butler Yeats

Baylis family, c.1905

PART ONE

TOT TO TWENTIES

PARISH OF
SOUTHAMPTON

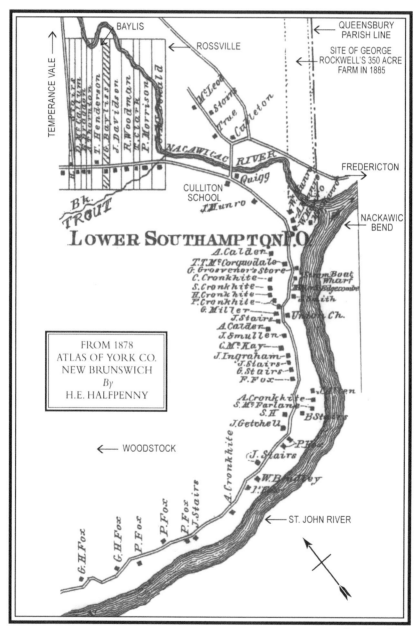

BAYLIS

ROSSVILLE

QUEENSBURY
PARISH LINE

SITE OF GEORGE
ROCKWELL'S 350 ACRE
FARM IN 1885

TEMPERANCE VALE

FREDERICTON

NACAWIC BEND

CULLITON
SCHOOL

LOWER SOUTHAMPTON P.O.

FROM 1878
ATLAS OF YORK CO.
NEW BRUNSWICH
By
H.E. HALFPENNY

WOODSTOCK

ST. JOHN RIVER

donahuedesign

8

CHAPTER ONE

The Beginning

Mother and Dad's wedding day

With Mom in delivery (Dads stayed in the waiting room then), Dr. Kelleher brought me into the world at Woburn, Massachusetts' Choate Memorial Hospital on Monday, July 27, 1931. In concert with Mother's birth date of July 29, 1897, and Dad's on July 30, 1896, we were as close throughout life as those end-of-the-month dates. My parents, Lucy Anna Baylis and Charles Edward McGowan, were married on Wednesday, August 27, 1930, at St. Charles rectory in Woburn, Mass. by Rev. Fr. J. Francis Toomey. When I was baptized there, my oldest cousin, Loretto McGowan, stood in as proxy godmother, because Aunt Ruth Murphy was expecting my cousin Frankie.

Exactly how my parents met, I don't know. Many of us united with our spouses through pure coincidence, and that explanation will suffice here. It's Lucy and Charlie's personal history that provides the when, where, and how this story evolves. There are natural cycles and unexpected twists and turns.

My mother's New Brunswick, Canada birthplace is recorded as Pinder (Lower Temperance Vale) York County to Alexandria "Dandy" Munro Baylis 1875–1941 (who made her "X" mark on the birth certificate) and William "Willie" James Baylis 1870–1930. She was actually born in the nearby hamlet of Rossville as were six Baylis siblings: Mabel Violet, Jean Dessa, Ella Pearl, George Rockwell, Willa Christie Jane, and Ronald Kitchener.

Rossville is a small farming community in Southampton Parish, York County on a road just inland from a distinct bend the St. John River at Lower Southampton. It lies northwesterly on the outskirts of what today is the Town of Nackawic. Named after farmer Ross Fanning Woodman, 16 farm families numbered 100 in 1904 when Mother was seven. The adjoining hamlet of Culliton, or "Cullerton," had a one-room schoolhouse that Mother attended through eight readers (an annual progression of prescribed schoolbooks). While she was there, there were 37 pupils in 1906 and 62 in 1913.

To familiarize you with the area, I'll quote a Fredericton *Daily Gleaner* article, "Wedding in Lower Southampton," published one month before Mother was born. It detailed the guest and gift list of 100

Mother Lucy & Aunt Ruth Murphy

Mother, Sister, & Baylis horses, c.1915

family, friends, and neighbors attending the marriage of Mary Morrison and George Munro. It was an adult census of sorts since few in the small community missed a wedding or a funeral. Mother's grandfather, the family founding farmer George Baylis (b.1826), died at 71 years of age, on the day of her birth. Mother's arrival must have been a comfort to the grieving Baylis family. She was named after her aunt, Lucy Ann Baylis, who married Wilmot Fox, also from Southampton, in 1886 and had crossed the border to live and farm in Maine.

At age 17 in 1914, my mother left the farm and registered at the Provincial Normal School (PNS), a teacher's college in Fredericton. The small city's Coat of Arms characterized its status: crowned shields of the Union Jack and British sovereign Royal Arms, a cathedral city cross, and a fir tree symbolic of the prolific forest around it. Derived from the French "Ecole normale superieure," the PNS was a school to foster the arts of teaching and communicating. She boarded with Mrs. Alex McLeod at 666 Scully Street and was exposed to a Fredericton city style for two years. In an old photograph, she is posing between diverging tree trunks and wearing a fashionable knit pom-pom cap, heavy long sweater with two-tone collar and waistband, wool knickers, long socks, and laced low leather shoes. She looks handsome, happy, and confident. I have two other studio portraits where she has bouffant hair styles and is wearing a white satin or a black lace dress. Pictures on the farm, with her look-alike sisters, show country styles of dress.

Mother told me little of her past life, but said that she taught in Carleton County in one-room schoolhouses and boarded in local homes. In the Provincial Archives of New Brunswick *Schedule of Provincial Aid to Teachers 1916–1923*, Carleton and York County teacher records profiled "Lucy Baylis." "Annual salary" varied from $190 to $675, and "Years Taught," 7½ with a Class II "Teacher License." Among the "District" Parishes of Brighton, Hartfield, Lr. Southampton, Queensbury, Simonds, Wakefield, and Wilmot-Wicklow, her teaching days varied according to farm and weather variables: "Auth.

Lucy Baylis, c.1921

*Dad, U.S.Navy,
c.1918*

Days School in Operation" 80 to 122 and "No. of Pupils" 15 to 48.

She first crossed the border by train at Vanceboro, Maine, July 23, 1923, seeking employment through a Mrs. John Hurley in Middleton, Massachusetts. On February 23, 1924, with 18 year old cousin Gwen Trail, she came to work in Massachusetts as a nursing assistant at the geriatric unit of Danvers State Hospital, called the Middleton Colony, and remained there until 1930. Her siblings remained in New Brunswick.

Dad Charlie, whose native city of Woburn is ten miles north of Boston, Massachusetts, and known for its tanneries, grew up there and, for a short time, in Milford, New Hampshire. His father, John, formulated the "Liquors" used in the tanning process. Grandma Bridget McGowan emigrated from Clonmanny, County Donegal, on the North Sea of Ireland. Dad's paternal grandparents, Patrick and Ellen (Hamilton), emigrated from Manor Hamilton, County Leitrim, Ireland to Woburn. Dad and siblings, older brother Thomas, younger sister Ruth, and youngest brother Norman lived on 24 Lake Avenue not far from Winchester, where I was raised. In World War I, Dad enlisted in the U.S. Naval Reserve serving as an aviation machinist mate on active duty in Biloxi, Mississippi. Following discharge, he became a member of Woburn's American Legion Post 101. A short stint at Burdett Business College wasn't his calling. Prior to the Great Depression, as a veteran with an extended education, he applied for, and was accepted to, the position of a U.S. Postal Service mail carrier in Winchester. He was well-liked by fellow carriers and clerks and respected by those to whose homes he hand carried letters and parcels. He often spoke of an elderly woman, Mrs. Mortensen, who gave him coffee on one of his early routes, and "Patsy," a big dog that followed him around. I learned to look up to anyone in uniform, because I was proud of Dad's official dress and dedication to duty.

His faithful 17 mile trips between Woburn and Middleton, with a 1920s auto on winding narrow roads to court Lucy, paid off. My cousin, Ruth Murphy Smith, was born in 1926 and told me that she was Dad's favorite. He bought her gifts, and took her with him when he dated my mother. Mother's diamond ring (now worn by our daughter Laurie Ann) was from Daniel Low & Company in Salem, Mass. After their August, 1930 wedding, both looked delighted and dapper in front of Grandpa McGowan's new Reo Motor Car.

In spite of the Great Depression, they must have been ecstatic expecting me and having a new home built by Mr. Grayson on 63 Woodside Road, Winchester, Mass. (1930s postal address). Since Mother was a teacher and Dad grew up locally, Winchester's excellent school system and urban neighborhoods probably influenced their choosing. Along with God only knows what savings they had, a monthly mortgage in cash was dutifully paid at the Woburn Five

Our Winchester home, c.1940

Me, Charles, 1932

Cents Savings Bank. With full focus on my upbringing, their security was a nice home and Dad's steady job at the Winchester post office. I'm sure that their new yellow Chevrolet Roadster, was frosting on the cake.

I called my mother Mumma or Mum, consistent with our Scotch and English heritage. Dad was Daddy. Murphy cousins called me Charles Eugene; to Canadian family and my teachers, I was Charles; to chums, I was Charlie.

The single-residence homes on Woodside Road were amply spaced and mostly occupied by young families. I've a picture, taken by a photographer who came around annually, that shows me on a pony when I was a year old. Our gray stain, cedar shingled home sat on a knolled corner lot and had shuttered, white-curtained windows. Dad built a long stone wall along the street with steps leading up to the front door. He hand mixed cement for our walkways and excavated a long sloping driveway up to the one-car, two-door garage behind the house. An auto was his pride and joy, and he could do most of the maintenance. That first year, we ventured as far north as

North Sandwich, N.H.,
Dad, Me, Baby Ruth
Murphy, roadster. c.1931

my grandfather McGowan's vacation house in the White Mountains of New Hampshire.

Dad planted a six-foot spruce at the lower lot corner, arborvitae bushes around the foundation, and flowering hedge bushes all over the yard, some of which shed tiny white petals as if in a snowfall. When we went fishing, the yellow perch or "Kibbie" (sunfish) catch was buried next to his arborvitae for fertilizer. Those were the days when the lawn was cut with a two-wheel push-mower.

Our front entrance opened into the living room and had a clothes closet beside the front door, and an enclosed stairway to the second floor. Our side entrance had enough space for an electric refrigerator with a tiny freezer compartment, mostly for ice cubes. Mother could make ice cream without using the hand-crank machine that was necessary on the Baylis farm. The eat-in kitchen had an enameled cream and green gas stove, an enclosed sink under the back window, a counter, and storage cabinets for cooking utensils and groceries. A fold-down ironing board was cleverly enclosed behind a small door on the wall. The handy pantry was also a passage into our dining room that had a formal table, chairs, and buffet. Mum displayed her fragile dinnerware in a built-in china cabinet. The tall, striped, and multicolor summer-drink glasses with glass stirrers, were very special to me.

Except for the kitchen linoleum, our floors were varnished hardwood. Most were protected with oriental-type carpets. A novelty among our living room furniture was the dark brown wood, cabinet radio with an amber color lighted dial and a speaker concealed by woven cloth in back of an open-mesh frame. News, music, and programs were ours by merely turning knobs to adjust the needle to a selected station or regulate volume! The inner metal chassis had multiple tall and short, glass upright plug-in "Tubes," wiring, and whatever other components made it work.

Radio programs that kept me mesmerized were *The Shadow*, *Jack Armstrong All American Boy*, *Tom Mix*, *I Love a Mystery*, and *Mr. Keen, Tracer of Lost Persons*. I played out the "G Men" (FBI) type of program with my black, battery operated "Tommy-gun" that rattled and had a flickering red muzzle light when I pulled the trigger. *Asher Sizemore and Little Jimmy*, was a popular father and five-year old son program from Louisville, Kentucky. Dad sent for their songbook which contained "Chawin' Gum" and "As I Lay Me Down To Sleep." President Roosevelt held wartime *Fireside Chats* that drew families close to the radio set. Walter Winchell was another commentator whose byline was "Good evening Mr. and Mrs. America from border to border and coast to coast and all the ships at sea. Let's go to Press!" *Voice of America* had specialized short wave transmissions that reached out to embattled countries overseas. Live messages from children, safe in America from Nazi bombings, were broadcast home to anxious British parents.

A round, convex living room wall mirror, popular for the times, comes to mind. Golden balls about the size of marbles were encircled within the gold-painted frame, and an eagle with spread wings graced the top. Double living room French doors with glass knobs opened into the adjoining sun porch and dining room making the downstairs open and inviting.

We didn't have a telephone, and I never heard its absence enter conversation. We would use my grandparent's phone in Woburn if necessary. Our mail was hand delivered twice daily as Dad did on his mail route. Telegrams were used to convey messages quickly. News of Grammie Baylis' death came that way.

Upstairs, there were two bedrooms and a single bathroom with a tub. Dad was clean shaven, and used a straight-edge razor sharpened with a smooth stone and finished with what still is called a long pliable "Leather strop." He had a cup that held the shaving soap and a soft, round badger brush to liberally apply the foamy mix. From my parent's bedroom, there were stairs to the unfinished storage attic (where Christmas decorations were kept and my presents concealed). Its bare tented rafters and brown flooring smelled woody, and I imagined it to be my hideaway.

A stairway from the kitchen accessed the cement floor cellar. In that lower level, a coal furnace heated the house by circulating hot water through pipes to cast iron upright "Radiators" in each room. Radiators made a banging sound when too much steam got into the circulating water. A small valve near the top could be opened with a turnkey to let the excess steam escape. Removable winter storm windows shielded the inside sashes, and were sealed with felt strips on the edges. When the coal truck came to fill the bin through a cellar window, the roar going down the metal chute and the huge pile produced were wondrous to me. Tending to the coal furnace was not an easy chore. Using a cast iron handle, burnt coal was shaken down through grates to the bottom of the furnace. Any unburned coal was saved, and the solidified "Clinker-chunks" were discarded. Powdery ash leftovers were carried out in metal trash cans and spread on winter driveways and walks for traction.

Dad built a small workbench for me next to his. When challenged by a project or repair, he used his head and hands to get the job done. One example was constructing folding beach chairs for our lawn. The frames were oak, and the sling-seat green and orange striped canvass. I recall us driving to Charlestown, in the north section of Boston, to a canvass shop to buy the material. Dad had a cast metal pedestal and foot-form to repair his boots. When he used glue, the odor made his workbench smell like a cobbler shop. Working together in the cellar on a Cub Scout "Soapbox Derby" project, we built a racer to compete in a race on Wildwood Street Extension slope. The project and race was a small-town mimic of the popular national "All American Soapbox Derby" held in Akron, Ohio. I didn't win our race, but memory did. That smell of plywood, sawdust, and vision of my bright red racer are as real to me today as they were then.

Our clothes-washing soapstone sink was beside an enclosed

bulkhead stairway, handy to where Mother could carry the wash out to the backyard clothes-lines for drying. She used four inch wooden clothes-pins to secure the laundry to the rope lines; pranksters were known to cut neighborhood lines on Halloween. In autumn, I would secretly taste the kettle of mincemeat that she kept on the cool bulkhead steps.

Our garbage was put in a heavy-covered, below-ground pail container. Town workers emptied them once a week. Other trash was brought to the smoky, bad-smelling town dump. Many families burned whatever they could in 55 gallon barrels.

In summer, my American Flyer sled ("c. mcgowan '38" burned on the steering bar by Dad), skates, a hockey stick, and wood skis with bamboo poles were stored in the cellar. Skis were held on by single leather toe straps. In those days, we judged the proper length a ski by the distance from the ground to a finger-tip pointed straight toward the sky. We tried to mimic the newfangled metal spring bindings by stretching inner-tube elastic under our boot toe, past the leather strap, and onto the heel. It worked…to some degree. My bicycle was stored in the cellar in winter. My Spaulding tennis racquet was kept from warping by a wood press held together by four bolts and springs with wing-nut screws. Among stowed fishing equipment was a rod, line, and leader with a dangling fly. One cellar catch was Skippy, my dog, when he grabbed the fishing fly in his mouth!

I had three treasured musical instruments: a brass Boy Scout bugle, a six string guitar, and a harmonica. I could barely do justice to "Taps" (lowering the flag at dusk), "Reveille" (wake up), or "Call to the Colors" (flag-raising) with my bugle. Whether from finger-tip pain (excuse) on the frets or not dedicated to practice, my guitar playing was poor. My best efforts on the harmonica were "America" and "'Way Down South in Dixie." I loved music but wasn't musical.

When I was little, my parents took me to a favorite park, Salem Willows by the sea, and then we went to what I think was one of their courting places in an upstairs Chinese restaurant. I remember entering the dining area through beaded curtains. I was timid about unfamiliar cooking odors, hanging paper lanterns, dragon wall decorations, the dim interior, and waiters who looked and spoke in a different way than people that I knew.

The Stoneham Zoo, in the next town, had every jungle animal

and rare bird that I could imagine. The Harvard Museum of Natural History seemed like a round-the-world tour where my parents and I would view game mounts, glass flower displays, and dazzling mineral specimens. Before July Fourth, a trip to the fireworks stand beside the Big Bear store in Somerville was part of our red, white, and blue celebration. Boston Sears and Roebuck multi-floor store contained a huge variety of their "Good, Better, and Best" goods. When I sat on Santa's lap and watched model trains rattle and toot, the Christmas season came to life. We strolled through a miniature New England village at Sailor Tom restaurant in Reading. Some of the model buildings were scaled taller than me, and they were luminously decorated in winter and summer. Furthermore, we loved Sailor Tom fried clams. The Mohawk Trail to western North Adams was a much longer drive. The Hairpin Turn restaurant, gift shop, and observatory overlooking the city and valley made the trip worthwhile.

Our home atmosphere was happy, but I never saw my parents celebrate with liquor. To my knowledge, there was none in the house, and temperance, or lack thereof, was never discussed. On cold winter mornings, Dad filled an embossed clear glass pint wine-bottle with coffee. When at his sorting station in the post office, he put the bottle on a steam pipe to keep it hot when he walked his mail route.

We listened to radio broadcast news of Allies at war with German armies in Europe, and then in the Pacific, after Japan attacked Pearl Harbor on December 7, 1941. One week earlier than that date, Mother became a naturalized U.S. citizen. My parents worked a small "Victory" garden in keeping with the home-front war effort, and Mother preserved all that she could. Rationing included gas and tires, foods such as butter, sugar, coffee, and meats, clothing, and many goods made by factories converted to wartime production. Homes had window banners with proud blue stars for each member in the service of our country; a gold star memorialized a son lost in battle.

Even to us children, it was evident that we were at war. Blackouts were mandatory exercises when neighborhoods, towns, and cities turned off street lights, pulled down shades on windows, and masked auto headlights. Volunteer air-raid wardens walked our streets with official armbands and dimmed flashlights. I would close the door to my room, peek out into the dark, and watch massive searchlights sweeping the sky for mock military aircraft. There was a small U.S.

Army anti-aircraft artillery and searchlight detachment on Tenny's Hill across from my grandparent's home that made our country at war, a reality.

Anecdotal and actual, the soldiers took a liking to "Duke," a friendly South End fellow with the mind of a child. He walked Main Street greeting everyone and asking for money. Kids laughed when he chose a nickel over a dime, but he was crafty enough to know that if he took the dime, the opportunity to collect loose change again was less likely. Come winter, Duke was always dressed in warm Army clothing.

We listened to news of battles on the radio, saw black and white Paramount Pictures' movie war clips, collected scrapbooks of wartime planes, and built balsa wood replicas of military aircraft and ships. As Scouts, we paraded on Memorial Day to Wildwood and Calvary cemeteries to honor veterans by salute, flag, drumbeat, and Taps. Among many uniformed marchers, I remember those from World War I, and once saw two, probably 90 year-old, blue-uniformed Civil War vets riding in a parade car. To me, the day was a patriotic glory. To Rossville WWII soldier, William Davidson, in the European theatre and Cousin Ruth Smith's husband, "Bub," who fought with the Marines Corps in the South Pacific, combat was gory.

My first formal employment when 13, was working at Wildwood Cemetery in Winchester. Joe Duran was the superintendent who kept us on our toes. His office was in the gate building where our landscaping tools, artificial grass burial carpeting, and mechanisms to lower the casket were stored. That room had an odd, somewhat sweet, sanitary odor. I worked with friend Harold "Moe" Moran, who after his army service, assumed Joe Duran's job. We cut grass with push lawnmowers and trimmed around the gravestones with clippers that looked like sheep shears. Being so close to birth and death inscriptions, my subtraction was always in progress. Fall leaf raking never seemed to end. I helped to dig a grave where we hit the hollow corner of another rotting grave. I dared to put my hand in, but found nothing in the dark opening, but dampness.

CHAPTER TWO
HOMETOWN

My neighborhood was chock-full of children, and we had a variety of places to play. The chestnut tree across from our driveway fulfilled our climbing and tree hut instinct. Its "Pig" nut meat, after cracking the shells, was white and sweet. Beside that tree (now Ardley Road), we had our own hill for sledding or snow-sliding on sheets of cardboard. Streetlights illuminated neighborhood play places before suppertime when the days were short. In daylight or dusk, one of our favorite outdoor games was "Kick the Can." Players encircled a tin can and whoever was "It." After "It" covered his eyes, the others hid. "It" counted to ten and then sought the others. Given the chance, a hidden player would emerge and try to kick the can. If tagged first by "It", they would exchange places. If the runner kicked the can, "It" stayed for another round and so on.

Neighborhood mothers rang a hand bell when they wanted children to come home. Horn Pond "Mountain" was nearby with a CCC (Civilian Conservation Corps of Depression years) fire road leading up to the "Indian Bowl," a two foot wide bowl said carved in rock by the Algonquin Innitou tribe. The "Mountain" (to us) had a medium size ski-jump facing Pond Street and Big Winter Pond. Once when a jumper was injured, my dentist idol, Dr. Owen J. Logue, was the first to come to his assistance.

I was the center of my parent's life, and they were the center of mine. Undeniably blessed, my upbringing was "Je prend le gateau [I take the cake]." None-the-less, they quietly inspired me to strive for the best and enjoy what the world had to offer. Mother didn't drive, so we did things together travelling in our only car. I can't recall any home in the area with two cars. We went food shopping on Saturday night as did most families. There were two grocery-store shopping choices in Woburn center, The Great Atlantic and Pacific Tea

Uncle Tom &
Aunt Loretto

McGowan family,
Loretto, Martha,
Mary, Tom Jr., John.

Company (A&P) or the First National Store chain. Mother liked the A&P. I was happy when she bought cereal, because the boxes had mail-in coupons to for games or trading card prizes. While Mother was shopping, Dad and I would watch a large family burst in and out of front and back doors as soon as their mother and father walked out of sight in the direction of Main Street.

As a tiny lad, I remember a crowd at Woburn Common where someone was giving a political speech in front of City Hall. Mayor Kane was in office and fought with the teachers, denying them timely pay. To the firemen's chagrin, he put ten watt bulbs in the fire stations. He preached "God put the snow there, let him take it away." A police officer was sent to patrol East Woburn on an old mare. Those were his cures for the Great Depression years. To boot, he brought a circus wagon to the Common and threatened to put the drunks in it. I'm told that no one was put in the cage. The ventilator cowl from the U.S.S. Maine, sunk in 1898 in the Spanish American War, was preserved in a glass case on the Common.

In 1937, my 16 year old cousin Tom McGowan Jr. drowned at Squam Lake in Sandwich, New Hampshire. I only remember seeing Junior in a casket in their parlor, surrounded by baskets of flowers. That may have had an underlying effect on me, because I wasn't much of a swimmer. My Uncle Tom could not get over the loss and went to Junior's grave daily for many years. My Aunt Loretto grieved silently. They gave their row-boat to the town of Sandwich. A happy event in their family came when oldest daughter Loretto married Jerome Lynch. At eight, it was the first wedding that I attended, and the reception was held at the historic Shaker Glen House in Woburn.

Mother converted to Catholicism. She and I would walk over a mile to Father Fitzsimmons' rectory on Main Street in the North End of Winchester where she was instructed in the teachings of the church. Every night, in non-denominational prayer, Mother and I recited:

> Now I lay me down to sleep,
> I pray the Lord my soul to keep.
> If I should die before I wake,
> I pray the Lord my soul to take.

Dad and Mother brought me to church regularly and taught me to respect faith in any religion. Religious classes, sacraments, and Holy Day services were well attended at St. Mary's Church in Winchester Center. The teaching Order of St. Joseph nuns schooled us in Catechism, and I fortunately had one Sister who was motherly. When Ronny Purcell (of the Purcell pansy-grower family) and I would look at one another and laugh, a gaze from a holy sister quieted us down quickly. I had a bed-wetting flaw, and it happened a few times in church. The wet patch on my trousers was hard to conceal.

On Christmas morning, Santa Claus, *in whom I still believe*, brought gifts. I once got a green all metal truck with a box trailer that had "Spearmint" printed on the side. Two rear doors opened in the back just like on a real trailer. My Christmas-gift American Flyer train set got a lot of use on the living room carpet and on a sheet of plywood in the cellar for the rest of the year. Reels of cowboys and comedy scenes came with a Keystone movie projector. Other than black and white pictures, filter options were yellow, red, or blue. The film kept jumping off the projector sprockets or breaking. Mending broken film with a special kind of glue was not fun. Like those presents and so many others, each year had a highlight. As I got older, a yellow six string guitar gift was "Cool."

With aunts, uncles, and cousins, we gathered Sundays at Grandma McGowan's Lake Avenue house in Woburn and devoured her famous fried bread sprinkled with sugar. I spent one afternoon a week at Mrs. Lois Hersey's Winter Pond home learning crafts and earning Wolf, Bear, and Lion patches for my Cub Scout uniform. She was the Den Mother to her son Elliott, and eight of the rest of us. Mrs. Hersey had a "Secret" crawl-in-door installed for us to enter and exit the Scout "Den" room. We wore blue Cub Scout shirts and gold bandanas at meetings and in parades. Monthly Pack (all Dens combined) meetings were held at the Congregational Church hall in Winchester center where Reverend Mr. Chidley was pastor. After a salute to the Flag and formal business, blue and gold uniformed scouts were constantly running around the hall.

I had able and kind teachers at the Wyman Elementary School located about a mile from my Woodside Road home. In Miss Hawes kindergarten class, we took turns shaking a mason jar to churn butter

Charlie, 2nd row, middle, Cub Scouts Den 4 at Herseys, 1941

that was then put on saltine crackers. Mrs. Randlett taught first grade, Miss Follansbee second, Miss Lawry third, Miss Butterfield (later a patient in my surgical practice) fourth, Miss Chapman (my favorite) fifth, and Miss Wallace from Lexington, grade six. We wore tiny white tin clip-on Red Cross emblems when we contributed coins at a classroom collection. When report cards came out before summer vacation, the common query among classmates was "Did you pass?"

I remember that the dirt playground surface had lots of small hollows for marble-games. Marbles were the craze, colorful, and very collectible. Each was cradled in the curve of a forefinger and flicked with the thumb from a designated line hoping to land a tossed marble in the dirt bowl. I had one heavy three inch diameter prized marble at home, but I'd never bring it to school because of its chips and pitting. It was big!

Walking on Wildwood Street to or from the Wyman School with friends, I waded through piles of leaves in autumn, patted a dog along the way, stopped to skip stones in Big and Little Winter Ponds, or cautiously walked out on the ice at the edge to test the thickness.

I was playing on the shore of Little Winter Pond with friends one summer, and we were throwing stones in the water. When my stone hit John Burchard on the head and he started bleeding, I panicked, ran home, and told my parents what had happened. They promptly took me to his home to apologize. His parents were courteous and understanding. Mrs. Burchard was very friendly and known to sit on the curb and talk with the town street workers. When she brought me and John to visit Mr. Burchard, a Dean at Massachusetts Institute of Technology, I remember passing through an electric eye beam that opened the main entrance door.

My walk home from school sometimes meant meeting Dad who was delivering mail, and he would give me a coin or two to buy candy or ice cream. On one such day, he had no change, but looking down, he saw a coin on the ground, and we both were very happy!

I picked and sold blueberries to neighbors. Skippy, my brown cocker spaniel, went out on Winter Pond with me in an unbelievably small plywood boat when I gathered water lilies for sale. With friends, I took swimming lessons at Wedge Pond beach where the town had tennis courts and a building for changing clothes. I never saw Mother or Dad in a bathing suit. The tiny store had "Hoodsie" ice cream cups and small, flat wooden spoons, and summer-treat frozen "Milky Way" chocolate bars. In Horn Pond, there were ice cold springs that gave swimmers cramps and sometimes resulted in drownings.

I walked the shores of Big Winter and Horn Pond to fish in the summer and skate and ice-fish in the winter. Calendars from my parents insurance agency described both pond's history as part of the 1793–1851 Middlesex Canal barge and locks system from Lowell to Boston. Large snapping turtles terrified Cousin Frankie and me because it was said that they could break a broomstick with their jaws. With teenage friends on an upper bank at Horn Pond, we grabbed a rope-swing tied to an overhanging limb, bravely swung out, and dropped into the water. What fun!

Mr. Bill Cox, a neighbor from across the street on Woodside Road, drove me and his three children, Kathryn, Gerald, and William, to school many times in his Model A Ford roadster. When another

Rope swing at Horn Pond

Iver Johnson ad, 1938

neighbor, Mr. Berquist, drove his son Harold and daughter Norma, to the Wyman School, I was often included. As soon as I got in the car, I knew, by that familiar cooking odor, that he had bacon and eggs for breakfast.

I rode a popular Iver Johnson brand bike to school in the upper elementary grades and in Junior High. It was a 26 inch wheel model, and had a metal basket on the handle bars to carry books, whatever, or on occasion, little Bill Cox. The Iver Johnson factory was in Fitchburg, Massachusetts, and I have one of their 1938 ads for firearms, "Bicycles, Velocipedes, and Juniorcycles."

Our neighborhood was typical of most, where some residents came from other continents. Mrs. Theresa Loftus, who lived across the street, was Irish born. Down toward Winter Pond, the Mouradian family, in the oriental rug business, were from Armenia. Toward

Horn Pond, Mr. Kennedy and his shy Irish wife were generous when we kids peddled blueberries or sold Scout raffle tickets. So were Ned and Ella Fleming, a vibrant older (maybe in their 50s if that!) couple. Their stucco home, lawns, and bountiful summer gardens were always kept immaculate. The Kennedys and the Flemings had no children.

Bent-over Mrs. Davey, was a memorable and lovely old Irish woman. She lived two houses down from my house with her son John, who worked with Dad at the Winchester post office. At some point in life, she had severe facial injuries incurring loss of an eye, one-side facial paralysis, and a severely depressed cheekbone. Her kindness to me far exceeded her deformities.

Mother's cousin Gwen Trail settled in Gloucester on the North Shore and was a popular employee at W.G. Brown Department Store for many years. She married Martin Levy around 1940. They had no children but made a lot of me. I distinctly remember them giving me a metal top with geared spinner discs. When the spindle was pressed down, the spinning top created colorful kaleidoscopic images.

I remember visiting Mother's close friend, Almira Burns, who still worked at the Massachusetts State Colony nursing facility in Middleton. She was slight, prim, wore glasses, and spoke quietly and properly. Her favorite nephew, Spurgeon (I can't forget that name), also of Nova Scotian heritage, was mentioned in conversation quite often. When visiting us in Winchester, Almira brought me nice hard-covered children's books.

Comic book heroes Flash Gordon, Superman, Tarzan of the Apes, Dick Tracey, Roy Rogers, and Mickey Mouse captured my mind. There was a special hard cover comic book about four inches square and two inches thick. Along with text, its characters in an upper right page corner moved, like in moving pictures, when the pages were flipped from front to back.

When 12 and in junior high school, I joined Boy Scout Troop Seven in Winchester that met on Monday night at the Baptist church basement. I became friends with boys from all over town. While I was at a Scout meeting, my folks visited with Dad's postal co-worker, Frank Shaw and his wife Noni, who lived nearby. They played a card game called "Flinch." I remember going on a day trip with my folks and the Shaws to Nubble Light in York, Maine where we picked high-bush blueberries.

Boy Scouts required a 14-mile hike that took us to small, rustic Camp Lane in the Burlington, Massachusetts, woods. When our scoutmaster, Mr. John Casler, cooked pancakes not to our liking, we secretly passed them to fellow scout Frank Lawton, who could devour almost any quantity of food. I spent one week for a few summers at Scout Camp Fellsland on the Pow-Wow River in Amesbury. Activities that made us hardy, healthy, and not picky about food, were fishing, canoeing, swimming, saluting the flag to bugle calls at dusk and dawn, working to earn merit badges, and drinking "Bug juice" in the "Mess (dining) Hall."

Prior to summer vacation, Mr. Ray Hayward, my sophomore history teacher in high school asked if I might be interested in spending time with his family at their Maine camp helping with chores and rowing back and forth to the mainland. I took it as a compliment but separation from family and summer activities did not make the offer practical.

From my *Aberjona* high school year book, I recall being the football team assistant manager who carried the black bag for Dr. Barone onto the field when a player was injured. I was a Traffic Squad member who monitored the stairwells as students walked between classes and was on the Athletic Association exectutive board. Life at school was good!

Likeness of Dad buying my .22 rifle

When visiting Uncle Tom and Aunt Loretto McGowan in Woburn, I was intrigued when shown small caliber rifles that were locked in an upstairs gun cabinet. Cousin John was a ham radio operator and had the whole set-up, including a tower in their backyard. Uncle Tom would read us letters from John when he was serving as a navy hospital corpsman with the Marines in the South Pacific in WWII.

When on occasional trips to Boston, I enjoyed going to Iver Johnson Sporting Goods store on Washington Street. I doubt that I made many purchases, but the displays of camping, fishing, and hunting equipment always caught my eye.

My first gun was a chromed Daisy airgun that shot small lead or copper-coated pellets called "BB's." Dad taught me that the privilege to own a firearm also meant learning its safe and proper use. He bestowed the right of ownership in 1943 when he bought me a Remington .22 caliber Model 510 Targetmaster single shot rifle at Central Hardware in Woburn. It had a pre-war April 5, 1939 serial # 46472 and went with me to Boy Scout Camp Fellsland where I earned a merit badge in marksmanship. In 1945, Dad allowed me to bring it to New Brunswick where Warden Alec Ferguson issued a Scot's burr "Permut." I wouldn't say that he sprinkled his porridge with tacks, but he was strict. Bill and Hazel Ingraham and their ten children lived next to the Baylis farm. George and Arthur Ingraham, about my age, and I shot at tin cans and the occasional red squirrel. A catchy Canadian brand of a .22 caliber rifle was the "Cooey." I've kept that first "Targetmaster" as the most meaningful of my firearms.

One of my favorite places to visit, was Woburn Public Library where Uncle Tom McGowan was the librarian. After a bighearted greeting from him and his secretary, Agnes Cronin, the mysterious and magical alcoves of the castle-like interior were mine. It was exciting to see the drum used as a model in the Archibald Willard "Spirit of '76" painting and read about Woburn native, Benjamin Thompson b.1753. Because he was a Loyalist with diplomatic and scientific accomplishments, he was welcomed in Britain, and subsequently titled Count Rumford. The still efficient Rumford fireplace was his design. Woburnites erected his statue on their library lawn.

During high school, I worked as a landscaper for Irish born Mike Heggarty, a chap who bewildered his clients by constantly rushing around, working or not. After a hot days work on the Winchester West

Grandpa & Grandma McGowan, 1947

McGowan home, Woburn, Mass., 1920s

Side estates, a "Ballicky" swim from a secluded cove on Horn Pond to its tiny wooded island, made us feel like real men! Winter spending money was earned by shoveling snow on neighborhood walks and driveways and at the Boston Edison electrical distribution sub-station near Horn Pond. Along with academics, sports, and extracurricular activities in high school, I had no difficulty about working in my free time.

In 1945, my parents and I had a major change in daily living when we moved to Woburn to live with Dad's elderly parents. I was accustomed to staying on Lake Avenue overnight with my cousin Frankie Murphy whose family, Aunt Ruth, Uncle Frank, and his older sisters, Ruth and Norma, lived with Ma and Pa. Though Frankie was my age and good company, he did not mix well with fellow students at St. Charles parochial school. His sisters dubbed him "Yankee," probably because it rhymed with Frankie. The Murphys decided to move to Boston where Ruth and Norma were enrolled in the U.S. Cadet Nurse Corps program at St. Elizabeth's Hospital in Brighton. My grandparents would then be alone.

Uncle Tom, the oldest McGowan son, was a 1914 Harvard College graduate, attorney, and city alderman. He was looked upon for family advice, and I think that Tom advised my parents to sell their Winchester home to subsidize my future education and come to live with Ma and Pa McGowan. Our home sold for $8,800, and the new owner was Mr. Herbert Skerry, a Winchester High School teacher. My parents used the home sale income for tuition to complete my education in Winchester and attend Tufts College in Medford.

Our new Lake Avenue address was a front porch (Ma and Pa called it a piazza) neighborhood in summer. Grandma's Chinese glass wind-chimes tinkled in the warm breeze, and we watched passersby walk to and from the beach at Horn Pond. Elder McGowan cousins, Terry McGowan (who believed in ghosts) and Eddie Doherty (a Spanish-American War veteran who dressed in black), occasionally had a room in the attic. After school at first frost, I loved to feast on Concord grapes from the backyard vine. I made a space in the cellar where I could study and build model airplanes. I think of the whitewashed old stone foundation and shelf of Grandma's preserved grape juice. There was a big supply-drum of kerosene from which I refilled and carried a special container upstairs to the kitchen stove to fuel the burner wicks. My other chore was emptying the water drip-pan under the non-electrified ice-box. Food was kept cold by blocks of ice that were delivered as needed.

Grandpa, "Johnny" to friends and "Pa" to the family, was retired and quite a character. By day, he wore a suit and vest. A gold watch, with a dangling gold chain, decorated the front pocket of his vest. After supper, he listened to "Flash newses" by radio commentator Fulton Lewis, Jr., read the *Woburn Times* newspaper, and cut Mayo brand plug tobacco for his pipe, or spilled it on his clothing. Late in the evening on his way to the bathroom, he passed my room wearing a wool nightcap, long underwear, and pants that he held up with each suspender drooping. He wore full upper and lower dentures (sometimes) and attributed tooth loss to tasting the tanning liquids of his trade. In age and temperament, manual labor was not his strong point. When we visited the McGowan grave plot in my younger days, the grass was barely growing. I was told that Grandpa put salt on it to kill the weeds. It did…for many years. He walked down to the Electric Plant where the foreman gave him free electric-panel fuses to replace ones that had blown at home.

Pa had his way of teaching by example. He took me to Woburn District Court, Judge William Henchey presiding, to witness the goings on when people stepped outside the limits of the law. When Frankie and I were 14, he arranged to have us visit a Massachusetts state prison, the Concord Reformatory, where his cousin, Jack Algeo, was Deputy Superintendent. After the tour, we asked why so many innocent looking men were jailed. Frankie and I had some good times shooting at crows on the Algeo farm in Concord. The property now is occupied by Hanscom Field in adjoining Bedford.

Pa McGowan seldom missed a trip when my parents took Grandma shopping at the new A & P grocery store on lower Main Street in Woburn. As soon as they went in to buy groceries, Pa got out and cleverly weaved among the rows of parked autos to Doherty's liquor store. He tried to conceal the brown bag, but we soon caught on to his determined antics. Another one of his regular stops for prescriptions was Case Drug Store across from the A & P. He referred to the apothecary as "the pothecary."

When 20 at Tufts, I barbered his balding head and offered, in jest, to trim his moustache. The retort was always "No." His "Pleasure" in a bottle, sat on the floor between his chair and the window overlooking our back yard. I would sit across from him with a newspaper raised in front of me…and a small hole in it so that I could watch his movements. When thirst got the best of him, he would reach for the jug, and I would abort the mission by slowly lowering the paper. Mother once had some fun with him when he offered to help her decorate our Christmas tree. He returned repeatedly, because he knew that a "Swig" was the reward if he helped to hang and drape glass ornaments, golden garlands, and silver tinsel.

Pa called Grandma Bridget, "Beazie," and we called her "Ma" as did our parents. When Dr. Kelleher made a house visit to check on her health, Pa would ask "Doc, please take my blood pressure too." Ma was a mild-mannered elegant lady who always had a cookie for us grandchildren. She'd say "You should always be kind and say hello to other people even if you are not their friend." She was very hard of hearing, and the family bought her a hearing aid. When I commented that it was a good idea, her reply was "Heh?" With a detectable Donegal brogue, she called me "CHAR-les" till her passing at age 94. When I touch and smell lilacs or lilies of the valley like those that grew at home in Woburn, I think of my grandmother, and how grand she was!

I've a fond memory of Uncle Tom. I asked him to speak to our Holy Name Society at the Immaculate Conception Church that served the South End of Woburn and the North End of Winchester. Growing up in the South end, he spoke with ease and familiarity about the "Old days." The presentation was appreciated and well received. At its conclusion, he gave me his speech that was written in long-hand.

Everyone got along well in the two family household, but separation from her 14 years of homemaking in Winchester may have left its toll on Mother. Just before my 1949 high school graduation, she had a nervous breakdown and was hospitalized. Dad did more than fulfill his wedding vow of "For better or for worse." Electroshock treatments helped, but then came relapse with many repeat hospital admissions. I helped when I could, but the burden was mostly on Dad.

I was caught smoking on high school grounds and in confidence said that Mother's illness was bothering me. A kind ear, from an I-don't-remember-who in administration, calmed my worries and encouraged me to do my best. I did and became a National Honor Society student.

CHAPTER THREE

My New Brunswick Family

"**H**ow much longer before we get there?" must have driven my parents crazy when we frequently returned to visit my third generation Baylis family farm in Rossville, New Brunswick. Early on, I became immersed in their Atlantic Canada way of life, but knew not how my good fortune came to be.

I never asked, but I know now, and this is the story. Originally granted to disbanded loyal regimental soldiers from the American War of Independence, large York County tracts of Crown Lands were divided from Queensbury and Southampton parishes to the Carleton County line, and similar domains on the other side of the St. John River. The Crown also sold enormous tracts of land to British politically-connected investment groups to develop communities and attract settlers. Chartered by an act of Parliament in 1834, the New Brunswick and Nova Scotia (NB & NS) Land Company inexpensively acquired 589,000 acres for 2 shilling and 3 pence ($.56) per acre in York County providing $329,840 in welcome revenue for the scanty provincial treasury. Maps show Rossville parcels as part of that enterprise.

During The Clearances when upper-class landowners ejected Highland Scot crofters (small farmers) from their meager plots, many sought a better life in Maritime Canada. Grasping land grant opportunities, my maternal great-great grandfather, George Munro, came from Creich Parish in the Highland district of Sutherlandshire, Scotland. My great grandfather George Baylis came later, and possibly connected with the NB & NS Land Company headquarters when he lived in England. Each found a conquerable land with similar countryside and seasons as in their United Kingdom homelands.

By this time, you've often seen the given or baptismal name George regarding my great-great grandfather George Munro, great grandfather George Baylis, Uncle George Rockwell Baylis, Mother's

Uncle George Munro, and my friend George Ingraham (others will follow). King George V, Queen Victoria's grandson, must have made a big impression on British Empire mothers when it came to naming their sons! I'll do my best to label each along the way.

Refering back to the "Parish of Southampton" map on page 8, Great grandfather George Baylis petitioned for land grant acreage in the "Nackiewikiak" area on July 1, 1855. *Nackawic Bend* states that settlers bought land on Rossville Road under the auspices of the NB & NS Land Company. Peter Morrison and John Davidson were among the first Rossville landowners. In the process of Baylis land acquisition, census taking, or any document where their surname appears, spellings varied according to the record taker. In the 1861 New Brunswick Census, George Baylas was a farmer in Southampton. The *Hutchinson Directory of New Brunswick 1865–1868* lists George Bailes as a farmer in Nackawic. The *Lovell New Brunswick Directory, 1871* records George Baylis, farmer, Lower Southampton. In the *1878 Halfpenny Atlas*, G. Bayliss was among 12 families on Rossville Road. Of Ross F. Woodman, Sr. in the book *Temperance Vale*, "He settled on the Bayliss place. He and William [? meaning George] Bayliss traded places." I've no further explanation. Such exchanges of property were sometimes never legally registered. The 1881 Southampton Parish Canada Census registers George Bayles, a farmer, age 54, and names the members of his family.

While reading the following, the "Parish of Southampton" map at the beginning of Chapter One will be of aid. My great grandfather Baylis, was finally granted a deed from the NB & NS Land Co. in 1883: "being known as lot number six and containing fifty acres more or less." The successive deeded history of accumulated land was: George Baylis to William Baylis [my grandfather] February 16, 1894, original 50 acres; John Henderson [1864-1934, son of Thomas] to William Baylis, December 2, 1911 "adjacent to Baylis lot six and part of lot seven," 25 acres; John Henderson to William Baylis, April 26, 1926, remaining 75 acres of lot seven. Uncle George had a woodlot somewhere above the Upper Temperance Vale Road. I found it recorded as "Ross F. Woodman to William Baylis, October 7, 1902 lot 2 or the one-third of the Cliff Block, One Hundred and Fifteen acres." The Baylis land holdings then totaled 265 acres. A 1951 Southampton Assessment roll named the William Baylis estate as valued at $3,400: Lands $1,200 and Buildings $2,200.

In the Henderson/Baylis 1926 deed, the Baylis back boundary near Trout Brook abutted Uncle Dave Munro woodland for 30 rods; turned right angle northeasterly along the Jabez Bradbury line, crossing the Rossville Road, toward Nackawic stream; turned hard right again at the original N.B. & N.S Land Co. base line for another 30 rods, and went back again along the William Baylis lot to the point of origin.

My Baylis grandparents, William and Alexandria, were married in Woodstock by Presbyterian minister Mr. Ross on April 4, 1893. Grampy, 22, as son of Annie Munro, and Grammie, 17, daughter of Annie's brother John, were cousins. In the 1901 Census of Canada, I find my grandfather, William Bayles and family, listed between neighboring heads of household, Ross Fanning Woodman and Jabez Bradbury (*remember the name!*). By 1909, the Baylis family had grown to six children: Mabel, Jean, Lucy, Ella, George, and Willa. Willa Christy Jane was born on December 25, 1910 and died on October 17, 1913. She was named after Christy Jane MacCallum Munro, my great grandmother and first wife of my great grandfather, John Munro, both born in Scotland. I don't know anything else about Willa, or the cause of her death at age three, except that she has a stone in Munro Cemetery. Ronald was born in 1915.

My Baylis grandparents, c.1893

*Mabel Violet Baylis,
1918*

Over the next 18 years, three Baylis family members passed away. My aunt Ella, three years younger than Mother, clerked in a general store and married Justus James Stairs, a rural mail carrier. At age 24, she died of a cerebral embolism 11 days after giving birth on June 1, 1924 to my cousin Ella Miriam Stairs. Newborn Ella came to live at the Baylis farm. Her father, "Joe," later remarried, lived nearby in Lower Southampton, and was always around to support Ella.

Grandfather William died at age 59 on January 12, 1930 at the Victoria Public Hospital. He had a finger injury while logging and developed streptococcus septicemia (blood poisoning). His body was taken by Valley train to Pinder, and the funeral was held at home on January 15th with burial in Lower Southampton Munro cemetery.

Aunt Jean died on July 15, 1933 at Victoria Public Hospital. I vaguely recall being at her bedside with Mother. She had surgery for an intestinal obstruction, but died five days later of "Strangulated Mesentery," according to the cause of death report. She left husband, Russell McElwain, and young sons, Earle and Alton. Uncle Russell later married school teacher Leola Fox, and they had two boys, Arden and Lynne. I liked Leola and knew a few of her students from three generations. All spoke well of her. I'm told that Leola possessed the healing gift of being able to stop bleeding through the magical power of prayer. Our family talks about their good sense of humor. In one instance, Russell mistook dishwater on the stove for soup. He and Leola laughed about it too.

A March 17, 1941 telegram came to Winchester bringing news of Grammie Baylis' death. She contracted pneumonia from the flu. Mother, Dad, and I immediately drove up for the funeral. After crossing the Houlton border, Dad's 1939 Chevrolet did a 360 degree spin between high snow banks on the road to Woodstock. Fortunately there were no other cars on the road. Upon arrival, we were brought into the front parlor where I panicked (maybe she was not laid-out in a casket) and ran out crying. In the midst of extreme wintry weather and deep frost, her grave was hand-dug by family friends. The funeral service at home and burial in the old Munro Cemetery in Lower Southampton, was directed by Frederick Roy Flewelling. The little nearby Reformed Baptist Church church constructed well before 1900 was often used for funeral services by other denominations. The Baylis family was Presbyterian.

I loved my Aunt Mabel and my uncles, George, and Ronald from the time that I was born. My uncles would rub their bristly beards against my face to my childhood amusement. I always appreciated being noticed.

Aunt Mabel was Baylis' first-born on June 12, 1893. She remained at home after schooling and did not marry. I never saw her drive, smoke, or drink, nor did I ever hear her curse. Her comfort was keeping house in Rossville for my grandparents and uncles, and visiting the neighbors. Her unusual phobia, since childhood, was being deathly afraid of kittens! She occasionally went to town for a day, but I don't recall that she ever came to see us in Winchester.

The light of her life was her niece, my cousin Ella Stairs, who came as an infant in 1924 and had wonderful Mabel to nurture her. As surviving sisters, Mother and Mabel's love and letters kept them close between visits.

Mabel, I think, was very shy and humble. Kind to me, she was always bustling around in a housedress and apron doing the household tasks of feeding the wood stove for cooking, baking, washing and ironing; churning and butter making; cleaning; quilting and mending; making trips to and from the clothesline; and making beds and carrying chamber pots to the workshop privy. There was a foot

Mabel & Ella Stairs, 1926

Grampy & Grammie Baylis, 1926

treadle Singer sewing machine in her room over the kitchen. Photos show her nicely groomed, well-dressed, and strong. The Baylis home had many visitors including uncles, aunts, and cousins in the Munro and Trail families, my cousins Alton and Earle McElwain and Ella Stairs Briggs, the Ingraham girls from up the road, next door neighbor, young Bertram Stairs, and a cousin from Maine.

I heard the Baylis folks talk about Arden Bull, a second cousin from over in Mapleton, Maine, who enjoyed visiting with them (he and Edith had a family of 13). His mother, Nettie Rose Fox, was born in Lower Temperance Vale, and a first cousin to the Baylis siblings. She came over the lines to Perham, Maine with her parents, Aunt Lucy and Uncle Wilmot Fox in about 1894. Nettie married Edward Bull in 1910, and became the mother of nine. She was named Maine Mother of the Year in 1957, met Governor Muskie and his family at the State House, and went to a "Mothers of the Year" convention in New York. It was said that the Fox and descendant families made their mark in farming in Perham, Washburn, and Mapleton in Aroostook County. I was told that they looked upon Mabel as a favorite cousin.

Mabel's social contacts gradually faded. After my grandparents died, Cousin Ella got married in 1942, and Uncle Ronald married in 1946, it left her and George alone to manage the home and farm. In later years, she became slightly bent over, frail, and appeared to

Mabel & Grammie, 1939

be constantly fretting. At the time of her death on March 2, 1953 at age 59, Mabel was described by neighbors as "A peaceful soul." Uncle George found her dead on the ground, having fallen off the back porch at the clothesline. RCMP investigation, autopsy, and inquest followed. D.J. Anderson, Chief Coroner, wrote "Head Injuries and Skull fracture (Accidental) yard of home." I was in college at Tufts, and Mother and Dad immediately came up for the services which were held at the farm. A choir, accompanied by the parlor organ, sang "Rock of Ages" and "Abide With Me." In Mabel's mind, I think that her simple outlook on life and dedication to family was sufficient.

Uncle George's middle name was Rockwell, an unfamiliar surname to those of us who are living. As well as having quite a few photos of George at different ages, I found his description in a September 1929 Ft. Fairfield, Maine, border crossing manifest: "Via Presque Isle, Canadian Pacific Railroad from Fredericton, 4th time to pick potatoes in Caribou, Maine, height 5'9", medium complexion, amber hair, grey eyes and $20 in hand." His Aunt Lucy Baylis Fox and husband, Wilmot, had relocated to that area, and one of their sons was named George Baylis Fox. The common Rossville expression for crossing the border was "Going over the lines." It was said simply, and in the same casual way as "Going to the store." My uncle could use a horse-drawn potato digger or hand harvest potatoes into half-bushel ash baskets.

Uncle George haying, 1950

"GB" marked his potato barrels in Rossville, but funny neighbor Billy Morrison had another version for the initials. When visiting in the autumn, we always came home with a full burlap sack of "Spuds" or "Taters." I also recall returning home with Grammie and Mabel's home-knit mittens and socks for winter wear. When the farmers spoke of potato varieties, a name that I remember best is "Katartin." Long before, in 1804, the first "Yankee" ascent of Mt. Katahdin was made by a surveyor named Charles Turner, Jr. who called it "Catardin." In any case, it's a northern Maine potato and mountain peak attribute.

George was reared and farmed the old way, with horses only. When he was planting or harvesting hay, grain, and potatoes, or hauling wood or gravel, the team responded to right, left, back-up, and stop commands by "Gee," "Haw," "Back," and "Whoa." Farms without stands of hard and softwood often had woodlots elsewhere for cutting firewood and pulp. Uncle George had one a half-mile up on Rossville Road somewhere above the Upper Temperance Vale road corner.

Cousin Ella's son, Weldon Briggs, recalls one of George's smart horses, sometimes without reins, twitching fallen logs to a common work area called a "Yard." George loved to work his horses. I now realize that horses didn't harm new growth like petrol-powered equipment. Whether single or as a team, in field or in woods, his horses adapted to the task at hand. Merlin Fox told me that Uncle George and Roy Davidson were working in the woods beside Trout Brook, when the horse broke through the ice, was badly injured, and had to be put down. On a walk through the upper fields, George once told me of his fondness for farming. When I admired his leather jacket, he gave it to me.

I think of the two-foot "Spud" that Uncle George used to peel or strip bark off a spruce or poplar log for pulpwood. In those days, pulp had to be peeled of its bark before going to mill. The ash handle, covered with pitch, was set in a steel socket that tapered to a shovel-shaped sharp 2¼ inch edge. Peeling lasted through May, June, and July (and so did the pesky black-fly time). Peeled logs were left to dry because they were cleaner and easier to cut and haul away. He cut four-foot standard lengths with a crosscut or buck saw and later a chainsaw. My uncles used a short, hand-held pulp hook to grab one end of a pulp stick. With a gloved hand on the other end, they tossed the four-footers onto a pile at the yard, on a wagon, or into a boxcar.

I recall driving three miles with George by sloven (low loading centered platform) wagon to Perley Fox' blacksmith shop in Temperance Vale to get the team shod. Blacksmiths were farm metal workers who shoed horses, repaired wagons, and forged tools. In the barnyard or at work, neither the horses nor I were edgy, but in the stall we were more uncomfortable, maybe because of our size difference or just lack of familiarity.

After Uncle Ronald left the farm, George did most of the haying alone. I relive the full flavor of horse and wagon haying, when I listen to the first two verses (and the whole nine yards) of "The Haying Song" lyrics by David Mallett. Dave was raised in Sebec, Piscataquis County, Maine, and knows old-time farming.

When the raspberries burst from the woodbine,
And the summer lies close to the ground,
And the porch is the fit place for young boys to sleep,
And the brook in the hollow dies down;

Then with straw hats and wagons and horses
Like young Tim and tired old Dan,
We head for the fields to the creak of the wheels
With a pitchfork that blisters your hand.

Haying in Rossville usually involved a crew to mow, rake, pitch on, and build a load on the wagon before driving it to the barn. Gender was not an issue to Bill Ingraham and Bill Morrison, since their girls could bring in hay as well as their boys. No matter who or where, thirst accompanied haying in the hot clear days of summer. Few fields had much shade or a cold spring nearby. To remedy the problem, farm wives like Daisy Davidson would prepare an 1800s remedy called "Haymaker punch" or "Switchel" that was brought out to the fields in a pail. Daisy made use of a concoction of cold pump water, vinegar, brown sugar, and oatmeal.

Uncle George Baylis' sickle-bar mowing machine cut five foot swaths on each trip around the hayfield. He scythed around the edges and kept the blade sharp with a narrow ten inch hand-held whetstone. A single horse-drawn, two-wheel dump rake with long curved steel teeth rolled cut-hay into what the farmers called "Winrows" before it was pitch-forked onto the hayrack. The hay-load was then driven on to the barn floor (drive floor, threshing floor) which was between and below the "Mows" (upper-level hay storage spaces: sounds like "Cows"). Suspended from a trolley track on the ridge beam, a rope-and-pulley system lowered a two pronged hay-fork or a grapple fork to grab a bunch of hay. A rope, hitched to a horse, was then pulled to lift the bunch of hay up into the mow. When in the right position along the trolley track, a small trip-line rope was jerked to release the forkful. I've walked the horse and slack rope, with a grab hook on the end, back to be hitched again and again to pull another forkful until the wagon was empty. There was no cure for being covered with sweat, dust, and chaff while putting hay away. It was get it done fast, climb down a ladder, and get a cold drink of water!

Harvesting grain on a small farm was like haying, but a horse-drawn binder with sickle bar was used to cut the stalks. A rotating reel with wooden cross-bars swept the stalks and grain onto a canvas bed. Then, a conveyor mechanism gathered and tied bunches before discharging them onto the field. The tied bundles were "Stooked" upright in small groups for drying and wagon pick-up. Once under cover, a traveling "Thrashing" (threshing) machine arrived to separate bedding straw from grain. The air rattled and the chaff flew and blew! George grew and cut enough hay and oats to feed his horses for the year.

George kept the pulp-peeling spud, axe, saws, and hay-mower bar sharp with a file or hand-stone. When he used the mounted grind-stone wheel, I cranked and watered it for him on occasion. I have and hold his two and three tined hayforks respecting the labor that they represent. Their tines, like his double-bitted (bit is the cutting edge) super sharp axe, were burnished shiny smooth from service. My light chain saw is no comparison to the weight of his first heavy one.

As "Dog Street Barber," his hair parlor was on the back porch in warm weather. He had a high stool, shoulder drape, scissors, comb, hand clippers, fragrant hair tonic, and talc as if a professional. Hair-cuts for boys around a farm were few and far between. When I went to a professional barber after a summer vacation, he asked "Did you just come out of the bush?"

Frank Murphy, my traveling salesman uncle, had a large territory that included northern Maine. He was good to me, but an outspoken, a city-type-of-guy. He had a strong Boston accent, and argued with Grandpa McGowan about presidential politics, saying "My theory is etc., etc." Pa would put the framed President Roosevelt picture up on the wall, and Frank would take it down (or visa-versa). When Frank drove George Baylis down here once, George said that he had never been so frightened.

Around 1945, George took me to visit Bobby Lowe, a legendary woodsman, trapper, and guide in backwoods Allandale. Bobby showed us a box half full of bear paws. He told us that his health improved after cooking meat over an open fire to get rid of the fat drippings. I noticed copies of *National Geographic* magazine on the table. Bobby said that they were left by American hunters that he guided.

Dad came in one night quite uneasy after a trip to Woodstock with George, who had gone to the house of a woman who sold alcohol after the provincial liquor store closed. While there, the Mounties arrived to investigate and evidently left with no consequence. My father, being very quiet, was extremely tense with what had happened.

Uncle Ronald was born during World War I, and had the middle name, Kitchener, after an English military hero. I recall that the only book on the Baylis kitchen shelf was *Lord Kitchener and the Great*

Uncle Ronald & team, 1937

Me on Baylis horse, 1937

War. As a child, I assumed that it was a family keepsake, not knowing Ronald's full name.

Ronald was fair with freckles, always wore glasses, and inherited red hair from my grandmother. He farmed with George, sometimes for Mike Cronkhite, and worked for Alfred Fox racking potatoes and loading pulp in boxcars. At age 23 in September 1938, he flew from northern Maine to visit us (a thrilling rarity for a young farmer). Boston-Maine Airways was called "The Flying Yankee of the Air." I've two memories of that trip. We met him at the Boston Airport terminal on the black asphalt tarmac (the runway was cinders). It's the present 2400 acre Logan International Airport that extends out into Boston Harbor. While with us or shortly afterward, the September 21st Great New England Hurricane devastated the northeast with high winds, extreme flooding, and loss of life. Ronald had a lot to tell the folks when he got back home.

Ice cream making on a summer Sunday afternoon was an exciting event. By horse and wagon for ice, Ronald and I went up to the unoccupied old Henderson farm next door that my grandfather owned.

The empty granary was the Baylis ice-house. It was exciting to open the door and see a pile of sawdust, knowing that ice was buried somewhere in it. Ronald dug and prodded with a barn shovel until he hit a preserved stream-cut block which we brought home with all eyes upon us!

The ice cream maker, about the size of a pail, had wooden staves joined on the outside and a central metal container to hold the liquid ingredients. When the handle was cranked, a gear on top turned the cylinder and its internal mixing paddles. For ice cream making, we used the best of heavy cream from the Baylis Jersey cows. Maple "Honey" (syrup) was a favorite flavoring. I think that Mabel also combined sugar, eggs, and cornstarch with the mixture, but I'm not sure. Ronald put ice chips and rock salt, to lower the water temperature, in the tub around the container. Refilling the ice and rock salt, and turning the crank handle to rotate the container, was no easy task, but everyone liked to have a try at it. When the turning finally became difficult, the ice cream was ready to eat. We held our breath when

Ronald & Ella Baylis wedding, 1946

*Cousin Ella &
Haldean Briggs,
c1943*

the canister was opened, because the salty cold water could spoil the whole thing if it spilled into the ice cream. Ronald's reward was licking the ice cream off the wood mixing paddles.

It's hard for me to remember more bits and pieces about Ronald, but here goes. When he married Ella M. Colwell in 1946, they moved to Water Street in Woodstock. He worked in the feed mill. Daughter Brenda was born in 1949 and inherited Ronald's red hair. I knew Ella's single sister, Irene Colwell, who was employed in a bookstore on Main Street. Dad and Ronald thoroughly enjoyed each other's company. Cousin Joyce Jones recalls "Ronald's jolly laugh." When asked at table or treat, Ronald's acceptance was "Don't mind if I do." I quote it often.

Cousin Ella Stairs and I always remained close. Her warm personality, good morals, and strong work ethic were influenced by Mabel's upbringing. Ella first crossed the lines to visit our Winchester home around 1940. At age 16 and accustomed to drying her hair over a wood stove, she scorched it over our stovetop gas burner! She married Haldean Briggs, from a fine farming family in Temperance Vale, in 1942. Their children, Weldon, Joyce, and Gwendolyn "Gwen" were born in 1944, 1949, and 1951. Hal farmed his parent's acreage, and Ella managed the home and children along with raising hundreds of chickens for eggs and poultry. She was conscientious about keeping in touch with Mabel, George, and Ronald and visiting with us when we were on vacation. That pretty much sums up our Canadian clan.

A hallowed part of life, along with birth and being, are our perpetual graveyard monuments. Our Munro family cemetery holds long-lasting stones that tell of age from birth to death. All were Presbyterians, and their church (Kirk to the Scot's) was built in 1891. Baylis affiliation is found in *Register of Baptisms* for "Wm. J. Baylis & Alexandra his wife" and lists "Mabel V., Jean Dessa, Lucy Anna, Ella Pearl, George, Willa Christie Jane, and Ronald Kitchener." I've not found anything about my great grandfather, George Baylis' English past. In retrospect, I wonder if my grandfather, William James Baylis, or his sister, great aunt Lucy Ann Baylis, came by their names from great grandfather's English relatives. Maybe my mother, or aunts, given or middle names, Mabel Violet, Jean Dessa, Lucy Anna, Ella Pearl, or Willa Christie Jane were those of English kinfolk.

Neighbors in the *Register of Baptisms* are Ross and Isabella Woodman, Barbara and Jabez Bradbury and John and Isabella Davidson. *Nackawic Bend* writers Jean Burden and Shirley Scott noted that William Baylis, John Culliton, Thomas Trail, and W.J. Smullin were elected to the Kirk's board of managers in 1906.

The Baylis small front parlor, a very formal room, had a pump organ. I looked at the hymnal and recognized "When the Roll is Called Up Yonder" and "In the Sweet By and By." My friend George Cliff's father, Clarence, was known by his "Whatever suits will be grand" expression and winter-time mitten and sock knitting. He once took me to Baptist Sunday school in a horse and carriage. The Sabbath was kept free from labor among farmers. I can assert that Rossville was not a cursing community, but I never knew who was a church-goer and who wasn't. Hazel Ingraham, mother of ten, walked all the way to Lower Southampton from Rossville for Sunday school. Spiritual respect was exercised in baptism, marriage, and at death. Uncle George served as a pallbearer at many Rossville funerals.

CHAPTER FOUR
How It All Happened

Cross-border circumstance brought Americans north to Canada, later enticed Anglo and French Canadians south to New England, and, through family, gave me reason to go back and forth between Massachusetts and New Brunswick via Maine.

The War of Independence, called the "Glorious cause," or American Revolutionary War, lingered from 1775–1783. East Coast Americans loyal to the Crown were looked upon as sympathizers and not accepted by the liberated "Patriot" population of the thirteen colonies from South Carolina to Maine. Those aristocrats, farmers, and disbanded soldiers of British-American regiments who wished to pursue life under British rule, according to "Fear God and Honor the King," left from East Coast seaports as Loyalists to relocate in the closest British North American territories of Nova Scotia and New Brunswick. The latter was founded in 1784 as a separate colonial province with the provincial motto of Spem Reduxit, "Hope Restored." Present generations of Loyalists, listed in the United Empire Loyalists' Association of Canada directory, reside in the River Valley countryside.

In contrast to the Loyalist migration to eastern Canada after the War of Independence, my mother's generation joined the spirited 1920s Maritimes-to-the-States movement. There used to be a New England saying that "The best cooks and nurses come down from the Maritimes." *The Daily Gleaner* and *Woodstock Sentinel* obituary and community columns frequently named relatives who were living in New England. "Massachusetts is the smallest Province of Canada" was another common cross-border quotation.

After coming from a farm, attending a school of education in the city of Fredericton, and boarding-out to teach at one-room schoolhouses, Mother took notice of chums and kinfolk who had gone Stateside where jobs were more plentiful and the money was good.

American managers were known to hire people recommended by competent Canadian employees, and probably prompted Mother to cross the border and seek work.

The Great North Woods became an idyllic out-of-doors paradise for fishing, hunting, and camping. Those urban sportsmen, adventurous women, and families who owned a camp, could pack up and go according to season and quest. For those with clan connections like me, travel to and accommodations in northern Maine and the Maritime provinces was relaxed. Visits to the Baylis farm set the pace, and year-round open space activities at home provided encouragement. Because I was a young relative and only fished for trout with my Canadian friends in Rossville's little brooks, I didn't buy a provincial fishing license.

An annual event in the 1930s and '40s that brought the North Country south to Boston was The New England Sportsmen's Show. It brought city folks whatever of the out-of-doors that Maine and the Maritimes had to offer. Dad dutifully did his best to get me there. The old, 1881 Mechanics Hall Building on Huntington Avenue was the site of the show until it was razed in 1959 for the present Prudential Center. The various exhibits and events were more exciting to me than was the circus. Sporting outfitters had replicas of camp porches dotting the hall with taxidermy, photos, brochures, sign-up trip sheets, and tales of trophy fish and game.

A large waist-deep pool was centered in the hall. Birling (log rolling) was a pool contest in which, a lumberjack on each end of a free-floating log, used fast footwork and frisky movement to spin the log in an effort to dupe and dunk the other guy. In the two-canoe sparring event, each had a paddler and a standing jouster. The latter held a long pole with a padded end to prod, push, and knock an opponent into the tank. Wood-chopping competitions sent chips flying all over the stage.

Ted Williams Hall of Fame Red Sox hitter and boxer Jack Sharkey demonstrated fly casting in the pool. Among "The greatest" that fished with Ted were, prizefighter Sharkey, Bob Smith of "Howdy Doody" TV, fisherman Stu Apte, and bandleader Benny Goodman. Ted's "Greatest" were his children Bobby-Jo, John Henry, and Claudia, and down-home guides and their families on the Miramichi where Ted had a camp. Ted told a young fly fishing admirer at a show booth: "Practice, dammit, practice."

*1950s Boston Sportsmen's
Show poster & Ted Williams*

Arthur Sullivan, "Sports Afield" columnist for the *Boston Herald American* memorializing the passing of Orvis Company rod maker "Wes" Jordan in 1975, recalled a show incident that demonstrated how respected Wes was in international fishing circles. Ted Williams, Wes, and Charles Ritz of the famed hotel family, author of a fine fishing book, and rod designer, were at the show pool discussing rods that they were using and how the action could be made better or worse. "Both Williams and Ritz let Jordan have the last say for he certainly was a master rod-maker with bamboo."

In an April 1982 *Yankee Magazine*, Red Sox legend Ted Williams, while fishing, was quoted as saying: "And you have to know your limits…don't cast more than you can handle,"…he could handle a lengthy 80 feet! Ted promoted the conservation of his beloved Atlantic Salmon, and relished his times on New Brunswick's Miramichi and Cains rivers. Sports-writers often got Ted's goat, but he was at ease among most fishermen. While the statisticians recorded his feats on the field, Ted kept a log of his salmon, bonefish, and tarpon catch (most released I'll bet, though 1000 each…a Triple Crown!).

An article in *American Fly Fisher* has a 1985 photo of Ted and locals relaxing on the porch rail of the Veazie Salmon Club above Bangor. At a Boston Atlantic Salmon event, I literally and figuratively looked up to "The Greatest Hitter That Ever Lived," and our chat was about fishing in New Brunswick. Unbeknownst to each of us, we both excelled at the same game of going to Beans. Long-time employee, Carlene Griffin, quoted Ted as saying: "I've always liked Bean's. They've been great to me." His foot size differed from right to left (or was it from left to right?), and the boys at Beans had no problem in fitting him to shoes (or was it boots?).

Ralph "Bud" Leavitt, the "Outdoors" columnist for the *Bangor Daily News* from 1948 to 1994 and "Bud Leavitt Show" TV host, first met Ted, young like himself, when on assignment for the *Bangor Daily Commercial* at Fenway Park in 1939. Ted was tall, talented, and talkative. He taunted Bud calling him "Bush" as a Maine bush-leaguer, but really wanted to talk about fishing. That they did for decades, and Bud, big as life, became the state's most popular outdoors writer. Their magnet was Maine and New Brunswick; their friendship was fishing; their zeal was conservation. Viewers enjoyed their '80s and '90s series of Nissen Bakery commercials for TV. Undoubtedly their personal chats included some colorful cussin', but their angling philosophies were cast-out on lines from Sir Walter Scott.

> Along the silver streams of Tweed,
> Tis blithe the mimic fly to lead,
>
> When to the hook the salmon springs,
> And the line whistles through the rings,
>
> The boiling eddy see him try,
> Then dashing from the current high,
>
> Till watchful eye and cautious hand
> Have led his wasted strength to land.

Ted and his bantering buddy "Porky" Leavitt came over the lines to Doaktown and Ted's White Birch Lodge in Blackville on the Main S. W. Miramichi River for many years. It was a "'Til death do us part" relationship between the two, Bud passing in 1994 and Ted in 2002. At Leavitt's in Hampden, Maine, Ted loved Barbara's lemon pie. Bud's daughter tactfully said that Ted's presence could be boisterous. Ted often brought his son, John Henry, and daughter Claudia to New Brunswick as Claudia has written in her recently published *Ted Williams, My Father*. Dr. Martyn Vickers of Maine and the Cains River wrote, "My family is from New Brunswick and they are work-in-the-woods, very simple people and he always treated them with respect." Though baseball sports writers criticized Ted's attitude about interviews, and fans objected to his not tipping his hat to them, I respected his enthusiasm and expertise in fishing. His patriotism prevailed having served on active duty twice with the Marine Corps. Ted was dedicated to supporting the Jimmy Fund in Boston for children with cancer. The 13 year old anonymous "Jimmy," a 1948 patient of Dr. Sidney Farber, was Einar Gustafson, son of a potato farmer in the Aroostook town of New Sweden, Maine. Ted met him at a 1998 Red Sox-Yankee game when Einar threw out the first pitch. Ted said "This is the biggest thrill of my trip, right here."

The Sportsmen's Show booths fortified my fever for the wilderness with whatever fascinated me. Penobscot Indians from Old Town Island, in traditional dress, put native crafts up for sale. I treasured a decorated miniature ash longbow. The Paine Company sold little log cabins with tin chimneys to burn balsam incense for a whiff of the Maine Woods. The New Brunswick and Maine Departments of Natural Resource had booths with uniformed (and informed) game wardens to attract tourism. For entertainment, the province of New Brunswick brought Don Messer and his "Lumberjacks" musical group to the Show in 1936 and 1937. Jim Witherell, author of a book on L.L.Bean, said the company had a booth there, but I either missed it (doubtful) or it was prior to my time. Not much was left to the imagination, as I recall that vivid scene in Mechanics Hall.

Between the shows, outings, and stops at L.L.Bean in Freeport, Maine, sporting magazines like *Field and Stream* and *Out Door Life* were my favorite source of advice on "Where, when, and how-to," as well as adventurous stories of fact and fiction.

Even though I was American, Rossville friends never called me a Yankee (in the Maine sense, I guess I'm not!), and Canadian acquaintances never singled out my citizenship or suggested that I was from away. Crossing the border was uncomplicated and incidental. When my parents spoke of "Downeast," we were simply going to or coming back from coastal Maine and Atlantic Canada. The term's been around since 1825, when ships from Boston sailed downwind to those eastern ports. When they returned, against the wind, they were said to sail "Up to Boston." Though our land route through Portland, Bangor, Houlton, Woodstock, and Rossville is inland, we still considered it "Downeast."

CHAPTER FIVE

MY MAGNETIC NORTH

"**E**verything in life is somewhere else, and you get there in a car" wrote author E.B. White, who, by the way, is buried in Brooklin, Maine. In the days when a compass was the most common directional device, its magnetic north was also mine. I'll do my best to define the familiar landmarks along the route of our trips north.

The 400 mile journey from our home in Winchester, Massachusetts, took two days in the 1930s. Always anxious to get there, the long drive was a pleasure because we got to know so many places along the way. Upon reaching each, we knew that progress was in the making. Though Dad's two-seater 1931 yellow roadster had a rear fold-down, open-air "Rumble-seat" for two more, it was not practical for the distance or changes in weather conditions. He then bought a four-door dark-green 1929 Buick sedan that had wooden spoke wheels and a rear-mounted spare tire. The chassis was high off the ground requiring a long footstep on each side called a "Running board" to get in or out of the front or back seats.

Hilly Route 1 followed the coastline of Massachusetts, leveling off along New Hampshire coastal wetlands, to the old port city of Portsmouth. Dad paid a ten cent toll to cross a two lane Piscatiqua River bridge into Kittery, Maine. The present turnpike sign, "Welcome to Maine, The Way Life Should Be," says in words what we always felt. On the Pierce Island, Maine side of the Harbor, we could see the government-gray Portsmouth Naval Shipyard and the imposing, yellow concrete Portsmouth Naval Prison. They stood out in contrast to the vintage brick wharf structures and church spired building district on the hill across the harbor. The prison impressed me because I had seen lines of shackled sailors in Boston's North Station in transport to Portsmouth.

Passing through Cape Neddick, I remembered once visiting George "Pete" Hutchins' home. He was a Winchester classmate whose family came from York, Maine.

L.L.Bean Store, Main St., Freeport, Maine, c.1939

The Ogunquit Playhouse, white-with-green-trim, and hub-of-the-universe traffic on summer weekends were transient attractions on U.S. Route 1 as we headed farther north.

Three places in Portland seemed special to me. The name Baxter Boulevard suggested a privileged avenue of upscale homes. The B & M Baked Bean factory canned beans for our table and had a stack that never stopped puffing steam. The brick and stone U.S. Marine Hospital, built to care for merchant mariners and the Coast Guard, sat staunch on Martin's Point before the narrow Casco Bay tide-water bridge to Falmouth Foreside. "Foreside" was another captivating name, and after passing through Cumberland Foreside, I had a double dose of satisfaction. A rather annoying fact (at least to me) was the cement road surface in the area. Seams between concrete pours would cause the car tires to incessantly echo, "Bump-thump, Bump-Thump."

As we drove north on Route 1 along Main Street in Freeport, the L.L.Bean factory store was on the left over the post office. It was not uncommon in the fall to see deer or bear on the fenders or roofs of cars parked in front. How Dad happened to stop there in the first place I never knew, but to me, it was a store stocked with all the wonders of camping, fishing, and hunting. From my small boy perspective, the sales room was more like a shelved stockroom. It smelled of leather and held racks of clothes to be worn in the woods or at fishing grounds. I'm pretty sure Beans sold State of Maine fishing and hunting licenses. White signs on the tables and racks displayed product and price. I've learned since over the years that the sales people know all the details of what those signs represent. Everything in the store in the 1930s was wide open for the eyes to see.

I climbed the long, enclosed flight of Beans worn stairs when I was eight or maybe earlier. The shellacked stairwell walls were smooth and shiny. I'm certain that I recall the image of Mr. Bean sometimes standing at the showroom entrance! When I see smiling full-face pictures of him now, it's obvious that he had what's known in the dental trade as a "Diastema," a mid-line space between his upper two front teeth. Stacks in full view held the merchandise, and large tables served for display and transaction. Subsequently at the head of the stairs, portly Major Briggs, brother of Don in the fishing department, worked the night shift with a breast pocket chock full of pens and pencils. Open 24 hours every day except for a stretch during WWII up until 1951, it became my bragging rite to say that I had been to Beans! Each catalog was as good as reading an outdoor magazine, and one of my favorite books was the 1942 L. L. Bean authored *Hunting-Fishing and Camping.*

Our Pine Acres overnight cabin, Vassalboro, Maine, 1930s

Burma Shave and Bean-Hole Bean signs, along with every countrified poster imaginable, dotted our roadside route. Burma Shave
Cream advertising had rectangular signs spaced at intervals. One was
"A peach looks good"…"With lots of fuzz"…"But man's no peach"…
"And never 'wuz'"…"Burma Shave." Like coastal clambakes, bean-hole
baked beans are the famous food of farm and forest folk methodically
cooked underground in a covered cast iron pot or crock. Mother's
oven bean-pot was made of ceramic ware that was light brown on
the bottom two-thirds and dark brown on the top third and cover.
Her baked beans bubbled and were crowned with a piece of salt pork.
Sight and smell were the appetizers!

Travel scenes, halfway to Canada, were marked by Augusta's
copper-green State House dome and gold-sculptured crown, mountainous pulpwood piles beside Kennebec River pulp and paper mills,
and post-war barrack-like dorms on the Colby College first campus
in downtown Waterville. The citizens of Waterville gifted Colby 500
acres of land at Mayflower Hill for a new campus. As Dad did the
driving for the entire 400 mile trip, we stopped for an overnight at
Pine Acres' rustic, log cabins in Vassalboro, between Augusta and
Waterville. We always commented on fox farms, in the area, that had
distinctive shingled towers. Before Bangor, in Etna, I was awe-struck
by a religious spiritual encampment that my folks said were a group of
people who believed in ghosts.

While passing through the center of downtown Bangor, I always
remember the story that my parents told about the 1937 gun-battle
between federal agents and the notorious Al Brady Gang. The gang-
sters had committed robbery, murder, and escaped from an Indiana
jail. In the Bangor standoff, Brady and Shaffer were killed, and Dal-
hover captured, tried, and executed for Midwest murders. Brady's
unclaimed body was placed in an unmarked grave in Bangor's Mt.
Hope cemetery. Farm folks that I knew would refer to that gang as
"Bad pups."

Leaving the city at Eastern Maine General Hospital, we drove
upriver to Orono. At the University of Maine campus, on an island
between the Penobscot and Stillwater streams, I once saw carved ice
sculptures in front of mansion-type houses with odd (Greek) letters over each front entrance. My parents explained that the sculptures were probably a contest between fraternity houses. The word

fraternity describing mansion-like houses didn't mean much to me, but the ice sculptures froze in my memory.

In 1936, an impassable Penobscot River ice-jam flooded Old Town and the road to Lincoln. Dad had to detour back through Bangor and over to St. Stephen, New Brunswick, once guided by lanterns to cross a bridge covered with flowing water.

I have three memorable anecdotes from above Old Town. Approaching Lincoln, there was no question about a pulp mill's presence. As soon as the sulfite "Aroma" got inside the car, whether daylight or dark, it interrupted conversation. The smell can be described as a four letter word that rhymes with art. Next, we waved and honked our horn whenever we met a Massachusetts car in upper Penobscot or Aroostook Counties. Lastly, Dad asked a young boy tending a small store, somewhere on Route 2, what kind of pies they had. "Rawsberrie" was the singular, simple reply.

Past Mattawamkeag's (Matah-**WAHM**-keg's) rail junction, the Military Road forked off on 2A at Macwahoc (Mak-**QUAH**-hock). I took the name, "Military Road," at face value, but it was constructed as a troop and supply route in an 1839–1842 British (Canada) and American (Maine) border dispute. At Haynesville settlement, one small store with a gas pump serviced an almost uninhabited 40 mile stretch, called the "Haynesville Woods."

Potato houses, beside large growing fields, were built half in the ground for storage, and an indication that we were getting closer to Houlton. In grim economic times, we once saw a line of railroad cars loaded with spoiling potatoes, sitting idle, and going nowhere.

My Houlton county-seat, attractions after leaving forest and fields were the Aroostook County Jail (youthful fascination because of bars on the windows), the Northland Hotel where Uncle Frank Murphy stayed as a "Drummer or Sam Slick" (traveling salesman) in the '40s, and the Madigan Hospital, where Laurie's father, Dr. Laurence J. Louis from Boston, came up to do surgery on friend Dr. Joseph A. Donovan's wife. Laurie and I called on Dr. Donovan (Houlton born, Bates College, Harvard Medical School 1912) in the late 1950's and remember him smoking a cigar while conversing with us on Market Square. At the border, Houlton's general aviation airport was an Army Air Base and a prisoner of war compound during WWII.

Before entering Canada, a stop at U.S. Customs was not required.

U.S. Customs & Immigration Station, Houlton, Maine, 1950s

Canadian Customs, Woodstock, New Brunswick, 1930s

The Woodstock Canadian border personnel were courteous, and we had no problem bringing gifts and goods to family. When returning to the U.S., we passed Canadian Customs and drove in under a portico at the white U.S. border station in Houlton. Checking in, we often renewed acquaintance with Mr. Glidden, a border officer that we got to know over many years.

After crossing to Woodstock on the St. John River, I was relieved to finally be about 30 miles from Rossville. Passing the Indian reservation on Old River Road, it was common to see someone pounding water-soaked black ash small poles and saplings to make the growth rings come apart for splits that were shaved and made into baskets. Indians along the border sold potato-picking baskets to New Brunswick and Maine farmers for many years. The dozen small gray cedar shingled houses were humble, and I wondered what hardships caused them to be different from most of the homes in Woodstock. I figured that they were not the same tribe as the Old Town Penobscots who came to the Boston Sportsmen's Show.

Driving downriver, we passed Valley farms, fields, and forest. White steeple churches and roadside graveyards marked settlements along the Meductic, Temple, and Ritchie route. Pokiok (POE-kee-ock) was an important landmark, because it was where we crossed the 1907 steel three section long arched Hawkshaw Bridge that would bring us within eight miles of Rossville. The 1906 cost estimate was

Pokiok Bridge, St. John River, Lower Southampton, N.B.

Pokiok Falls, 1940

$60,000-$70,000, and the big blocks of granite for the three piers was quarried at Pokiok.

Pokiok Falls was the most prominent sightseer attraction on the 63 miles between Woodstock and Fredericton. For over 50 years, it was featured in most tourist brochures. The Pokiok Lodge overnight cabins and dining room were beside the highway bridge where travelers and local folks stopped to view the 20 foot-wide gorge. It had sheer 75 foot dark red granite walls and a series of tumbling, frothy waterfalls. At one time, a series of wooden stairs went down to the river. I went there with friends on many summer Sundays and had a candy bar or ice cream cone at a snack bar that my friends called a "Canteen." Legend has it that an Indian maiden leaped across the chasm to escape captors. In another fable, a stranger on horseback in a rainstorm, crossed the washed out bridge unknowingly on its few remaining two narrow timbers in total darkness.

The Southampton side of the Pokiok bridge road snaked up the hill past my mother's Aunt Hughena and Uncle Charlie Allen's farm. At last! We were on the Lower Southampton road and in home territory as we passed Berley MacDonald's store, Flewelling Funeral Home, Fraser Flewelling's garage and gas pumps across the street, the small Otis rail-bed terminus and station, and the telephone office with the sloping roof and front porch. After a church and graveyard further along the flat, there was a water tower that serviced the steam trains. In 1948, the new white wooden Southampton Regional High School stood out along the road. After it burned in 1952, the red brick high school replaced it until demolished prior to the 1967 flooding (now 15 feet under the cove water).

The white-spired United Church was just before Mother's uncle Dave, and son Austin, Munro's farm that sat up in the fields to the left. Way back, I remember Uncle Dave as bent over but spry ('cause when I get tired and a bit bent over, I think of him). Austin followed suit in his own mild way. At first, that Lot 34 of 700 acres was granted to Captain John Mackay of the Loyalist Queen's Rangers in 1786, then it came down to his widowed sister Catherine Munro of Creich parish, Scotland, and through her, to my great great-grandfather George Munro. My great grandfather, John, built that farm in 1868, and the fields across the road sloped down to the Munro cemetery at riverside. It was there that I recall my grandmother Baylis' wintry March burial in 1941. Getting closer to the Baylis farm, I knew that behind "Munro Ridge" (my label) was Trout Brook and Rossville Road.

Next along the way, was the home of Donald, Mary, John, and Andrew Cronkhite at the top of Culliton Hill that led down to the Culliton schoolhouse and covered bridge corner. Donnie was always in the lumbering and sawmill business. The graveled road to the left led to Rossville, Campbell Settlement, and Temperance Vale. When we crossed over Trout Brook culvert and drove up Woodman Hill, the back side of Munro Ridge came into view with dark green patches of uncut timber. Beneath it, we saw our beloved Baylis farm. Within minutes, we were greeted by Grammie, Mabel, George, Ronald, and cousin Ella Stairs with open arms and kisses. They helped us unload gear and gifts, and Dad parked the Buick on the side of the house near the outbuildings and barnyard.

CHAPTER SIX

THE BAYLIS FARM

Baylis farm, Rossville Road

And this life is just that from beginning to end:
It's a camp, and a hike, and a camp.
It is greeting a stranger, farewell to a friend,
Ev'ry morning new timber to tramp.

For we can not remain and we can not return,
We must follow old Time in his track;
But the campfires of old in our memory burn—
And we stop and we take a look back.

Tote-Road and Trail, Douglas Malloch

Looking back at my farm visits in the 1930s, I will never forget kerosene lamps for night light, water carried in pails from a spring or wellhouse, split wood to fuel stoves, haying with horses, and firm friendships renewed.

The landscape was as meaningful to me as seeing the house and barns. Three stately elms bordered Rossville Road, and century-old zig-zag cedar-pole fencing enclosed some boundaries and the pasture

67

Ella Stairs, Baylis farm, Henderson farm in background,c.1927

land within. Hay and grain fields across the road crested at the horizon and became "Back fields" with woods sloping down to the Nackawic Stream. Familiar neighboring farms framed that image of what I regarded as a part of me.

Next farm up, on the same side of Rossvile Road, was the Ingraham farm where I spent a lot of time with the boys and the family. I really didn't know anything about the property (lot eight) except that older maps labeled it as belonging to Alfred Thornton, and a Baylis deed referred to it as later owned by Jabez Bradbury. It was above the John Henderson farm of 100 acres (lot seven) that my grandfather Baylis bought from him in 1911 and 1926. Hazel Henderson Ingraham and her brothers, John and Myles, were brought up there. I remember the old Henderson house as quiet and empty except for a flail surrounded by dry bean pods on a downstairs floor. If I had to describe the smell, it was not stagnant, but storied. In an upstairs room, there were two spinning wheels said to belong to Annie Munro Baylis, my great grandmother. The one that I was given is called the

"High, Great, Walking," or "Wool" wheel. It's labeled as made in Spofford, New Hampshire, by the Frederick B. Pierce Co. (between 1868 and 1882). One leg is not factory turned, but whittled and functional. I hesitate to replace it.

Coming back to the appearance of the Baylis farmhouse, I thought it looked more like homes seen in town. When they said that neighbor Ross Woodman was the builder, I thought of Ross' snow-white hair, meticulous dress, courteous manner, and how they matched the careful construction. I don't know when it was built to replace the first

George, Lucy, & Ronald Baylis beside touring car, 1928

Uncle George & Dad, Studebaker Champion, c.1950

home that burned, but I speculate somewhere around 1906. The neat barns had gray-weathered spruce siding and white cedar shingled roofs. The outbuildings were shingled from top to bottom. The farm sat solid, and was in good working order.

Turning into the circular drive, we saw the mail box where our letters arrived, and Mabel's were picked up for posting to Winchester. At that entrance, a Harvey Creamery Co-op truck regularly picked up my uncles' cream in two and a half foot galvanized cans with covers. Apple trees and a gray shingled one car garage with red trim were beside the drive. I have a picture of George, Mother, and Ronald standing there in front of a, perhaps 1928, new touring car. I read that only 14 cars were registered in the province in 1905. The "G`radge" (as in badge) had a plank floor and early New Brunswick number plates nailed to the inside walls. Back then, the license plate motto was "Picture Province." Uncle George had a 1949 Studebaker Champion, but I can't recall the make of car that Ronald drove.

The farmhouse had two right-angle gables with a chimney on each ridge. Window and gable trim were painted white, and sidewalls were gray clapboard. In a picture, I note that the front gable has a window at the peak. That mystifies me, because an attic would have been a wonderful place for me to explore! A roofed front porch faced the road and extended across the entire house to include a section that we referred to as a veranda. Dad screened that in for a sitting area. When on vacation, he was happiest when occupied with painting or fixing anything that needed repair.

In country fashion, the grass in front was tended with a push lawnmower but not trimmed. In preparation for winter, my uncles banked the foundation with fir boughs or pit gravel shoveled into plank troughs for insulation.

Mabel or Grammie planted pretty nasturtiums beside the steps. A big barrel under a porch valley collected soft rainwater to wash clothing. When we walked in the front kitchen door, all images and smells that we retained since the previous visit became welcome realities. Grammie, when older and feeble, might be sitting quietly in the rocking chair but always managed a smile and a "Hello Charles." Rossville Road neighbor, Pearl Cliff (who had ten children), sometimes came in to help with Grammie's care.

The black-and-chrome kitchen woodstove provided heat, cooked

Baylis farmhouse

Kitchen woodstove

food, heated irons to press clothing, and kept warm water for washing or bathing in its copper reservoir. I can't recall the brand, but it was the mainstay of the room. Aunt Mabel baked "Soldier" beans in the wood stove. Slices of oven baked brown bread were a treat in smell, sight, and taste. I loved molasses whether dribbled on bread, cooked with beans, or in cookies. I found this quote, maybe from Mrs. Beavan, about the kitchen stove: "Bore on its polished surface shining evidence of the housewife's care."

In wet or wintry weather, damp and cold outer clothing, woolen socks, and mittens were hung to drip and dry behind the stove on hooks over the wood box. Dad made a creative wire bread-toaster to use over the open stove-lid. My constant chore was keeping the wood box full. It had a clean hardwood smell. Smaller splits of scented cedar were used for kindling. At first, the Sad (meaning heavy) laundry-press irons and handles were solid cast metal. Later they had a removable wooden handle to change to an alternate hot iron on the stove-top.

I recall a teapot boiling on the stove at all meals. Baylis' favorite teas were Red Rose or King Cole. Mabel's chopper for frying boiled potato leftovers at breakfast was a small hand sized round tin can with a sharp top edge.

One of their kitchen devices, most practical in summer, was the long handled wire mesh fly swatter. Chase and swat were ongoing. Less arduous solutions were yellow gooey ribbons of flypaper that hung from the ceiling. Contact with our hair was to be avoided! When hung in the milk-shed, there soon were more trapped flies visible than sticky paper. A swatter of sorts for parlor or bedroom was the larger wire rug-beater. Another beater was the long wooden spoon that mothers used for cooking and on unruly boys and girls.

They didn't need a kitchen wastebasket, because they didn't waste anything! Worn fabrics became salvage material. Whatever didn't burn went to the dump down in back.

Prior to an electric water pump, two galvanized pails of cool clear water sat beside the soapstone drain-sink. We drank from a metal dipper with a long handle. Next to the kitchen sink on the inside of the back porch door, an endless cotton towel hung from a rotating one-inch dowel. The towel always smelled fresh and was changed frequently.

The kitchen cot, or couch, had a single-spring mattress covered with a wool blanket. After a hard day's work, my uncles could lounge or have a nap on it. We boys sat there when waiting for supper or while just plain socializing. Clothing on hooks above the cot pleasingly gave off their odors of labor and comfort. Beside the cot and a few steps up, a door opened to stairs leading up to Mabel's room.

A three inch jew's-harp (mouth harp, jaw harp) hung on the adjoining kitchen shelf. I tried to play the lyre shaped metal instrument by holding it between my left thumb and forefinger, placing the metal bars between my front teeth, and plucking the flexible metal reed with my right thumb. While breathing in and out for resonation, I could only produce a hum-drum twang!

In periods of silence throughout the day and night, there was always a rhythmic presence of the ticking clock on the wall. I believe that its wind-up piece was the only key in the house.

The Rexall calendar from Ross Drug in Fredericton hung on the wall. Each month had a drugstore theme. The January 1950 page showed a pigtailed little girl in a frocked dress shyly showing the pharmacist the arm that had broken off a doll that she was cradling. Except for the Sabbath dates in faded red, work days were in bold black print that could be read from across the room. Fine print was everywhere else. Each day had predicted weather, sun and moon rise and sets, and gendered star positions. On the back of each month's page, there was a health product ad such as toothpaste or baby products, and a chart for keeping records of milk and egg production, household and farm expenses, and farm receipts. The last leaf was full length blue with printed Astronomical Data, The Zodiac, First Aid, Weather Indicators, and a coupon for next year's calendar. The back had Annual Inventory of Your Assets, Simple Disorders and How to Relieve the Accompanying Discomfort, Breeding Table with Average Gestation for Farm Animals, Minimum Weights of Produce, Weights and Measures, and Rates of Postage. We were often at the farm in haying season and could celebrate my birthday on July 27th.

Before the area code 506 was established in 1955, the Baylis crank telephone number, 94 ring 4, remained in my mind. A rectangular oak box was wall mounted with an angled bottom shelf below a projecting black speaker piece. At the top, a magnetic clapper whacked two round ringer bells. The centered speaker cone stuck out like a daffodil

*Crank telephone,
cream separator,
tumble churn*

in bloom. On the left side, the handheld ear-piece, hung on a u-shaped lever when not in use. On the right side, what looked like the handle on a fishing reel was cranked to "Get on the line" and connect with the telephone office. Connecting with the operator at Otis also meant that the conversation would be open to whoever wished to listen in on the party line. Myrtle Davidson Grant told me that the Davidson telephone number was 94 ring 11.

After my uncles milked their Jersey cattle, raw milk was pail-poured into a large metal bowl on top of the red separator that sat beside the kitchen stove. When hand cranked, a mechanism separated cream and skim milk that were each funneled into separate metal bowls. Skim milk was used to feed the calves, pigs, and barn-cats. If not used for cooking or for sale, the cream was allowed to sour a bit before churning it into butter. Butter had a market value in that it could be traded for goods at the Culliton general store. On a grand scale, butter was an important provincial export product.

A wooden barrel butter-churn mounted on a metal frame sat on the side porch in summer. A hand operated rocker or foot treadle made it tumble to churn. The top was secured by a metal clamp and had a small glass port to check the process. In an oblong wooden trencher bowl on the kitchen table after churning, a paddle was used to press buttermilk out and work salt in. The bowl tipped easily to drain off the buttermilk. Dad duplicated a broken wooden butter paddle for Mabel. Finished butter was pressed into pounds and wrapped in special paper for home use or sale at the store.

The long farm table and chairs were beside the window that faced the road. An adjacent cupboard with button-latch doors for dishes and bowls had a wooden lift-top counter below it to access a flour barrel and yeast.

White or brown bread, and bun dough, kneaded on the breadboard, raised and slowly came to life as a loaf when covered with a white dish towel. After baking, they smelled and tasted so good. Fresh bread seemed best when it was dribbled with molasses.

Their divided wooden tray for knives, forks, and spoons had an upright handle. Dad repainted it black and decorated it with white and red stripes. It's still in our family,

Kerosene lamps cast a soft glow in the evening. Above the glass base which held the fuel, a brass burner collar lifted or lowered the tightly woven wick to adjust light intensity. Vertical prongs or a fancy ring supported the flared clear glass chimney. If adjusted too high, the chimney glass got smoky and smelled of kerosene. Reading beside a kerosene lamp was not easy, and the traditional position for school work was hunched over and up close. At night, we carried them over the stairs to the bedrooms.

A kitchen door opened into the dining room and front hall. When the dining room table was not being used for Grammie and Mabel's quilting frame, a cut glass condiment-set in a silver holder sat on the lace tablecloth. There was a fancy breakfront (buffet) with an upright mirror and drawers, and decorative glass and porcelain pieces that sat on a lace runner. Once when sleep-walking, I woke up under that table.

I've shown the picture, of Grampy and Grammie handsomely dressed. It hung in a beautiful oval frame (also reproduced in *Nackawic Bend*). With a bouffant coiffure, she is wearing a crinkled black crepe dress with white buttons and laced high collar. He's dressed in a suit, vest, shirt, and tie. I would guess that it might be a wedding portrait. I detect a sense of humor in my grandfather's eyes and facial expression. There was a low dining room wall cubbyhole where a bearskin robe and large, cuffed black driving gloves were kept from the days of horse and sleigh rides.

George slept in an adjoining bedroom next to the pantry. A round pantry tin held Aunt Mabel's memorable and enormous molasses cookies. Cousin Joyce Jones said it well: "The pantry was always filled with good cooking." Joyce remembers the home's "Nice dark hardwood floors." There was a wood burning heater to warm up the downstairs hall and parlor. It was black, round, and chrome trimmed, and the fancy finial was a lot taller than me.

I played with the stops on the parlor pump organ or looked through an old stereoscope at exotic palace scenes from India. From the time that it was in fashion when Mother was in her twenties, her Edison phonograph player in a mahogany veneer cabinet sat on the upstairs hall varnished floor. Recordings on the grooved surface of hollow hard celluloid cylinders were slid on a metal tube that rotated when cranked, and a worm-gear stylus (needle) engaged the grooves to reproduced sound. I listened to catchy, scratchy music and vocals, and made me feel as if I was living in a magical past. Pearl and Cora Ingraham from the next farm played it when they came down to visit Mabel on Saturdays. That cylinder type of player was replaced by flat, round, what we call "records" played on a turntable with a floating stylus. The common name for any hand-cranked phonograph was "Victrola."

I slept in the front bedroom brass bed, enveloped in a supple goose down coverlet that we called a feather tick. I remember my Cousin Ella's tiny porcelain tea set in that room. My folks had a back bedroom. After electricity was installed, hanging ceiling lights turned on and off with pull-strings conveniently connected to headboards. Mabel's room and a small room with a tin bathtub were over the kitchen. Pails of warm bath water were carried over the stairs and poured into the tub which had a round and very slippery bottom. In bedrooms, a wash-stand might be oak or walnut. On or under each cabinet there was a tall pitcher for water, a matching round ceramic basin, and a chamber pot, which was the only indoor toilet facility.

Whether coming in from hanging clothes or going out to the barnyard, the back door between the kitchen and porch was used more than the front. The connecting side porch had an oblong copper tub on a wood stand used for large washes. The woodshed, filled to the top before winter, was close by and convenient for fetching firewood. The purpose of a woodshed was to season the split sticks by keeping them dry and frost free.

A garden, with fresh vegetables for the table, was between the woodshed and side boundary. Two verses of the "Garden Song" composed and sung by Maine's David Mallett come to mind:

Inch by inch, row by row,
Someone bless these seeds I sow,
Someone warm them from below,
'Till the rain comes tumblin' down.

Plant your rows straight and long,
Temper them with prayer and song,
Mother Earth will make you strong
If you give her loving care.

I can't forget the summer servings of fresh peas or carrots in cream with boiled new potatoes, meat, and fresh buttered buns. Summer garden bouquets were rows of white potato blossoms. Mustard pickles and the like were preserved for the winter. A back porch door led down to a small cellar with stone walls without mortar and a dirt floor where potatoes, turnips, carrots, and apples were kept cool. A barrel of brine (concentrated salt water) preserved pork.

There was always a broom, the simple symbol of cleanliness, at the back porch to sweep barn scraps or snow off boots or shoes. The long cable clothesline went out from the porch corner to a high pulley on a pole. Washes flew from it, frozen stiff in winter. In a field behind the porch and clothesline pole, a cedar- pole, snake-fence separated the pasture and tiny spring-house on the edge of the alder growth and woods.

We have a back porch photo of Ella's friends, Irma and Alice Stairs, posing on a ladder. Daughters of Ralph and Mildred Davidson Stairs, they lived halfway down Woodman Hill next-door where William and Marie Davidson later brought up their children, Aubrey, Alleen (Love), and Dena (Wortman). I wonder if Ross Woodman may have built that house, because it was a duplicate of the Baylis home except it had no side porch, and did have a two story addition with a gable window.

Between the Baylis house and outbuildings, was a growing wood-pile destined for the winter woodshed, a chopping block, and a grindstone wheel. The two foot diameter grindstone, with a centered axel, was vertically mounted on a wood frame at about chair-seat level. Sometimes in summer, I'd crank it and pour water on the grindstone while George sharpened his mower cutter-bar blades and logging tools. He told me that anyone who could whittle a good ax-helve (handle) of White Ash or Rock Maple was highly regarded.

The first outbuilding was a cedar-shingled workshop and pig pen with a bump-out privy in the back. The sliding workplace door hung on an overhead trolley-bar. On the workbench were George's tools and a wooden box for hay wire and old nails, straightened and saved, to repair anything that needed fixing. "Fix it up, wear it out, make do, or do without" was the mindset of Rossville farm-folk.

A small screened window in the privy could be opened in summer for ventilation. With two satin smooth adult and one child size butternut wood cutouts, we could comfortably review Canadian history on a big Confederation Life calendar or flip through the pages of an Eaton catalog. "Going outside" meant just that! A few excerpts from James Whitcomb Riley's "Passing of the Back-House" confirm the feeling.

When memory keeps me company and moves to smiles or tears,
A weather-beaten object looms through the mist of years.

That dear old country landmark; I've tramped around a bit.
And in the lap of luxury my lot has been to sit.

A very large round metal cauldron with a conical top and an overhead brick chimney sat in the middle of the workshop. It was used when a pig was slaughtered to remove the hair. A visit to the shop meant a visit with the pigs even when not filling their feed trough. A huge sow with her piglets was quite a sight and sound when she grunted and they squealed anticipating mash feed or skim milk.

Me on pony, 1929 Buick, Baylis outbuildings, 1939

Harold Davidson on Mike Cronkhite's pony

Lucy & Charlie McGowan, Rossville, 1950

I have pictures taken in front of that shed in the summer of 1939. The black and white pony was loaned by Uncle Ronald's friend, Mike Cronkhite. Behind me is Dad's Buick and a hand-trip, single-horse hay rake. Harold Davidson, came up to ride on the pony. Another picture shows Cousin Ella and me holding the pony's reins while seated in a two-wheel, rubber-tire pony cart.

The small building next to the workshop was a shingled granary. As I remember it, it didn't have a window, but maybe had one in back. It's a background to a 1950 photo of Dad and our dog Penney. The wooden bins were dry, clean, and contained oats and grain. Dry mash-feed was stored in cloth bags. Next, inside the gated barnyard, was a small well-house with a hand-pump. A full bucket of water was kept there to "Prime" the pump if there was not enough suction to lift the water to the surface. If there was too much barnyard runoff from rain or melting snow, spring water was carried for house use.

The granary, well-house, two gates, and two barns enclosed the circular barnyard. The horse and cow barns were gabled and attached at right angles. They sheltered wagons, straw, hay, feed, horses, harness, and milk cattle. Centered on the broad side of each barn, were a pair of large hinged doors that allowed a high wagonload of hay to enter the barn floor passageway. There was little or no storage space below the dry stone foundations. The roofs were cedar shingles, and the vertical plank barn-board siding was unpainted and weathered gray. Dust, chaff, and spider webs screened the few windows. The barn frames, built by or for my great grandfather Baylis, had hand hewn, honey-brown beams and rafters. The bracing beams were secured with hardwood pegs pounded into matched auger-bit holes. In Grandfather and Uncle's time, sliding doors on tracks and rollers were added to the horse-stall and cow-barn entry ways. A dusty old sleigh, with the front kicked in by a frisky horse, was stowed in the back of one barn.

Hay was pitched down from mows, high on either side of the barn floor, and forked through leather hinged wood flaps in front of each stall to feed the horses. Each horse eagerly gobbled its measured share of oats and drank from a pail of water that George carried into the stall. There was a box of tools to repair harness behind one stall, as was a long handle, four-tined stall fork to clean out the manure. Heavy sets of leather harness were hung on high wooden pegs behind the stalls. The team stood patiently as George lifted, draped, and strapped each harness in place. When led by their halters into the barnyard, they seemed happy to get outdoors for work.

A small section of the cow barn had stalls where the cows were tied, bed-down in straw, fed, and milked. That barn had a pair of doors on each end granting through-and-through wagon passage either way. The wide doors opposite the barnyard, faced Rossville Road, and were convenient for hay-wagon or threshing machine access.

I liked a horse barn's smell of beams, old wood stalls, the team, oats, hay, and harness or the cow barn odor of cattle, straw, and manure. Milking stools had round seats and short legs, to position my uncles' forearms level with a cow's teats. The rhythmic streams of milk rang clear as each hit the metal bottom of the empty pail. The tone went down as the milk level got higher.

There were few machine-made latches on outbuildings. Other than forged hooks and hasps, the most common object to keep a door closed was a wooden button latch. It's a flat and rectangular block of wood positioned on a door-jam opposite the hinges. A hole in the center for a nail, allows it to spin. Those on cabinets in the house, rotate on a small screw. A simple vertical twist allows the closed door to open, and when placed horizontal, holds it shut. Whenever coarse barn-board, usually spruce, of any size was subjected to frequent friction, the fine yellow sheen of bare fir caught the eye and felt silky smooth. That makes me think of the waxen barn floor planks beneath the mows. They were shiny from the shuffle of boots, the constant sweep of hay being moved around, and the press of the hoof and wagon wheel.

A hen pen was attached to the cow barn. Inside, it smelled of feed and nest straw. Sometimes, when I went in to fetch eggs, the hens were reluctant to move over. The sight and feeling of warm, fresh eggs made the chore quite pleasant. I often wondered if an egg in the basket might have a double yolk. That wonderment carried over to patches of clover in the grass outside. Might I find one with four leafs?

There was an extraordinary fear of fire in tinder-dry barns. The original Baylis farmhouse loss, c.1905, and fire destruction in general, called for strict rules for cigarette, match, and lantern use. The reason for keeping a ladder on the roof of a home was to get at a chimney fire quickly. Lightning strikes occasionally claimed structures, but few had lightning rods to divert the bolt from the storm clouds into the ground.

> Now crash like a sound like I never have heard,
> Like a cannon from Uncle John's war.
> My father and brother, they head for the stairway,
> And I shudder and head for the door.
>
> And there's fire, fire, out in the barn, Father,
> Fire in the chicken house, too.
> And the flames run so high they are scorchin' the sky.
> And there's not a damn thing we can do.
>
> Verses from "Fire" by David Mallett

Getting back to landscape around the Baylis farm, alder-tree thickets prevailed along Trout Brook, and in field and forest wetlands behind the house. Bushy "weed trees" of no commercial value, they protected wildlife, prevented erosion, and supplied boys with sling shots, whistles, and fishing rods. The book, *Temperance Vale*, quoted: "When alder leaves were the size of a squirrel's ear, it was supposed to be time to fish." Along the alders in the pasture behind the Baylis house, old tin cans and medicine bottles, oil and axel-grease containers, broken cookware, and rusty farm implement fragments were dumped in out-of-sight piles. I wish I could paw through one now for glass, pottery, and iron relics.

Nearby, the weathered springhouse covered a hogshead barrel sunk into a clear, bubbling, cold spring-hole. When I was very young, some kind soul put a big trout in the spring for me to catch. In turn, trout fishing caught me. When the spring-house door was left open, and an old sow pig fell in, there was hell to pay as to who did it. The Ingraham boys and I were prime suspects!

CHAPTER SEVEN
AMUSEMENT A'PLENTY

"With many a quiet touch of wit, the natives possess a great original fund." A natural knack for lightheartedness among the inhabitants of the backwoods of New Brunswick was observed by English-born author, Mrs. F. Beavan, who lived among them as early as 1845.

I never sensed lack of sparkle or signs of boredom among families along Rossville Road. When it came to entertainment, they supplied their own or sought it out. Residents relished the humor of the hamlet as when one farmer, in keeping with the necessary frugality of the times, bragged of buying a window display suit in Fredericton for a good price. Neighbors were quick to notice that the "Giveaway" was faded in the front!

Elderly Mary Woodman was a meticulous housekeeper for her bachelor brothers, Ross and Johnny. She put paper down on the kitchen couch so that they would not soil the cover fabric. Mary spoke precisely. When talking about news of the times, I heard her pronounce "**CHE**Micals [as in _ch_urch]." After she died, Rossy did the cooking and housework, and Johnny did the chores and tended the garden. Both got in the crop and did the haying. The aging brothers maintained their farm as best they could. Rossville folks joked about Ross and John's horse standing in its stall with hind legs higher than front due to an accumulated pile of manure.

While on the subject of John "Johnny" Woodman, I'll pull ashore from mainstream humor and tell about his pleasure as a river-man on the upper St. John river-steamer, "Aberdeen." At age 88 in July 1967, the _Saint John Telegraph-Journal_ published an interview titled "The Riverboat Era: A Trip into its Colorful Past" relating John's years on the 165 foot shallow draft, sternwheeler from 1894 to 1906. As a fire-man or freight agent, he made three trips weekly between Fredericton and Woodstock. "One spot that gave more than a little trouble was the swift water at Shogomoc [Meductic Rapids]." His father, Ross Sr., and other farmers along the river owned shares in the company. In that 13 hour run, 18 stops were made. One was the steamboat landing at Lower Southampton across from the Grosvenor store that sold "Groceries, Provisions, Dry Goods, Boots, Shoes, Hats, Caps, Clothing, and Country Produce."

The "Aberdeen" deckhands earned a dollar a day with meals and living quarters aboard for their rugged work; "The captain didn't want to lose any time." From Fredericton, the boat carried both passengers and freight, such as farm implements, manufactured supplies, and barrels of flour and molasses. The downriver passenger run brought local farm food, grains, hides and leather, and animals to market. A drum of molasses cost 25 cents for freight. John Woodman remembered that the "Aberdeen" once carried 50 molasses hogsheads out of Fredericton. Passengers were served meals in a space on board. He told another tale about stopping ashore to help extinguish a house fire. When the steamer remained overnight in Woodstock, Saturday moonlight excursions to Meductic and back were very popular. Johnny was an "Aberdeen" deck hand on its final Woodstock riverrun in 1906. The freight and passenger river service gave way to the advent of the railroad.

Now that Johnny's "Aberdeen" tales have been told, I'll push offshore out into the comedy current again. There's a joke (not to the participants) about a local lady who was waiting for the mail driver to pass by and pick her up out on Rossville Road. He took folks to town and did errands for others while there. The woman's husband didn't want her to go and tackled her to the snow-bank until the driver went by.

Rossville was dubbed "Dog Street" for some bygone reason and set the tone for comical comments. Some of my treasured, old blackand-white photos are labeled "Hunting on Dog Street" wherein the Ingraham boys and I are postured (so obvious!) holding and aiming a rifle (at nothing) in the middle of an open field. I have a confession to make, but forget it as soon as you've read it. Though Rossville is crucial to my tales, I honestly don't think that I ever heard "Rossville" spoken locally, but names like "Dog Street," "Cullerton," and "The Vale," were commonplace.

A favorite pastime was looking out the Baylis kitchen window to determine whose car was going up or down the road (seldom saw two in a row). Folks told of an old timer who spotted a motorcycle speeding on a country road. He described the rare episode as "The devil with smoke coming out his arse!" When high snow banks blocked a clear view of the road, the only car sightings from the house were through narrow shoveled drive-entrances. Rubbernecking had to wait until snow melt.

Roy St. Peter, who lost a leg in WWI, frequently traveled between home on upper Rossville Road and the Royal Canadian Legion Hall in Culliton. His Model A Ford, negotiated both roadway and culvert. Roy had a ruddy complexion, ready smile, and I recall that he was usually outfitted in an engineer's cap and wore suspenders. He rolled his own cigarettes by cupping the paper lengthwise under his index finger and filling the crease with loose tobacco (or spilling some of it on his shirt or lap). With a finger twist and a lick of his tongue to seal one end, it was ready to smoke, and smoke he did! While cigarettes were mostly hand rolled, store-bought "Sweet Caporal" or "Players" were saved for Saturday night or work-free Sunday. Matches were the wooden stick kind. I learned to ignite them with a single friction swipe on the seat of my britches. It meant raising one leg slightly with knee bent to get rid of any slack in the seat fabric before the swipe.

Hazel Ingraham's bachelor brother Myles Henderson often visited on his "Wheel" (bicycle). One Sunday, my uncles repeatedly prompted him to pump-up a patched tire tube "One more time," until the tube exploded leaving poor Myles "fit to be tied."

Dad, as a practical joker, would bring harmless explosive smoke bombs for uncles Ronald and George to secretly wire on a visiting friend's engine. Upon hitting the starter, a bang with smoke pouring out from under the hood brought the terrified driver out on the run to the delight of the pranksters.

Neighboring farmer Vern Grass, would hire out his "Thrashing" machine in late summer, bringing it to the Baylis barn door to separate oats and straw. Being quite short, Vern's nose was barely over the flapping drive belt, and his voice was as high pitched as the engine whine. Vern would say "His'n," "Her'n," or "Your'n." When Vern brought his wife's specimen to a doctor in Woodstock, a nurse amazed at the quantity in a jug, asked if it was urine. Vern's reply was "No, It's her'n!" Myrtle Davidson Grant said that Vern was a welcome sight, because new straw meant fresh bedding for the livestock and fresh straw stuffing for their mattress covers. She also said that goose down pillow stuffing was changed spring and fall.

I'm told that old timers held social gatherings in their homes called "Sings" or "Sing-alongs." When a farmer had a barn-raising with neighbors help, the host and wife would hold a social gathering, called a "Frolic," with supper for the work-party.

When the Fredericton *Daily Gleaner* newspaper was delivered by mail, we focused on happenings in and around Southampton. The *Gleaner* had it all: Who visited whom, who travelled where for a day or longer, were crops poor or plentiful, who participated in pageants, who was sick or recovering, as well as recent births, marriages, or deaths. Hostility overseas and war effort stories made frequent news in the 1940s.

With one kitchen radio in 1939, we faithfully listened to *Don Messer and His Islander's* program on CFCY, Charlottetown, PEI. Their sprightly opening "Barndance" tune was a mix of "Fireman's Reel, Lamplighter's Hornpipe, and Soldier's Joy."

Don was born near Harvey Station, New Brunswick. He crossed the border at 16 to stay at his Aunt Mary's boarding house and find work in Boston. He got a job at Woolworth Five and Ten Cent Store and met a violin teacher, Professor Davis, who taught him formal music. Either the Great Depression, homesickness, or both brought

Marg Osburne, Don Messer, and Charlie Chamberlain, 1948

him back home to begin the climb from local to national fiddle fame.

In addition to Don and his famous fiddle, each band member was a household name. Charlie Chamberlain, on guitar, sang in English, French, and harmonized with Marg Osburne, a lively, lovely, Moncton-born vocalist. Duke Neilson played bass and Warren MacRae, drums. Cecil MacEachern mastered both guitar and fiddle. Waldo Monro pounded the piano, and Johnny Forrest squeezed the accordion. Rae Simmons played the clarinet or sax.

CBC Television broadcast *Don Messer's Jubilee* at CBHT, Halifax, from 1957–1969. Jack Scott, in the October 11, 1960 Vancouver *Sun*, said of the production: "It is to television what Grandma Moses is to art." I look at the titles of his compositions and know that they are provincial in detail and dominion in breadth: "Crossing on the Ferry," "Little Burnt Potato Jig," "Country Waltz," "Snow Deer," "Joys of Quebec," "Red River Waltz," "Red Wing," "What's the Matter with Father," "Mouth of the Tobique," "Mother's Reel," "Flowers of Edinburgh," "Rippling Water Jig," "St. Anne's Reel," "Silver and Gold Two Step," "Atlantic Polka," "Logger's Breakdown," "Happy Time Schottische," "Maple Sugar Two Step," "The Rose Upon the Bible," "On the Road to Boston," "Western Reel," "Bowing the Strings," "Buckwheat Batter," "The Girl I Left Behind," "Grant Lambs Breakdown," "Big John MacNeil," and so, so many others that represent the heart and soul of old-time Maritime Canada music.

My catchy favorite is Bathurst-born Charlie Chamberlain, the "Singing Lumberjack," booming rat-a-tat verses in French of "The Old Man and the Old Woman." Messer renditions are the down-home, hymnal recipes of Canadian culture. Rough roads, as life goes, were smoothed and soothed with uplifting Messer music. In tribute, Don's melodies are perpetuated on CD and YouTube video and played by generations of North American fiddlers in dance halls, festivals, and kitchen parties.

I listened to two Nova Scotia-born balladeers that performed throughout the Maritimes on their roads to fame: Wilf Carter, "Montana Slim," singing "Blue Canadian Rockies," or Hank Snow, "The Singing Ranger," who wrote and recorded "I'm Movin' On." I bought their 78rpm records. Each passed away cross-border; Wilf in Scottsdale, Arizona, and Hank in Madison, Tennessee.

With teenage friends, I would occasionally drive out to Millville on a summer night. We enjoyed sitting in the car outside the Pentecostal church listening to the music, but were too far away to hear the preaching and testimonies. Another good pastime was playing cards in the evening with Corbett and Marie McGuire who lived across from the Baylis farm. Corbett farmed and ran the road grader. Wounded in WWII, he and Marie were active in the Southampton Canadian Legion Post.

General conversation was as entertaining as the radio. The ring of a Rossville farmer's greeting "How ya livin?" puts into words, a genealogical query of times past or when seeking present circumstance. I enjoyed hearing local pronunciations of "Coocumber," "Coolie dog," "Cal`ate," "G`radge," and "Massatoosits." Passé are "Gee Hover," "Jeasly," and "Sonofa'hore," but "Frig" or "Friggin" didn't go out of style. Admittedly, I frig around with historical trivia (offering found facts that I *must* save and not delete). For instance, a Parish is only recognized as a civil division in New Brunswick and the State of Louisiana. Did you know that New Brunswick law, according to existing British Commonwealth rules, made it mandatory to drive on the left? In 1922, a new law changed it to the right. To complicate matters for a while, Nova Scotia kept the British rule to drive on the left. A bit of travel trivia is that bilingual New Brunswick has provincial highway signs in English and French. In like manner, Ireland requires them in English and Gaelic.

A wonderful word that conveyed the innate generosity of my New Brunswick family and friends was "Treat." To those who gave and those who received, "Treat" might be a Christmas present, a "Lunch-on-me," a trinket for a child, a piece of pie, or hand-outs at newly-wed chivarees. Their telling is my treat!

Folks told tales of a fabled "Indian Devil." It probably was an eastern mountain lion. Hair-raising, hard to authenticate stories of their eerie screech, following people in the woods, and seldom seen tracks made children…and men, true believers.

Visiting was entertainment. Cousins Earle and Alton McElwain often visited the Baylis farm, walking four miles or so from Temperance Vale, and staying for a few days. When I visited the McElwain farm, Alton impressed me with his .45-70 caliber rifle that had a massive muzzle bore. Always easy to be with, and aiming to please, he took me to see a dog-driven treadmill that was used to power a cream separator. Earle and Alton were good company.

I went to a logging camp in back of Trout Brook where Earle was a "Cookee," assisting camp cook Donald MacIntosh. Since loggers needed twice the calories of a city worker, he cut a pie in quarter portions to satisfy their appetites. Returning from overseas duty with the Army, Earle taught me the words to the soldier and sailor sung "North Atlantic Squadron." After marriage, he relocated to Sudbury, Ontario, eventually went west to Duncan, British Columbia, and finally passed away in Woodstock. I called and visited him in the hospital. As I think of it, both Earle and Alton inherited a twinkle of the eye like that of their father, Russell.

CHAPTER EIGHT
ROSSVILLE AND CULLITON

Y ou might call the Cliff, St. Peter, Grant, Ingraham, Baylis, McGuire, Woodman, two Davidson, Mooers, and three Morrison families a clan of sorts on the one road Rossville settlement. They were close-knit and helped one another when needed. I saw that happen when Bill and Nina Morrison had an old fashioned barn-raising just below where Trout Brook passed under the Rossville Road.

Among farmers in Rossville, Guy Hazen Davidson was unquestionably qualified to write about the Southampton area of the St. John River Valley. He was born, bred, betrothed, beloved, and buried at Lower Southampton. His first wife, Florence Cronkhite Davidson, died leaving Guy with two sons, Roy and William. Guy was slow spoken and wise in human and Mother nature. Daisy was an energetically expressive wife, dear mother to my friends Harold and Myrtle, and certainly an example to me. At table, her "Bless this food to our good" remains righteous.

Daisy was a teacher with a talent for music, In *Nackawic Bend,* she gave credit to her one-room school curriculum and to the teacher who "corrected us for manners, to say please and thank you, and to be kind to older people." She entered Provincial Normal School in 1916, two years after Mother, and shared the value of education with students, "For I always loved school work." It was while teaching school in Culliton that she met Guy, and they married in September 1929.

I have a 1940s or '50s Christmas card photo with greetings from the Davidson family. Guy is behind a big bear standing on its hind legs with an apple in its mouth and a rifle cradled across its front legs: a perfect example of his hunting expertise and clever connection to nature. A cedar-fenced orchard is in the background.

At age 65 in 1956, he expressed a sense of place in poetry. I think that there's a hint of Daisy's approval in the composition. Among many verses, *homespun from the heart*, I chose those most pertinent to Lower Southampton from Guys "Life Along the St. John River."

> It's springtime and the songbirds have arrived from the south.
> The ice has left the rivers and streams from the lakes down to
>   the mouth.
> All nature teams with gladness as anyone can see,
> And life along the St. John River is good enough for me.

Guy & Daisy Davidson Christmas Card, 1940s

There's daisies on the hillside now, trout and salmon in the
 streams.
There's plenty of moose and deer to make this land a dream.
While the beaver, mink, and muskrat by the brooks rest
 peacefully,
Life along the St. John River is good enough for me.

Now all you good people from distant points outside,
Who cross the Quebec border or from Maine to this side.
The scenery here is wonderful, the atmosphere is free.
So give me the St. John River its good enough for me.

My latch string hangs out on the door for friends who may pass by
See the mounted birds and animals [in their home], they are
 pleasing to the eye.
While the kettle boils o'er the fire, and the smoke rolls out so free,
Life along the St. John River is good enough for me.

Among his "Friends who may pass by" was my Aunt Mabel.
According to Guy's daughter, Myrtle, Mabel would call out "Is the
rooster in [the pen]?" and hasten to the door before it chased her.
Myrtle remembers, and still has a large milk pitcher keep-sake, that
Mabel gave her for a wedding present. While my mother lived at the
Baylis farm in the late 1950s, she too often walked down Rossville
Road to call on Daisy and Guy.

Rossville's gathering place was adjacent Culliton, a little more than
a mile away. Across the covered bridge from the one-room schoolhouse, were the Farmer's Co-op general store, Angus and Myrl Dunlop's garage, the railroad crossing, and the Royal Canadian Legion Hall.
After WWII, the RCL hall sat on flatland next to the railway bridge over
the Nackawic "Crick" (creek). Most roads were gravel, and only Route
2 along the St. John River was paved. Big road graders kept the gravel
surface smooth and were fitted for plows in winter.

Dating back to 1912, the store was acquired by the Co-op in the
late 1920s and managed by Tommy Stairs. I remember him when, as
a child, I was known as "Lucy's boy." It sold to Donnie Cronkhite in
1945. Stanley Stairs bought it on April 20, 1947, and ran it as "Stanley
E. Stairs and Son" with son Earle, and his wife, Marjorie, and daughter

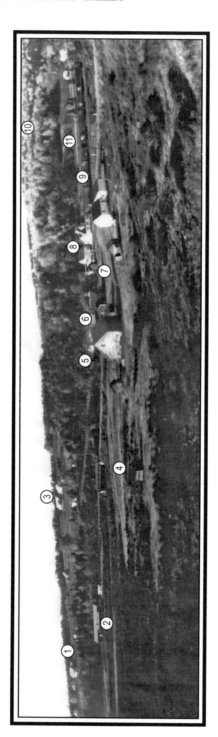

CULLITON
BEFORE 1966

1. ROAD FROM L.R. SOUTHAMPTON
2. ROYAL CANADIAN LEGION HALL
3. AUSTIN & LEONA MUNRO FARM
4. RAILROAD BRIDGE
5. CULLITON SCHOOL
6. DUNLOP'S GARAGE
7. "CULLERTON" RAILSTOP
8. STANLEY STAIRS & SON STORE
9. LINE OF FREIGHT CARS
10. MUNRO RIDGE
11. ROAD TO ROSSVILLE

donahuedesign

Helen, until April 20, 1967 when the Mactaquac Dam headwater was about to submerge Culliton.

Stanley's goods were the kind that the farmers couldn't produce. Essentials such as tea, spices, flour, sugar, and molasses accompanied hardware, pots and pans, textiles, and a multitude of other manufactured items. Bought goods were usually wrapped in brown paper and tied with white string; there were no paper bags. Bulk flour and feed were kept in cloth bags; farmwives sewed those for flour into children's underwear and pillow cases. Irving gas pumps were out in front of the store. Our 1937 Irving Oil *Road Map of Eastern Canada* advertised "Know where you are, Watch the Irving Signs" and "Clean Rest Rooms." We knew where we were without a sign, because we never went far from Rossville or Culliton. I can't remember a rest room at the store, but among us boys, behind a tree or under the bridge worked fine!

Service garages like Angus and Myrl Dunlop's had a stand-up pit to repair under-chassis needs or change oil since there were no hydraulic lifts. Gasoline smelled pleasant to me then. Up into the 1950s, tires had rubber inner tubes so that patching kits and hand inflation pumps were standard emergency equipment. Tire chains were often required for winter travel.

Angus and Georgie Dunlop's home was between the railroad crossing and his auto repair business. His family was known for its musical talent. Zenus played guitar and sisters Arlene, Uda, and Janet, harmonized songs and hymns. Haldean was my age. Robert, who had a wonderful sense of humor, went on to become a minister serving a congregation in Moncton.

Rossville's railroad link was a shed marked "Cullerton" and a freight platform. I'm amazed that I was young enough to remember when the line was operating and old enough to learn about its history from beginning to end. In 1913, a 13 mile "Short Line" Southampton branch joined the main Canadian Pacific Rail line south of Millville to connect with scheduled Fredericton or Woodstock trains. The point where the spur connected with the main line was called a "Wye" for turning single end cars; it was shaped like a "Y" or martini glass and stem (Right, Ms. E.?) with the rim as the main line. Stops along the subdivision were Maple Ridge, Caverhill, Pinder, Culliton, the terminus at Otis, or anywhere along the way by flagging. Passengers, like my mother in teachers' college, could travel to or from Fredericton.

PERSERVING CULLITON

CULLITON SCHOOL & CLASS, 1898

COVERED BRIDGE, ICE DAM WITH FLOODING, 1936

CULLITON CROSSROADS, CEMENT BRIDGE, STAIRS' STORE, DUNLOP'S GARAGE, 1950s

CULLITON SCHOOL, 1950s

RAILROAD BRIDGE& LEGION HALL, 1950s

donahuedesign

Railway right of ways and timber holdings were sold to K.C. Irving, Ltd. in 1941. After passenger and freight service dwindled around 1950, and the train made its last trip to Otis on July 25, 1966. The line again became active from 1967 to 1970 delivering construction material for Nackawic's St. Anne Pulp Mill. The last train run, operated by the Canadian Atlantic Railway, was November 29, 1993.

Meanwhile, Dan and Dave Dineen, Jim Robertson, and friends formed the New Brunswick Recreational Rail Riders in 1998 and prepared to maintain the abandoned rails for historic Railroad Motorcar use. A government five-year Crown Lands Lease was issued but was terminated in December 2010 to convert the rail bed into the recreational SentierNB Trail network. The track was torn up for salvage, and the 80 year service from Millville to Otis ended. The echoing clickety-clack and whistle warnings at Culliton Crossing became a vanishing memory.

The timber-framed covered bridge dividing Culliton crossed the Nackawic Stream. A wooden bridge covered with a roof and siding lasted about 80 years, and one without, only 20. Most were of the Howe Truss Design (patented in 1840 by Spencer, Massachusetts millwright William Howe). Out of 300 in the past, only 62 are left in New Brunswick. Six were recently lost, and two are new.

I suppose horses thought it was like walking into a barn that was open at both ends. To me, the interior was cathedral-like with barn swallows in the rafters. High enough for a wagon load of hay or logs, it also bore trucks and cars. The worn floor planks rattled and echoed from hooves, wagon wheels, and vehicles. If only the writings and carvings on the walls were recorded, they would jangle memories of those who crossed and courted! Once from the bridge entrance, I saw baptismal candidates immersed (sometimes called "Dipping") in the "Crick". That bridge was replaced by an open cement structure c.1950.

That leads to a remarkable tale of "Waste not, want not." I would never have known that the old Culliton covered bridge was not torn down when the concrete bridge replaced it except for a July, 1984 printout in the Nackawic CD that was organized as a major memorabilia project to times before and during the Mactaquac Dam impact on the community. Percy and Joyce Jones obtained a copy from Wendell Flewelling for me. Seems that the old bridge was actually *moved* to cross the Becaguimec Stream off route 104 between Millville and

CULLITON RITUALS

SCHOOL RECESS

ROSSVILLE ROAD TO CULLITON

MRYL DUNLOP & TEDDY

STANLEY & RICHARD STAIRS AT STORE

GRADER & MRYL'S GARAGE

ZENUS DUNLOP & RONALD NASON
AT RAILROAD CROSSING

BAPTISM BY IMMERSION
IN THE NACKAWIC STREAM

donahuedesign

Hartland! If it's still there, and all the old boards and beams haven't been replaced, I'd like to see the original scribblings and carved names.

The schoolhouse, playground, and girl's and boy's outhouses were across the covered bridge from the store. The one-room Culliton school was built c.1867 on land donated by John William Culliton. From an 1878 School Register where my grandfather William and great aunt Lucy Baylis were listed, family names familiar to me included Woodman, Morrison, Munro, Davidson, and Bragdon. About100 years old, the school served three or four generations of families.

In 1948, after eight years at Dist. No.1 Culliton School, most Rossville young folks worked for family, hired out, or got married. Myrtle Davidson and a few others went to the nearest high school in Meductic.

The Ingraham boys laughed about disciplined raps from a teacher's ruler. They said that the best defense was putting their hands inside the desk. A young lad named Charlie was tempted, like Eve in Eden, and stopped at an apple tree on his way to school. He was stricken with the "Green apple two-step" known to loggers as "The flying axe handles." His father was working on the road near the school and was introduced to the "Situation." With the results in his trousers and his father periodically prodding him along, they miserably marched homeward. Mother was a witness of that dreadful trek.

My 1937 Irving Oil road map has "Woodstock to Fredericton, 63.4miles." Highway No. 2, on the west side of the river, was recently paved then. We referred to hard-paved roads as "Macadam," meaning asphalt. Within that mid—Valley distance, there were three bridges crossing the river: Woodstock, Pokiok, and Fredericton. Four ferry crossings, all below Pokiok, were Davidson, Parent, McNalley, and McGinley. Mother, Dad, and I once crossed the St. John on one of those one-car cable ferries. In leaner Depression and war years, 30 mile drives on Saturday nights to Woodstock's Farmer's Store (with two floors of merchandise!) was quite a treat, and so were their ice cream cones. If a family didn't have a car, or gas rationing was a problem, rides on trucks with long benches cost 25 cents. Forty mile visits to Fredericton usually involved only the older folks. My favorite when there was James S. Neill and Sons sporting goods store on Queen

Street opposite City Hall. I would gaze in wonder at the extensive artificial trout and salmon fly selection, I think in a glass case. There was a picture of Babe Ruth in a big raccoon coat. Babe was a celebrity in 1940 when he visited Neill's, signed baseballs for fans, and bought hunting supplies.

Dr. Marcus Lorne Jewett of Millville was the physician who most farm families used. He might pull an aching tooth if he wasn't out on the summer or winter country roads tending to patients. Otherwise, the option was going to a dentist in Woodstock or Fredericton. Doctor Jewett, according to *Nackawic Bend,* had a special sled built for the railroad between Millville and Otis for winter travel since the tracks were cleared before the roads. His by-line was "Oh, by the way now." Applying his diagnostic know-how to a young man pleading for medicine for a "Friend with a dose," the Doctor's reply was "Oh, by the way now, take your friend out, and let's have a look at him."

He saved Myrtle Davidson's life in 1945. When Daisy called, he came right in from Millville and immediately saw that Myrtle had appendicitis. They had no auto, and Bill Morrison rushed her and Daisy to Fredericton 40 miles downriver where Dr. Chalmers removed the ruptured appendix. Versatile and practical, Guy finished baking the bread that Daisy had started! Myrtle was hospitalized for one month.

As a coroner for York County, Dr. Jewett had sad occasion to file death certificates. One, as reported in the *Daily Gleaner,* was Rossville neighbor Ray Morrison, who had gone to school with my mother. Unloading logs Feb. 10, 1940, at Culliton Hill, the team bolted, frightened by a train whistle sound from across the river, dislodging the load. Ray was crushed, dying instantly. It was his 43rd birthday, leaving wife Margaret and children, Elmer, Nellie, Shirley, Carol, Lorna, and Marion. Some were nearby at the Culliton School. Another Culliton fatality was Georgie and Angus Dunlop's son Zenus, age17, who Dr. Jewett wrote "As Coroner, 24 January 1944, Fractured Skull, Multiple Scalp Wounds, Auto collided with Engine of train" at "Railway Crossing." Dr. Jewett was also a Justice of the Peace. His son, Dr. "Buddy," pursued his father's medical career as a surgeon in Fredericton.

Uncle George Baylis wore a groin support under his clothing called a "Truss" consisting of a metal belt with an oval leather pad to hold in a bulging intestinal herniation. That medical device, to hold in what the locals called a "Rupture," is no longer used. The boys laughingly told a hernia-related story of Johnny Woodman. It seems that he had the habit of kicking stones off the gravel road as he walked along. Because of his "Rupture," he would cup one hand and lift his crotch with each kick. Speaking of Johnny, a New Brunswick newspaper printed a picture of him, when he was 79 in 1958, holding a giant turnip that weighed 20 pounds and had a 31-inch circumference.

Among health matters, the poliomyelitis epidemics 1937–1952 were frightening. Schools, in 1937, were closed until November first, and children were kept from public meetings. Charles Culliton, a courageous victim of paralysis, walked with the aid of leg braces and crutches. It did not destroy his happy personality. The Victoria Public Hospital in Fredericton was relocated, built, and named after Dr. G. Everett Chalmers, a popular Valley surgeon. In the 1950s, I had an infected black-fly bite between my left hand's thumb and forefinger. It was painful, red, and swollen, and I went for help to Dr. Peter Bramstrup, Nackawic's general practitioner. He skillfully and successfully froze the skin with ethyl chloride anesthetic spray, and incised and drained the abscess. I still have the scar (and a healthy hand) to prove it.

Speaking of incisions, I saw Uncle George puncture the side of a cow bloated with gas using a pocket knife that had leather stops on the blade to limit its depth of penetration. He kept horse liniment on hand for the team's chafes and cuts.

Home remedies for us included cold mud from a spring applied to soothe a bee sting, and barn spider webs put on an open wound to help stop bleeding. Moist herbal poultice dressings drew out infections. I'm skeptical about the home remedy of a red string tied around the neck to hinder bleeding from the face or scalp. I do know, however, that a teabag moistened in cold water will control excessive bleeding from a tooth socket because of tea's tannic acid content. Clarence "Pa" Cliff used kerosene on cuts. Daisy Davidson applied salt pork from the cellar brine barrel to Myrtle and Harold's bruises, and they said that the brine application "Did smart!" Flowers of sulfur powder and black-strap molasses were a "Spring tonic" for intestinal cleansing. In every home, cod liver oil, containing vitamins A and D, was dispensed to children by the spoonful.

Our Baylis family traveled to Ross Drug on Queen Street in

Fredericton for prescribed medications. That's where we bought Rawleigh's "Medicated Ointment." Sold in a round silver and blue tin, it
smells of soothing camphor and comforts tissues whether applied to
the skin as balm, inhaled, or swallowed. From cuts to colds, earaches
to headaches, or itching piles to aching joints, Rawleigh's ointment
was advertised to do the trick! I've kept a tin, if for nothing else, to
open it and smell the memories.

Raleigh Ointment, Ross Drug, Fredericton, 1940s

CHAPTER NINE
BOYHOOD MEDLEY

Best of Friends: Charles & George and Arthur Ingraham

My constant New Brunswick boyhood companions were George and Arthur Ingraham up the road from the Baylis farm and Harold Davidson, from down the road. All gone now, I pay them happy homage with a wordy but crystal-clear recollection.

> Many a vision, long buried deep,
> Was waked again from its dreamless sleep.
> Thoughts whose light was dim before,
> Lived in their pristine truth once more.
> "The Mignionette," 1845

Early on, we made lean-to camps with peeled pulp bark. We cut wooden cart wheels from spruce pulp log butts and pounded a nail

Best of Friends: Charles and Harold Davidson

through the center into a wooden axle. As children, we balanced a long board on a log to make a teeter-totter (see-saw). The boys' comparison in later years was "A long plank for a good teeter." Arthur and I watched George attempt a very short-lived rodeo ride on a calf in their milk yard. While farm folk in general would call cows in from the pasture to be milked, by hollering "CO-boss, CO-boss, CO-boss," the Ingrahams just said to their dog, "Buster, go get the cows!"

When the boys came down to the Baylis farm, Uncle Ronald teased George Ingraham by calling him "Massey," after Massey-Harris farm tractors. In response, George said "Don't call me those funny names" often backed up by fake strikes with Cousin Ella's old rubber jump rope. George could, and would at length, recite passages memorized from Culliton schoolhouse lessons. He was an erect, sandy Scot through Henderson heritage. Arthur was shorter and the spitting image of his Dad and Ingraham uncles. The Ingraham boys taught me that their Canadian alphabet ended in x, y, "Zed," the old British form.

As young boys, being taught good manners, they took off their hats when coming into the Baylis kitchen and sat quietly on the cot until spoken to. Their feet got hardened in summer when they didn't wear shoes. They could run over sharp field stubble with no discomfort after hay was cut. They wore "Braces" (British for suspenders) to hold up their trousers. Being fair skinned, they wore caps or hats summer and winter. Every Rossville man and boy carried a pocket knife as a handy, practical tool. A favorite boy's pastime was trading knives and pocket watches.

The Ingraham boys set brass-wire snares on saplings over rabbit tracks in winter for pelts, to earn extra money. In 1940, a five-dollar bounty was reinstated on bears, but my friends were too young to hunt or trap bears. When there was a ten cent bounty on porcupines with the nose as proof, some folks split paws sliced to resemble a nose to up the ante. After a while, the wardens became aware of the shenanigans.

We dug what the boys called "Angle worms" (L.L.Bean sold Angle Worm Food) with a dung fork in manure piles or in dark moist dirt behind the barn. That wiggly bait, carried in a tin can, truly tempted

Laurie's Trout Brook Watercolor, 1955

trout. We mostly fished on Trout Brook behind the Baylis and Ingraham fields with a fresh-cut alder pole, green line, and black hook. At that time, I didn't know Trout Brook's perfect name. Hanging beside me in the den, and pictured on the front cover, is a watercolor that Laurie painted. It's my favorite old-beaver-dam trout pool with an overhanging and partially uprooted tree. Dappled patches of summer sun beam on every land and water surface.

Catching the occasional eel was a flash of hard pull when one coiled tight under a rock. When retrieved, it was squirming terror since they were black and slimy and looked like a snake. We had to step on them to remove the hook. The brook trout havens from which to dash out for food, were underneath a rock or sunken log, in upper pool ripples, or beneath a shady bank among alder roots exposed from freshets.

Should one dart into submerged branches or under a log, a jerk on my part might hang up the hook, and I would lose the fish and the hook. Most of the time, I brought a trout out on the graveled edge of the brook or flung it high up on the grassy bank. Locally, the length of a trout was demonstrated by pointing one forefinger outward, and with the other hand's forefinger, moving up the forearm from the first fingertip to stop at the mark of measurement.

The image of a fragile, lush, brook-side plant returns to me. When caught in the current, its small leaves reflect a shimmering silvery surface. I vividly rekindle the joie de vivre of Trout Brook as I read Tennyson's poem, "The Brook."

> I wind about in and out, with here a blossom sailing,
> And here and there a lusty trout, and here and there a
> grayling.
>
> And here and there a foamy flake upon me as I travel,
> With many a silvery water-break above the golden gravel.
>
> I chatter, chatter, as I flow to join the brimming river.
> For men may come and men may go, but I go on forever.

While fishing, we covered the catch with ferns to keep them cool. The beauties were carried home strung through gills on a jack-knife

*Charles With Trout
and Rod, 1937*

cut thin alder branch that looked like a big check mark. They were so
easy to clean using a single incision on the belly to remove the intes-
tines. With heads and tails often left on, they were simply dipped in
flour or cornmeal and fried in butter Those "pan trout" are so delicious, when cooked crisp, brown, and juicy! Fiddlehead ferns, gathered in the spring and served with brook trout, make for a tasty New
Brunswick traditional dish.

A good place to find berries, was alongside an old zigzag, cedar-
rail fence. Blueberry picking was fun with the Ingrahams. Their dog
Buster, would try to chew through a hollow rail to get at a red squirrel. Small round black chokecherries puckered our mouths and didn't
seem right for jelly or jam. A gooseberry bush produced small, semi-
transparent, and lime colored oval berries.

We gathered raspberries that grew well among patches of logging overgrowth. Bears loved them, but they mauled the canes in
their quest. Summer-so-sweet wild strawberries showed bright red
through their shadowed foliage of grass or clover. When picking, not

every berry went into the pail. If bush to hand and hand to mouth, raspberries and strawberries were revealing, because both fingers and lips were red. Two clues as to who ate the most berries, were crimson color around lips and least berries in a bucket. "Little fellers" were the most susceptible to "Pick and eat."

Early Yellow Transparent apples, from a tree beside the Ingraham farmhouse, were soft, good eating, and of course free for our taking. Another first-to-ripen, was called the "Early Scarlet." In summer, the Ingraham's cook stove sat in a room toward the barnyard and was moved into the dining room in winter. The Ingraham boys always washed their hands and face and combed their hair before meals. Their kitchen washstand was a small four-legged table with a circle cut out of the top to hold a china or tin basin and had a place to hang a hand towel. I often sat at Billy and Hazel Ingraham's happy table for 12, with always room for one more. I relished the company, table-food, and her never-to-be-forgotten raspberry sheet pie. Kitchen dish or hand-wash water was emptied out the back door on the grass near their small smoke-house. Behind it was a convenient clear, "Deer" view (in Bill's mind) of the back field. I don't remember the Ingraham's having pigs or hens. I do remember the leather hinges on their backhouse door! A five-or six-inch section of worn out horse harness was perfect to make hinges. Once the door was leveled enough to swing, the harness hinges were simply nailed in place.

Guy Davidson had a woodlot on Upper Temperance Vale road that had a good stand of sugar maples. Myrtle told me that he delighted going out to the camp each spring to tap the trees. When the sap evaporated to a certain point, he brought pails of concentrate in for Daisy to "Finish off" on the stove. When that was done, she'd pour it through white wool underwear cloth to filter out impurities before it was bottled.

In summer, an Ingraham group and I walked a mile or so out to visit old Nathan Stairs who lived in Guy's tidy camp on Buttermilk Brook. He married and left Southampton long before, to work and guide in Stillwater, Maine, but he came back home to spend his elder years, wintering out with various families. He possibly was an Ingraham relative. Nate had a comical disposition and enjoyed children's company as much as we did his. He had treasure hunts for us in back of the wood lot near a spring. Nate set up the hunt and wrapped each tiny treasure (can't recall what they were) in a small piece of paper tied with string.

I hold dear, and make my daughter, Mary Ann, beam to a chorus of "Sweet Marie" (from 1893) that Old Nate taught me to sing. My Marie, (Laurie) of course, is "Sweet Marie."

> Come to me sweet Marie,
> Sweet Marie come to me.
> Not because your face is fair, Love, to see.
>
> But your soul, so pure and sweet,
> Makes my happiness complete.
> Makes me falter at your feet, Sweet Marie.

We were never bored growing up. Most playtime material was available at no cost, but it required practical application. Have you ever tried chewing what you thought was spruce gum after scraping a fresh resinous glob from black spruce bark…and discovered that it was actually pitch? A solidified sap, pitch has a distasteful turpentine-like difference and won't turn to chewing gum unless it has hardened for about four years. The boys were pretty good at choosing the right stuff, but my teacher was Trial and Error. Of historical interest, Thoreau's Maine Indian guide, Joe Aitteon, chewed it when hunting moose, loggers brought it home as a gift, and when steamed and filtered for gum and medicines, spruce gum had a good market value from 1900 to the 1920s. As kids, we simply knew that it was cheaper than Spearmint gum or penny candy.

Four-inch alder-bush whistles were easy to make by freeing the soft bark (late spring and early summer) by tapping it with the back of a jackknife handle After twisting and sliding it off the stick, a half-inch long notch was cut halfway through the bare wood near one end. When a thin, reed-like shaving was whittled between the notch and the short end, it became the mouthpiece after replacing the tube and cutting a narrow tapered opening over the notch. Then, the maker could be the tooter.

We also had fun making finger rings out of horseshoe nails. After contouring a nail-shank to finger size, the bent up nail head looked like a gem setting.

Here are a few recalls of being in New Brunswick with my friends as we were growing up. In summer, we didn't go swimming; I never saw George, Arthur, or Harold swim or go out on a boat. The local term for any kind of boating was to "Go for a sail." In our mid-teens, George, Arthur, and I made brew in a crock in a deserted Henderson farm outbuilding. We used potatoes, sugar, yeast, and anything that would ferment. We secretly (it tasted nobler) consumed the frothy, cloudy, brown beverage. I later learned that home brew was called "Cockaninny" up on the Miramichi.

On clear, dark nights in late autumn, we walked the Rossville road watching shooting, multicolored Northern Lights that seemed to be within reach overhead. There were no streetlights, few farmhouse lights, and almost no vehicular traffic to offset the sky works.

As young men, the Ingraham boys told me of working in the winter logging woods in back of Pokiok. While driving out on weekends, they occasionally had to stop for a stubborn moose between the narrow high snow banks. It was just sit and wait with the headlights out until it left the road. Another winter tale that they shared was about standing quietly beside a backfield fence under a full moon on a cold clear winter night. The sound of crunching snow from deer lured to apple bait meant fresh meat for the table.

One March, in a sugar lot (maple grove), I saw sap being boiled down in a big iron kettle to make syrup. Local folks called it "Maple honey," because I think, syrup to them meant medicine.

George and Arthur's father, Bill Ingraham, was a proud man and full of life. Verna, my cousin Alton McElwain's wife, said that Billy worked in the woods for her father, Frank Moorcroft, and could be heard from a distance hollering at the team, hallooing, and singing at the top of his lungs. All of the Ingraham children in my generation went to the Culliton School, and Bill had served as trustee and secretary.

Alec Ferguson spoke with a Scot's burr and walked his Game Warden route carrying a backpack. Bill did Alec's haying, and that may have been Bill's savior. Alec, passing by on patrol, asked to see Bill's rifle. I was there with the boys and knew where it hung behind the stove in the summer kitchen. I hastily retrieved it for inspection. An old model with an octagonal barrel, Bill's .30.30 caliber carbine had a bullet in the chamber! "Oh Deer, Deer!"

With a new car in the dooryard, Bill once did an eloquent "Show and tell" to those of us circled around it. I've heard Billy yell while haying, "Arthur, what ails you?" If anyone was getting too frisky, he'd say "Stop acting out the fool." George and Arthur's younger brother, Charles, would tag along behind us calling "Aufie, wait for me." Carl was the "Little feller." Sisters Ethel, Evelyn, Dorothy, Bessie, Pearl, and Cora were lovely like Hazel, always pleasant "With smiling browe and happy hearts" (from Mrs. Beavan in 1845).

One of my teen-time special events in New Brunswick happened when Dorothy married Arnold Bradley from Maple Ridge, and I went to a celebration called a "Chivaree." On the evening of the wedding ceremony, it was traditional for a crowd of well-wishers to gather, hoot, bang pots, and cheer when the young couple made an appearance. At the Ingraham's dooryard, it was hosted by the new bride's parents, Bill and Hazel. After Bessie married Arnold's brother, Ivan, the Bradley boys and their Ingraham brides brought up families on Maple Ridge farms.

When I wasn't with the Ingraham boys, I was down the road at the Davidson farm. Harold and I were the same age, and I liked to hear him sing and play the guitar. If we teased his sister Myrtle too much, she would chase us until we climbed in with the pigs. After a span of about 60 years, I've contacted Myrtle Davidson Grant in Moncton. In our conversations of precious recall, more vivid facts and visions come to light. She spoke the bountiful display of morning glories that climbed up their porch posts. Of interest to me, their mother Daisy made her own soap by dissolving stove ashes in water aimed at making lye, and then she combined it with animal grease. They, like most families of the times, sat down and ate together. Daisy always said a blessing at meals.

Guy Davidson both farmed and kept long mink pens in back of his barn with breeding data on each cage. We were told not to put our fingers near the wire. Mink give off an odor similar to a skunk but not as pungent. Guy had a root cellar beneath one of the pens to protect garden foods over the winter. On the coldest of January nights, he would fill an iron kettle with glowing hardwood coals, cover it with tin to prevent sparks from flying, and set it in the root cellar to prevent the vegetables from freezing. Usually, some coals were still burning in the morning. As well as using the granary beside their house for grain

Davidson Farmhouse and Barns, Summer & Winter

storage, he buried pork and beef deep in the grain that stayed frozen into the summer.

Guy was an excellent woodsman and hunter and enjoyed having small animals as pets. I recall a raccoon in a spacious chicken wire enclosure that he fed milk and homemade bread. In the house, a red squirrel made a round treadmill go lickety-split in its cage made out of wire and twigs.

A mischievous prank that Harold and I concocted began in Woodman's dooryard. I was disguised in a straw hat, a big false rubber nose attached to heavy fake black rimmed glasses, and a red bandana sticking out of my pants pocket. This curious sight drew Johnny and Ross outside, as the "Stranger" proceeded over the hill to Davidson's. There, I met Guy coming in from the barn who greeted me with a "How do sir." I moved along and sat on a distant cedar-fence rail waving my red bandana and got kind returns from Guy and from Daisy who came out to see what was going on. Harold, privy to the occasion, said their comment was "Must be some poor fellow home from the war." Watching my movements, Guy became quite uneasy when I opened Harold's parked car door down the hill near the road. Anything about an auto was Harold Davidson's pleasure.

On summer Saturday nights after haying, we went to dances at the Culliton Legion Hall. When an auto trunk was up outside the hall, the boys were probably passing a bottle around. It was a "More beer and wider roads" rite. A dance hall at Stone Ridge had a rowdy reputation where, I'm told, a Mountie lost his hat.

In contra-dance sets, two lines of couples faced each other and danced to popular tunes like "Lady of the Lake." Each couple would repeat a step a few times, cross to the other line, repeat the steps with another couple, and so on, until each twosome danced with all the others.

One of Culliton's older gents, as was often the custom, might perform a solo whoop-it-up step-dance. His fuel might be fire-water! There were variations to the step-dance whether to a Legion Hall trio or in logging camps when a fiddle, guitar, harmonica, accordion, or jew's-harp was on hand. The step-dancer stood erect with arms at side or waving chest high while legs, and especially feet, made aerial contortions. Leather soles sporadically struck the floor in rhythm to frenzied fiddling.

My magnetic attraction to the north was rewarded by a 1947 Christmas present for a flight on Northeast Airlines, the successor to Boston-Maine Airways, to visit family in Rossville. It was the year that Bar Harbor burned black in October. In the late '40s and early'50s,

Royal Canadian Legion, Branch 27, Culliton

Boston based Northeast Airlines had scheduled flight service to 12 Maine destinations, Moncton and Saint John in New Brunswick, and Montreal in Quebec. I recall the plane's abrupt landing in Portland that knocked the galley's coffee thermos off its holder. It rolled down the aisle and clearly upset the stewardess but not me, because her perfume hit me like a rock! Impressively high snow-banks lined the Lewiston runway as the 21 seat Douglas DC-3 landed and took-off on our flight up to Aroostook County. Strangely, I can't recall anything except that it was a delight to make the trip. Uncle Ronald and Aunt Ella kindly took me to the Presque Isle airport for my return flight to Boston. Later that March, a massive and heavy snowfall took down most of the hydroelectric and telephone poles and lines, disabling the area.

Northeast Airlines DC-3, 1947

CHAPTER TEN
CROSS-BORDER IN WWII

The *National Geographic Magazine* of May, 1941 set the stage for European war concerns and unity between Canada, already involved, and the U.S., on stand-by. The opening advertisement was "Look to Lockheed for Leadership. For peace or military use they're proving their stamina...[Lockheed Hudson bomber] distinguished itself for valor with the R.A.F. in England." M. L. Mackenzie King, Prime Minister of Canada had a full page letter "To the Citizens of the United States:" extending uninterrupted hospitality to cross the border for friendship, travel, and freedom. An article "New Brunswick Down by the Sea," features history and landscape, but at the same time, shows a picture of a massive pile of peeled logs awaiting shipment overseas for British mine and Air Raid Shelter construction.

The U.S., as "Neutral" early in the European war, produced planes secretly destined for the British and Canadian forces overseas. The aircraft were ferried to the Houlton, Maine, Army Air Base, and Maine farmers towed the planes on their wheels across the border. Using the Woodstock road as a runway, Canadian pilots flew them to a port where they were dismantled and "Cocooned" for shipping to Liverpool.

By the early '40s when our troops were fighting wars in Europe and the Pacific, every boy's toys were scale-model cast metal soldiers and sailors in some form of action. We played paratroopers by knotting four equal lengths of string on each corner of a handkerchief, tying the other ends together on something heavy, maybe a stone, and, tossing the collapsed handful as high as we could into the air, we watched the parachute float to earth. Nazi Germany's Hitler and Japan's General Tojo were scoundrels on comic book covers. Every community patriotically backed the war effort.

In New Brunswick, I saw soldiers from the Carleton and York

Houlton Maine farmer helps tow american war planes into Canada!

*U.S. Planes Ferried
to Canada Through
Houlton,1939*

John Deer tractors with Houlton farmers at the controls carefully but quickly wisk helldiver planes into Canada which had been flown into Houlton Army Air Base which is on the News Brunswick border. Neutrality treaties with Germany/Italy/Japan forbid flying the planes into Canada, a dominion of England. But the loop hole said nothing about "driving" or dragging them in by locals, helped America help England that was getting hammered early on. The German POW's that were interned in Houlton harvested crops, were well cared for and a few even moved here years later due to the kind treatment.

Regiment crowding the streets of Woodstock on Saturday nights. Mobilized in 1939 for WWII training, they were barracked on Island Park before departing for overseas. Regimental history stated that the recruits were "Largely farmers, fishermen, and woods workers committed to irregular and unpredictable hours of work, concentration and adherence to training schedules were difficult." They left Woodstock for Halifax in late November and landed in Greenock, near Glasgow, Scotland in early December.

In 1942, when food and gas were rationed, the reality of involvement in a war had impacted labor and family. Almost half of the province's 94,000 males age 18 to 45 had entered the Canadian armed forces during WWII. My friend Myrtle Davidson Grant told me that her husband, Neil, and her step-brother, William, were in the allied invasion at Normandy in June, 1944.

Driving north through Portland past Baxter Boulevard with Dad and Mother one year, we saw a convoy of naval and supply ships in Casco Bay at dawn awaiting overseas deployment.

Since my first airplane ride in Concord, N.H., gratis Dad and Mother in 1937, aircraft have intrigued me. Of note in my collection, is a first day cover of an airmail sent from Houlton on a 1937 northern Boston-Maine Airways flight. Note the proud presence of the Aroostook potato stamped on the front. In 1940, we passed by the U.S. Army Air Corps field under construction in Bangor that would send troops and equipment to the European war zone. Named Dow Army Airfield in 1942 with 7,000-foot runways, it became an Air Transport Command group strategic to ferrying military aircraft to and from the United Kingdom. In 1947, the Army Air Corps transitioned into the U.S. Air Force, and Dow was part of the Strategic Air Command. At the 1948 point in our "Cold War" with Russia, a jet-capable runway was constructed, and F84 Thunderjets were deployed from Dow. As we passed taxiways, camouflaged B-52 aircraft, in ready alert, had long wingspans with each wing tip unbelievably close to the ground. They were similar to those of a Canada goose starting to beat down to achieve altitude. The Pilots Grill eatery beside the airfield captured my interest and imagination. It stood witness to military personnel and landscape changes at Dow Field.

On July 4, 1941, the Houlton Town Council voted to sell its airport to the federal government for $1 to build an army airfield as the U. S. entered WWII. On July 1, 1944, Prisoner of War Camp Houlton received 299 German POWs from Camp Edwards, Cape Cod, Mass.,

olor titled U.S. Airmail, 1st Day Cover, 1937

then 600 more followed, and eventually almost 3,000. Prisoners came by train to the compound located next to the airfield on the international border. Guarded by a military police battalion, the prisoners were put to work until the 1945 victory in Europe. They were treated humanely and received monthly salaries that they spent in the canteen for cigarettes, beer, and candy. Some helped fill the farm labor shortage, but those that we saw picking blueberries at roadside with POW printed on their clothing, were delegated to woods work.

Gasoline was rationed, and Dad saved coupons for the 1939 Chevrolet's long trip to New Brunswick and back home. He hid tins of gas in an isolated Haynesville Woods section of Rte. 2A. Leaving the deep woods and approaching Houlton, we welcomed Township signs, open fields, and buildings.

The Women's Institute was active in every community on the New Brunswick home front. The Women's Institutes of Carleton County, encouraged by Mrs. Andrew D. (Laura) McCain's efforts, compiled *The Victory Cook Book* in 1942. A cover quotation qualifies the contents:

> We may live without poetry, music, and art,
> We may live without conscience,
> We may live without heart.
>
> We may live without friends,
> We may live without books,
> But civilized man cannot live without cooks.

Laura McCain not only served her wartime community, but managed McCain Produce Co. Ltd., after her husband died in 1953. She was the mother of Wallace and Harrison McCain who developed the frozen food business.

G.E. Barbour, Ltd., of Sussex, New Brunswick, perpetuated the wartime *Victory Cook Book* original by printing a replica edition in 1954, titled *Barbour's Cook Book, An outstanding collection of favorite home recipes from the Atlantic Provinces.* Three editions followed.

In Mrs. Beavan's 1845 book of early settlement, she said "When they pilgrimized to New Brunswick, I am certain they retained the precepts of the cookery book." Laurie carried *The Victory Cook Book* back to Massachusetts. As Daisy Davidson said at mealtime thanksgiving, Laurie put its recipes, "To our good use."

Among many *Daily Gleaner* war articles, three in January 1945 featured a story of local wounded coming home and home-front support by the Women's Institute. Among "Twenty-nine New Brunswick men aboard the hospital ship that landed at Halifax this afternoon with wounded and sick soldiers from the fighting forces in Europe," one was "Pte. A. L. McFarlane, Canterbury." Two spoke of Otis Women's Institute war effort work. The first read: "$2.50 was sent to the prisoner of war fund. There have been five quilts pieced and quilted during the month." In the second commentary, "It was moved and seconded that $10.00 be sent to the Queen's Fund. $2.50 was sent to the prisoner of war fund as usual. Two quilts and two baby quilts have been quilted during the month. The two baby quilts are to be sent overseas."

When down at Guy and Daisy Davidson's with Harold in 1945, I unforgettably watched a soldier walk up their winding drive to the dooryard. William John Davidson emotionally reunited with his grandmother Alwilda (widow of Guy's father John W.) who had brought him, and brother Roy, up after Guy's first wife died. Bill's Carleton and York Regiment suffered heavy losses in the European battlefield. Regimental history addressed it as "A reminder of adventure and terror to those who survived." Alwilda, almost 89, died soon after of pneumonia on October 25, 1945 (according to grand-daughter Myrtle). Alwilda was known to tend the sick or act as midwife.

Bill sold land to Legion Branch #27 for the Mactaquac project relocation of the hall. I remember him as a quiet man with a soft smile. Like Guy, he had the instinct of an Indian when in the woods.

Marlowe M. Fox, storekeeper for 27 years (except when in the Army), and son of Temperance Vale's blacksmith, Perley Fox, published *Pride in Our Past, Faith in Our Future: History of Lower Southampton Br. No.27, Royal Canadian Legion* in 1985 which documents activities of WWI and WWII veterans for 60 years. The Legion Hall burned in 1949, and a former POW recreation hall at Ripples was purchased, sections cut, transported, reassembled, and enlarged, all by members. Harry Corey, prominent in lumbering, gave a mortgage. Among Roy St. Peter from WWI and Southampton veterans of WWII, including my cousin Earle, I knew two generations of Royal

Canadian Legionnaires. My good friend, Major Bob Hutton, is a third generation Canadian veteran.

I didn't know them at the time, but sisters Sheila and Kathleen "Paddy" Hann, ages 7 and 13, came to live with Laurie's family in Newton, Massachusetts, during 1940s Luftwaffe incendiary blitz bombings in England.

In 1982, after a 36 year separation, Laurie reunited with Sheila Hann Hutton and husband, Bob, Canadian Forces Major, retired, in of all places, Fredericton, New Brunswick! Paddy settled in Amityville, N.Y. Bob has stories of Canadian Forces assignments that varied from a Greenland radar site, to the Middle East, and elsewhere. Conversation led to my questions, his answers, and a discussion of how Canada and the world often view America as know-it-all over other countries.

Bob and Sheila, and Laurie and I, rekindle 30 fortunate years of getting together, whether in Fredericton or Falmouth. Shared photos of the '40s are viewed with mutual delight. Each time we meet, "I wish we lived closer," always enters the conversation. Sheila's accounts of her youth in Weston-Super-Mare, England, on southwestern Bristol Bay captivate us. Her Canadian Army post teaching assignment at Camp Shilo, Manitoba, was where she and Bob met. Bob came from Winnipeg, where his father worked for the Canadian Pacific Railroad. In youth, Bob worked in the kitchen of a posh dining car of a train that crossed the western plains. He told us about his grandparent's prairie farmstead, where he learned the fundamentals of farming. I'll talk more about western farming when I tell tales of Rockwell and Grant family migration from Southampton, New Brunswick, to Saskatchewan in the west.

CLIMBING KATAHDIN

Eastern Profile of Mt. Katahdin

A high point in my life was free climbing Maine's highest peak, Mount Katahdin, situated smack within my northeast nesting ground! In travels between Lincoln and Houlton, I was constantly drawn to its signature silhouette over the western horizon. Katahdin is located within Baxter State Park in north central Maine's Piscataquis County, 99 miles north of Bangor, and 55 miles west of the New Brunswick border. On the Appalachian Trail, Baxter peak summit is 2150 miles north of the southern end at Spring Mountain, Georgia. Only 13 feet short of a mile at 5,267 feet above sea level, Katahdin has a timberline at about 3,500 feet, and sighting the gray granite or snow-white top is spectacular. In 1845, John Greenleaf Whittier penned Katahdin's unchanging image in "The Lumbermen."

Where through clouds are glimpses given of Katahdin's sides,—
Rock and forest piled to heaven, torn and ploughed by slides!
Far below, the Indian trapping, in the sunshine warm;
Far above, the snow-cloud wrapping half the peak in storm!

In July 1939, when I turned eight, everyone in America was following the saga (retold in a *Life* magazine article) of 12 year-old Donn Fendler's survival after nine days alone in the Katahdin wilderness. The New York lad, who had been lost on a camping trip with his family, was praised for his courage, faith, Scout training, and will to live. He was invited to meet with President Roosevelt. Another story of youthful stamina is that of Robert G. Page of Fort Kent, Maine. At age 15 in 1935, he climbed Katahdin in the winter. UMaine archives at Fort Kent have his memoir, *The Life of Robert G. Page.*

In the early 1950s, I was a college student at Tufts, living in Woburn, Mass., and was 275 miles south of Katahdin, as the crow flies. Twice with a friend, I camped and ascended the rock-strewn granite basin to experience Baxter Peak summit, the northern end of the Appalachian Trail. I now call it the "Beginning." To prepare, I read Henry David Thoreau's 1846 *The Maine Woods* to learn about primitive travel to "Ktaadn." His assessment described the cut-to-drive, log-to-lumber, and mill-to-market system presuming "The destiny of so many prostrate forests. The mission of men there seems to be, like so many busy demons, to drive the forest all out of the country, from every solitaire beaver-swamp and mountain-side, as soon as possible." Unknown to me at the time were my great uncle George Rockwell's last days in the winter and spring of 1886, spent when logging in that wilderness.

I made my first trip to Katahdin on June, 18 1951 with friend Frank Lawton. We took the Boston and Maine Railroad from North Station, Boston, to Millinocket, Maine, the closest rail connection to one of two roads that accessed the mountain from the east. Frank was an easygoing guy and never a complainer. Though he walked with a limp from a broken hip incurred in a fall from barn rafters, he was an eager and experienced camper. Frank was teased because of his simple innocence, but I liked his enthusiastic good nature and sincerity. He was proud that his father was a town garbage collector, because he said "It was an honest job."

I took planning and preparation seriously and constructed two backpack frames. They required two vertical and two steam-bent cross-pieces of thin oak slats bolted together. Across the bent cross-slats, I attached two 3-inch-wide canvas strips for comfortable back support. Adjustable, webbed shoulder straps, retrieved from back carried Indian Fire Pump tanks, sustained the total load. On each frame, we secured a knapsack, and used narrow cotton rope to lace a waterproof tent or poncho over our other gear. I sent for and paid $1.10 for a 1949, 73 page Appalachian Mountain Club *Katahdin Guide, A Guide to Paths on Katahdin and in the Adjacent Region*. The paths, we discovered, were not all foot paths but more often challenging steep, granite strewn mountain trails. The handbook, with foldout maps in the back, presented a lot of general information, regulations, mountain access points, trail and distance data, fire safety, and low-land campsite locations. Another valuable reference was my 1942 *Hunting Fishing and Camping* by L. L. Bean. His practical words of wisdom also referenced Baxter State Park benefactor, Governor Percival P. Baxter, as "The man who has literally given away mountains."

Frank and I worked out a menu for a week in the woods, and bought and gathered the supplies. We had a spreadsheet of planned meals and the makings. Most consumed were soup, tea, beans, oatmeal, stew, and pudding. Rice, spaghetti, flour, coffee, bacon, raisins and dried fruit, sugar, and powdered eggs and milk completed the list.

We put food, mess kits for cooking, and clothing in Boy Scout khaki knapsacks carried on the backpacks. Loggers would describe personal supplies carried in or out of the camps as their "Wangan." Our two war surplus, single-person "Pup" tents (more like triangular tarps) were waterproof overhead, but rain could seep in on the bare ground under our bough beds. The tents served as covers for rucksacks and rolled sleeping bags. Knives, canteens, and a compass were standard gear, as was my small camera.

As luck would have it, while walking the 25 mile road from Millinocket to our first campsite at Roaring Brook, Park Ranger Ralph Dolley stopped and gave us an appreciated ride. Ed Werler was the ranger at Roaring Brook who issued our camping permits. I've read since, that Ed had a pair of pack-burros, but I don't remember seeing them. Next morning, we trekked three miles past Basin Ponds to our base camp at Chimney Pond, altitude 2,900 feet, which is centered easterly below Katahdin's semicircular Great Basin. The first South Basin peak is Pamola, next is Chimney peak of like elevation, and then, South Peak along the Knife Edge trail to Baxter Peak summit. The North Basin Peaks have a two mile sloping "Saddle" from Baxter summit to Hamlin Peak. Granite slides were prominent in both basins. The Northwest Basin Trail from Hamlin peak to Russell Pond, which we would take later, bordered the Northwest Plateau. At Chimney Pond, we pitched our tents and cooked over a campfire. With Ranger Roland "Andy" Anderson, we watched clouds from the west cascading over the peaks and water-falling into the basin. What a sight! The ranger's log cabin was solid, neat, and had a homey appearance with a porch and flower beds in front.

Rangers were also hosts and often good storytellers. One was Leroy "Roy" Dudley, who evidently was among the best. His guiding days spanned the 1890s into the 1940s. Roy knew generations of outdoorsmen and hikers, and his prolific tales were legendary. The South Basin Dudley trail that we were taking to Pamola Peak was named to honor his mountaineering know-how.

The weather was favorable to cross the peaks and return back to Chimney Pond. As simple soldiers of fortune, we were not out to aggravate the Mountain Spirit Pamola, and wanted only to reach his peak's high perch. After a campfire breakfast, we scrubbed our

Charlie on Cusp of Pinnacle Rock, 1951

mess kits with Chimney Pond's gravely sand. Our fingertips again became sandpapered by tree and granite grasps on almost every step up. Climbing first among low-growth, we then scrambled through Humpty-Dumpty piles of boulders much larger than us. Along the granite strewn trail above the tree line, we came upon Pinnacle Rock that was also known as Index Rock. It stuck out like the shadow-casting part of a sundial. Scaled to my four inches short of six feet, the rock probably projected about 40 feet from base to tip. What a roost it was for either a mountain or mortal spirit! After I shinnied to the tip of the overhanging cusp (which angled at maybe 50 degrees), Frank took a picture with me waving in triumph and showing no fear of height. That gutsy agility now exists only in my mind.

From Pamola Peak at the southern end of the east-facing Great Basin, the panorama of northern Maine below us was magnificent. The land was laced with lakes and ponds. We took a few pictures of the A.M.C. trail sign "Knife Edge; Chimney Peak .1M, South Peak .8M, Baxter Peak 1.1M." A trail sign behind us read Dudley Trail, Pamola Caves, and Chimney Pond, about a mile back.

Between Pamola and Chimney Peaks, we came upon a gulley called "The Notch." As small as it looks on the horizon, it is not! Each of the Notch's 100-foot-plus chimney walls presented an extremely steep free climb challenge with "Thank-God" handholds placed in strategic places.

Pamola & Chimney Peaks and Knife Edge Trail

Charlie, Snow on Baxter Peak, June 1951

Frank Lawton at Summit of Mt.Katahdin,1951

At rest on Chimney Peak summit, we marveled at our Notch climb and looked ahead understanding why the notorious trail to the summit was called "Knife Edge," a geological arête. It was saw-toothed, narrow, and tortuous in keeping with the park's trail sign warning of "Dangerous in high winds." Unnerving to timid climbers in no wind, we were happy-go-lucky about traversing the Knife Edge to reach the summit. Finally at Baxter Peak rock cairn, the park sign read Northern terminus of the Appalachian Trail. I was on cloud nine with the world below! With the view scanned and snow on top in June, our next impulse was to make snowballs.

I wore a felt ranger-type bush hat and carried a small rucksack. Frank wore a baseball cap and carried the canteen. We were comfortable enough to have our shirt sleeves rolled up. Maine's high point was exclusively ours! Some say that Cadillac Mountain on the coast is the first place that the sun touches North America in the morning, but standing on Katahdin's peak, I *knew* it hits here first!

We left the summit on Saddle Trail and shortly cut off on the mile plus Cathedral Trail which is the most direct route to Chimney Pond. Descent was as hard if not harder than the climb up. Awful steep, with slides of small, loose rock on the upper trail, the bottom was a maze of big boulders and stunted trees. We had to scooch along on the seats of our pants as much as using our hands and feet for stability. Chimney Pond was a welcome sight.

Next day, we broke camp and then packed up the Saddle Trail to where it joined the Northwest Basin Trail. The upper part of the Saddle was steep and gravelly under foot. Once on top, we crossed the Northwest Plateau tableland, a high-altitude flat terrain with stunted alpine vegetation under foot. I recalled reading that caribou ranged the area in the early 1900s, and there was a failed attempt to reestablish a herd. At about a two and one half mile point on the high plateau, the trail looked down upon Davis Pond in the Northwest Basin, and we hiked down through rubble to that campground. The rock slides above the pond were reminiscent of those in the Great Basin. Like so many places on this journey, we were the only campers there.

The Davis Pond campsite was about five miles from our next campground at Russell Pond. We followed the tote road west bank of the upper main Wassataquoik (Wah-**SAT**-a-cook) Stream, sometimes crossing it on slippery rocks. Passing between pond-like Turner

STATE OF MAINE

BAXTER STATE PARK

№ 10919

Campground _Davis Pond_ Date _6/20_ 1951

Camping Fee .25

№ 10922

Campground _Russ Pd_ Date _6/21_ 1951

Camping Fee .25

Camping Receipts,
Katahdin Trip, 1951

№ 10009

Roaring Brook Campground

Campground _____ Date _JUN 22 1951_ 1951

Camping Fee .25

PLEASE OBSERVE RULES AND REGULATIONS
BE CAREFUL WITH FIRE
KEEP MAINE GREEN

Deadwater (except for scattered boulders and dead trees) and New City fields, an old logging depot, the trail went into the forest and became a mossy path of roots, ruts, a few blow-downs, and damp ground cover. Every so often there were massive decaying stumps left long ago by hurricane, fire, or logger. We were, no doubt, in one of the most remote spots in the northeast.

Anyone who walks the deep woods whether working, hiking, or hunting, has been lost, or knows a story of someone who has been. In this area, where the lay of the land flattens out, our compass was the best bet if disoriented, because bearings by sight are lost. We weren't that long out of Boy Scouts to recall that the sun's position or shadows, or moss on the north side of a tree were meaningful.

Ranger Ralph Dolley, who first gave us a ride in to Roaring Brook, was in charge at the Russell Pond Ranger Station. He and Ed Werler reopened the old Tracy Packhorse Trail from Roaring Brook. He told us that bears had walked among sleeping Boy Scouts. Searching for food, they left muddy paw marks on a bunkhouse wall. We must have made noise while hiking, because we didn't see any big game. When spotted by red squirrels, they chattered and scolded us for invading their domain.

On day five, it took us over three hours to hike eight and one-half miles down the valley. The trail ran due south past Sandy Stream Pond to Roaring Brook campground. Along with our paid camping receipts from Davis and Russell Ponds, our check-in receipt, as you can see, reads: "State of Maine, Baxter State Park, No.10009, Roaring Brook Campground, Camping fee .25, Jun 22 1951, Please Observe Rules and Regulations, Be Careful with Fire, Keep Maine Green." Next morning, it was off to Millinocket and home-bound for Boston and a bath.

On my second trip with Don Clark in mid-September, 1952, we hiked the same routes as the previous year. I've a picture of Don at the Chimney Pond ranger station where, since 1924, many a warden or ranger stood, including Roy Dudley. Among friends at home, rugged, red-headed Don was called "Elmer." He was good company and a capable companion. In continuity from the 1951 trip with Frank Lawton, I recorded details of my trip with Elmer on the back of an envelope that happened to have Frank's Air Force duty address "A/3c Francis T. Lawton 21290952, 1401 Installation Sqd., Andrews A.F.B., Washington 25 D.C." Elmer drove us up in his 1940s Ford, and we picked up a soldier in southern Maine who was heading north on

Don Clark at Chimney Pond Ranger Cabin, 1952

leave. By coincidence, we met the guy again at distant Russell Pond campground! I say "Distant," because it's actually in the middle of the park's wilderness.

Food for the trip stood us $12.52, gas $14.78 (maybe up and back to equal $.14 cents a gallon), tolls one-way totaled $1.10 (N.H. $.15, Portsmouth $.10, Portland $.75, and Augusta $.10), campgrounds cost $8.50, and miscellaneous $2.20. Odometer mileage was 356 miles up and 377 miles returning. The week's trip amounted to $20 each!

In 1904, Holman F. Day wrote a book called *Kin O' Ktaadn*. I consider myself a member of that climbing clan.

PART TWO

RAISING A FAMILY

CHAPTER ONE
MEANT TO BE

Two of my most life changing events skyrocketed in the early 1950s. *What a show!*

The first was career born. Since age six or so, I decided that I wanted to be a dentist. Woburn's Dr. Owen J. Logue was our family dentist and my childhood role model. After I told him about my ambition, he saved Tufts Dental alumni magazines for me. With that in mind, Winchester High prepared me for admission to Tufts College in nearby Medford. At my interview, Dean of Students, Dr. Wessell, challenged me with, "Why do you want to work on someone's mouth?" I can't recall my reply, but I was accepted. My folks did not make a hullabaloo of me going to college, because I think they knew that I had a good educational background and was motivated. Student loans were unknown to us, tuitions were reasonable, and my parents footed the entire cost. I commuted to Tufts in 1949 and wore the blue-and-brown freshman beanie. Classmates who had served in WWII didn't react well to that "Kid stuff," nor did they hesitate to question a professor's dubious declaration or conceited conduct.

To catch the train to Tufts in Medford, I ran through backyards and across Main Street to Cross Street Depot in Winchester's North End. One morning, old Mrs. Dooley was standing on her porch while smoke was pouring out from under the eaves. I alerted her to the situation, and she replied in a true brogue: "Sure and it goes up the chimney too." The fire department arrived, and I resumed my run. Steam-train commuting involved the acrid smell of burning coal, rattling on rails, and sitting on worn velour commuter seats. Conductors wore black uniforms adorned with gold trim, collected tickets, and announced each stop: "Winchester," "Wedgemere," "West Medford," and "Medford Hillside."

My campus life was attending class, eating a brown-bag lunch, studying beside Tufts' stuffed elephant, Jumbo, in Barnum Hall with Marine veteran Bob Collins from Reading (we became lifelong friends), and occasionally going to college sporting events. Friends at home fulfilled my social needs. With Jim McLaughlin, Art McGonagle, Jim Hession, Harold Moran, Bill Haggerty, Bill Thomas, John Scanlon, and the McCallion brothers, Joe and John, I went to the Lakeside Ballroom in Wakefield to meet girls and dance. "Happy" Hampton Beach bestowed weekend fun. Joe's Pizza on Main Street in Woburn was a favorite hang-out. With McLaughlin and McGonagle, I camped at Greeley Ponds in the White Mountain National Forest Pemigewasset Valley. I earned spending money ushering at the Woburn movie theater and working in a Malden metal plating shop for one summer. In the summer season of 1949, and a year or two thereafter, I handled hides at Beggs and Cobb Tannery in Winchester.

Two generations of McGowan's in leather-processing preceded my low-level entry into the tanning trade. I remember that the walls of a large commercial ice house on Horn Pond were insulated with tanbark from which tannin had been extracted. Woburn High sports teams were known as the "Tanners." Because the tannery work was hard, hot, and sweaty, they provided us with salt pills but disregarded the potential effects of the chemical effluent that was dumped into the Aberjona River. I remember it as a yellow scum. It, and other tannery runoffs, became implicated many years later as causing cancer! I recall sitting in on union meetings, where my Irish immigrant neighbors and Greek co-workers had little input. The owners could not agree with the union and sold out.

Running to the train was worth it as 1952 approached. After completing admission requirements in three undergraduate years, I was accepted to Tufts Dental School. Now I was speeding and swaying through Medford and Somerville on the sleek, silver, and self-powered B & M Buddliner coaches in my commute to Boston's North Station. From there, I walked to Tufts Medical Center in Chinatown.

What proved to be the biggest event in my life happened on a New Year's Eve. I previously brought friend Jim McLaughlin, to a party organized by Winchester High and Tufts classmate, John Morabito, where Jim met Margaret "Peg" Marshall; long story short, she became his wife. They were invited to his Aunt Ella and Uncle Dr. Larry Louis' Scituate home for New Year's Eve 1952. Unbeknown to their daughter,

*Laurie Louis
Portrait, 1938*

and only child Laurie, Jim was asked to bring a friend for her date. I was that friend! After that "Meant to be," there were phone calls and an occasional date over the next six months, but the details are blurry. Then came more frequent calls and letters, dates developed, and our relationship blossomed. To this day, that feeling has flourished.

Her early education was with the Madams of the Sacred Heart in Newton. From age ten, Laurie boarded at the Academy of Notre Dame in Tyngsboro, Massachusetts where she says that she learned discipline, and gained the stamina to raise our kids. After graduation in June 1952, Laurie entered Massachusetts College of Art in September. Her parents moved to Waban, Massachusetts, so that Laurie would have a reasonable commuting distance to college.

Her father grew up in Newport, Rhode Island, the son of a church organist and music teacher who was born in Lisbon, Portugal. Dr. Louis graduated from Holy Cross in 1910, Harvard Medical School in 1914, and was gradually retiring from a long successful surgical practice at St. Elizabeth's Hospital in Boston. Her mother, Ella Rushforth, was born in Ballston Spa, New York, moved with her family to Winchester, Massachusetts, and became a registered nurse at Carney Hospital in Boston. She and Dr. Louis met there when he was a third-year (exceptional training for that time) surgical resident. They were married in 1919.

Mrs. Louis' cousin, Mary Kelly, was brought up by the Rushforth family and was Jim McLaughlin's mother. Laurie, coincidentally, was at Jim and my Winchester High graduation in 1949 when neither she nor I knew that a 1952 blind date was in store for us!

Though commuting daily from Woburn to Tufts Dental School in Boston by train, I enjoyed social activities along with the academic and clinical. One, in 1953, was attending a school function at the Hotel Shelton at 91 Bay State Road near Kenmore Square where senior Paul McBride's father was a manager. As soon as I saw a tall, smiling, man stride confidentally through the lobby with an open shirt and in stocking feet, I knew that it was Ted Williams! After the Sportsman Show years, he remained the same guy to me, a great fly fisherman and Red Sox baseball star…still "The Kid" at 35. Ted lived there, a few blocks from Fenway Park, as did other famous names like playwright Eugene O'Neill and film actress Jeanette MacDonald. It became a BU dorm, "Shelton Hall" in 1954. I recall that Laurie and I went to a dance on the popular Shelton Roof.

When we dated between places named Waban, a section of Newton, Massachusetts, and Woburn, it was confusing to some. We managed the difference with no problem! Dr. Louis asked her "What does this mean?" when Laurie received my friendship ring. After asking Doctor Louis for her hand, he introduced me to Mr. Edward Levine,

Loretta Putnam & Laurie on June 9, 1956

the owner of Homer's Jewelry store on Winter Street in downtown Boston.

I presented her with a surprise engagement ring on North Scituate beach. Her parents gave us a wonderful catered engagement party in their backyard. We waited impatiently, but practically, until after graduation to get married. The good Doctor kept me busy working on the lawn and gardens and trimming the tall hedges in Newton and Scituate. The reward was Laurie and the fine Georgia cooking and close friendship of Loretta Putnam, their housekeeper. She prepared vegetables from their big Scituate garden, and we brought roses and gladiolas in from Dr. Louis' beloved flower beds. Loretta could also launder, press, and keep an ultraclean house. She enjoyed an apartment in Boston on days off, played cards with friends in Scituate, smoked Kool cigarettes, and loved the Boston Red Sox. She and Laurie adored one another.

Laurie's first trip to New Brunswick was in 1954. My folks were on vacation in Rossville, and we came up by Boston and Maine Railroad. Transferring to the Bangor and Aroostook Railroad at Northern Maine Junction, we had the pleasure of eating native brook trout in the dining car. Laurie mixed well with everyone in Rossville. She offered to help Dad wallpaper a slant-walled upstairs bedroom. Both were inexperienced at papering, and when frustrated, a coffee, donut, and smoke break motivated them to keep on working.

I took Laurie trout fishing in the intervale in back of Cliff's. It was a deadwater of smooth and slow-moving current, where Trout Brook meandered through a heavy growth of meadowland grass. The fishing was fun, but no-see-um gnats penetrated our long pants, shirt sleeves, and collars!

In 1955, we drove up to Rossville in Laurie's red convertible. She brought art supplies and did a watercolor of remote Allandale's deserted St. Dominic Church, built in 1878 by Catholics who settled the area. The local farmers called the steep, sharp roof peak "Hailsplitter." Turn back to the dedication page and see if it is a fit title. I've already mentioned (bragged about) her other watercolor of my favorite pool in Trout Brook behind the Baylis farm.

Saturday night dances were the flair, and I took her to Chateau St. Jean dance pavillion on the river flats below Woodstock. Nature called, and Laurie had to make a quick trip into the dark hayfield next

Our Wedding Portrait

to the Chateau. Relieved, she said something to the effect that the timothy hay was awful tall.

Back home in the city, Laurie and I went to see Mr. Levine about a wedding ring and met his protégé, Donald Cohen. Both men were meticulously dressed (always with tie pin and cuff links) and perfectly groomed. We welcomed their friendship and advice for many years. Marie Laurentine "Laurie" Louis and I were married at Saint Phillip Neri Church in Newton by Cardinal Richard J. Cushing on June 9, 1956. As Archbishop of Boston, we respected his presence at our sacrament. In his usual loud and friendly voice, he handed Laurie and me a Papal blessing and said: "Don't be afraid, it's not a bill!"

Among out of town guests, George Baylis and George Ingraham came down from Rossville. Before the wedding, I took both Georges to the Casino burlesque theater in Boston, only to find out many years later, that my "Shy" Dad also brought them there! A day after the wedding, Laurie graduated from Massachusetts College of Art and I graduated from Tufts College Dental School. On the next day, I took a State Board exam and qualified for licensure to practice in Massachusetts.

Honeymoon Bound!

After Laurie and I honeymooned on Cape Cod and in Quebec, I had orders, as an Ensign in the Navy Dental Reserve Corps since 1954, to report for active duty as a lieutenant at Boston's First Naval District. I worked among clinics at the active Charlestown Shipyard where the ancient U.S.S. Constitution was berthed, the South Boston Naval Annex, where WWII ships were in mothballs, and at the Fargo Building District Headquarters. My uniform was khaki in summer and blue in winter.

High school friend Bill Thomas was on guard duty at the Fargo Building. When he saluted me as I entered the gate, I said "Knock it off Billy!" My additional duties were taking alcohol and narcotics inventory and serving as a defense counsel for brig prisoners. Alcohol (the pure kind that we drink) came in pint tin cans. One medical captain with years of experience managed to taste it periodically and still not disturb the inventory. Morphine tablets came in small glass tubes, and the count was always correct. My lack of legal expertise didn't make much difference to the defendants who were "Before the mast" for minor infractions.

On one occasion in winter, the Captain assigned me to confirm the identity of a body that had been found in Boston Harbor. I had a missing sailor's dental records for comparison and went to a funeral home in Everett with mask, gloves, eugenol (oil of cloves) to counteract odor, and a dissecting kit. The findings matched the records, and some family had final closure.

Twenty-four years later on the morning of May 23, 1981, I had a call to verify the identity of Chris Currie, a friend of my son Chip and son of dentist L. Rodger Currie and wife Pat, who perished in a fiery plane crash on Cape Cod. He was accumulating in-flight hours for a multi-engine license, as a co-pilot on a Gull Air flight out of Hyannis to Nantucket at six a.m. with full fuel tanks. Apparently, the Beechcraft G18S was overloaded with freight, lost air-speed on takeoff, and crashed in the woods. I had operated on Chris' fractured jaw and brought the postoperative x-rays and my dissecting kit to the morgue at Cape Cod hospital. Sadly but surely, it was Chris. I recall standing at his burial site with Ted Kennedy, who was the Currie's Hyannis Port neighbor.

As newlyweds, Laurie and I had an apartment in a home at 191 Allerton Road in Newton Highlands. It was owned by Mr. and Mrs. MacDonald, natives of Nova Scotia, who were wonderful to us. Dad, retired in 1955, was alone at home as mother was hospitalized, and

Dad's Grave Marker, Woburn, Mass.

Lucy McGowan & grandniece

he enjoyed constructing a bedframe and a dining room table for us. With no bathroom upstairs, I reverted to farm days and got Laurie a "Thunder jug" for our bedroom. When her father came and saw the chamber pot, he must have thought that I had set his daughter back one hundred years. She developed a potentially life threatening staphylococcus pneumonia that summer, and Dr. Joseph Stanton, Jr. supervised her recovery at St. Elizabeth's Hospital. Our parents were thrilled with a November announcement that Laurie was due with our first child, and their first grandchild, in July 1957.

Dad, being a Navy veteran, enjoyed the Commissioned Officers Mess in Charlestown when we invited him for drinks and dinner. Just Laurie and I were there at dinner on Wednesday, February 27, 1957 when I had a phone call. It was Jim McLaughlin who said that he had bad news for me. I immediately thought of my hospitalized mother, but Jim said that my father had died. Dad collapsed while taking a barrel of coal ashes out of the cellar at 24 Lake Avenue, Woburn, and was discovered by Uncle Tom McGowan.

Grief-stricken at age 23, I went down the cellar stairs to the place where he had collapsed in front of the coal furnace. An old felt hat, that he wore when he was working at home, was on the floor, stained from the incident. I picked it up and kept it for a while. Mother came home for the funeral, dazed throughout. I felt bad for my widowed grandmother Bridget who, at age 89, was burying her 61 year-old son. I will not forget kissing him in the casket. As an only child, it was fortunate that I had Laurie's support and was stationed in Boston. Dr. and Mrs. Louis took in Dad's cherished little dog, Penny. They too, gave me a lot of sympathy and encouragement.

Laurie delivered our first child, Laurie Ann, on July 7, 1957. The obstetrician, Dr. Arthur Gorman, was a friend and fellow practitioner of Grandpa Louis at St. Elizabeth's Hospital in Brighton. By that time we had a house in Waban, and entered the world of bringing up kids. I completed naval service on July 1, 1958, and started a three-year program in oral and maxillofacial surgery at Boston City Hospital (BCH) and Tufts Medical and Dental schools.

My early career in doctoring had a New Brunswick connection. While an intern at Boston City Hospital in 1958, a young man from the province was admitted with a shattered lower jaw. His name was Arthur, a Mi'kmaq who had come to Boston as a construction worker. He had been out drinking and got in a fight that resulted in the trauma. Arthur and I became friendly. Surgery involved incisions through skin and muscle to approximate the splintered bone fragments before wiring his jaws shut for stabilized healing. Because he could only take liquids, he craved solid food. When I did Arthur's daily sterile dressing changes, nurses on the ward told me that he was stealing food from ophthalmology patients who had both eyes bandaged! After he was discharged and I was on call one weekend, he came in dressed in a shirt and tie to tell me that he was getting married. When I heard that he later had marital problems, I thought of New Brunswick and hoped that he returned to his senses and to his aboriginal homeland.

As my tales make headway, Ted Williams name keeps resurfacing. The E.R. at BCH had an x-ray room for orthopedic surgery called the Shortell Unit. Legend had it that Ted was diagnosed there for an elbow injury and successfully treated by Dr. Joseph Shortell...with whom he later fished.

Laurie kept Dr. Gorman busy as Charles E. McGowan Jr., "Chip," was born on January 8, 1959, and Jean Marie was welcomed on February 10, 1960. As a surgical resident with family obligations on the rise, my trips north were less frequent.

Among incidents that kept me connected, one unexpectedly happened when I met Dr. Donald Blackstone of Presque Isle, Maine at Tufts Dental in Boston in 1960. He was in the orthodontic training program, and I was in the middle year of my oral surgery program, mostly the second year medical school curriculum. He told me that he had been in the Navy in WWII, went to dental school, and was the first dentist in Maine to spend a year in the oral surgery program at Belleview Hospital in New York City. I told him about my great aunt Lucy Baylis Fox and husband Wilmot settling in Perham, Aroostook County, understood to be successful in farming, and raising a large family. Surprisingly, Donald's mother, Addie Fox Blackstone, was one of their children and a first cousin to my mother. Don and I were connected kin! Since then, he puts it well by saying that many of the County settlers and descendants like him have a "Foot on each side of the border."

In those early years, Canadian friends George and Evelyn Ingraham and Harold and Loverine Davidson honeymooned with us. The Ingraham's arrived with a hay-wired can still attached to their car by pranksters at their chivaree. The Davidsons took great pride in having

Wilmot & Lucy Fox Family, Perham, Maine, c. 1917

their picture taken in front of the Ford Motor plant in Somerville, Mass. In addition to staying in touch with relatives, I subscribed to the Fredericton *Daily Gleaner* to keep informed of New Brunswick happenings.

CHAPTER TWO
SIXTIES SUM-UP

Bob Moynihan, a dental school classmate, and I opened the first practice limited to oral surgery in Lowell, Massachusetts, a Yankee 1800s Industrial Revolution mill-town. I completed my residency at Boston City Hospital, and Bob his, at New York City Bellevue Hospital. Before we came, the textile industry moved south putting the city in an economic decline up into the 1950s. Lowell appealed to us because high-tech industry and cultural growth were on the upswing. It was being considered for a National Historic Park, and that happened in 1979. The city had three hospitals and a quarter-million ethnic mix of suburban residents: French Canadian, Greek, Italian, Polish, Portuguese, Jewish, and Irish. For quite a few years, we carried our surgical instruments from hospital to hospital for booked cases or inevitable trauma. For thirty years, we treated both hospital and office patients. Medically compromised and trauma patients kept us in daily contact with general, specialty, nursing, and ancillary hospital staffs. When we were asked to see a hospitalized patient, our first notation on the consultation sheet was "History and chart reviewed." We were team players in patient care.

In 1961, the same year that Bob and I opened our practice, Laurie and I bought a home at 17 Berkeley Drive in outlying residential Chelmsford, known for a good school system. As a young parent, I proudly brought Laurie Ann and Chip to meet my former teachers at Wyman Elementary School in Winchester. The principal, Miss Lawry who taught third grade, gave me parting advice on a child's upbringing, "Give children the chance to enjoy the things of childhood." With today's rush-around-world, I've never stopped quoting her wise words.

Mother recovered from a bout of illness and chose to move back to Rossville from Woburn to be with Uncle George, who had been alone since Mabel's death in 1953. Mom left Rossville 34 years prior, and it was her desire and joy to go back to her roots and cross-border family. I was comfortable with her choice.

Joyce Briggs Jones observed George as "Kind and giving but lonesome living alone," and that he seemed happier when Mother came to keep house. Gwen Briggs Bradbury said that one of her favorite family trips was taking Mother to or meeting her at the Houlton bus stop on trips to visit us in Massachusetts, and that she treated them with a lunch in appreciation. Gwen plays cards with Molly Trail whose husband, Gordon, was a Baylis cousin. Molly, 97, tells of visiting Mother, saying "She was a very soft spoken, gentle lady and when she smiled, she smiled with her eyes." Dad's sister, my Aunt Ruth Murphy, came up from Massachusetts for summer visits to see Mother and George. I think that Ruth and Mom had a strong sister-in-law relationship.

When Laurie and I first drove up to the Baylis farm from Chelmsford, with Laurie Ann, Chip, and Jean, we were sure to pack a thermos of coffee to accompany Laurie's delicious crabmeat sandwiches. One trip was an exhausting 12 hours on the road, not counting the time spent to repair a station wagon problem. Sherrill Munro Bradley, my second cousin, lent us a crib. We were afraid that our youngsters might touch the hot kitchen wood stove, but we were relieved when they were cautious. Laurie washed the diapers and clothing in woodstove heated water. Little Laurie Ann was fascinated with George's horse "Bill" and chatted constantly about him.

Easter Sunday, 1962, with Dr. and Mrs. Louis

Margaret Alicia, "Peg," was our next born on April 15, 1961, and Laurence Joseph, "Larry," on September 25, 1962. Dr. Gorman was still delivering our children at St. Elizabeth's Hospital in Boston. He prescribed castor oil to "Get Laurie going," and Larry was close to being born in Lexington on Route 128.

A very personal loss came in 1962, when we received the sad news of George Ingraham's death at age 31. He was electrocuted while working on a Hydro-Electric line. George and I had a brotherly bond. Evelyn was left with three small children, Frederick, Hazel, and David. She kindly sent us an announcement when she married Francis Hogan of Grand Bay-Westfield, New Brunswick on July 31, 1971. Other premature Rossville deaths were friend, farmer, and veteran Corbett McGuire at 44, and Aubrey Davidson, accidentally, in 1963.

After Uncle George called and said that Mother was ill again, I drove up to Rossville with 3½ year old Chip on Halloween, 1963, to bring her back to Chelmsford. We viewed snow-covered Mount Katahdin on the way up and learned that a climber, Mrs. Margaret Ivusic of Boston, died two days before from exposure in a ferocious mountain snowstorm. Her companion, Helen Mower of Concord, Massachusetts was a survivor. A second victim was Park Ranger Ralph Heath of Sherman, who perished in the rescue operation.

On that cold, first day of November, I took a picture of Chip,

Uncle George & Horse, Baylis Barnyard, Nov. 1, 1963

George, and his horse in the Baylis barnyard with snow on the ground. Laurie was busy at home anticipating the imminent arrival of our sixth child. She delivered Mary Ann on the next Thursday, November 7th. After Laurie experienced the long and harrowing trip to Boston to deliver Larry, Dr. Hugh Mahoney at St. Johns Hospital in Lowell was her obstetrician. One year later on November 12, 1964, he delivered Elizabeth. Fortunately, Laurie's prenatal exposure to German measles had not affected the pregnancy. Mary Ann, as Beth's everlasting room-mate, exclaimed and titled her sister as "Bethy."

Laurie and I, both only children, now had seven of our own (and more to come)! After the assassination of John F. Kennedy, we watched the Presidential funeral cortege on TV on the day of Mary's baptism. When she could talk and we said "Mary had a Little Lamb," she insisted "Ditherent Mary, Ditherent Mary!"

When Mother was well, she, Laurie, and I would visit her cousin Gwen and husband, Marty Levy, at their Beach Court home in Gloucester. It was formerly occupied by the Coast Guard in WWII and was located directly on the harbor of Gloucester's world-famous fishing fleet. I remember Gwen and Marty as funny and hospitable. Gwen referred to the reclining nude painting (not found in New Brunswick farmhouses) over their fireplace as Marty's "Hussy." She gave Laurie and me two new-vogue "Moscow Mule" copper cups in which vodka, ginger beer, and a lime were served over ice. Sadly, alcohol became too good a friend to Gwen. When combined with heavy smoking, it led to throat cancer and her demise.

In 1965, we crossed the border when Uncle Ronald prematurely passed away, on February 2nd at age 49, from kidney failure. We attended his funeral in Woodstock, not expecting that, in nine months, George would die and we would return again.

George gave in to liquor. He continued farming and was not isolated from family or friends, but imbibing, he tried to take his life with a rifle in the kitchen. Not successful, he landed in Fredericton's Victoria Hospital. I was getting my feet wet in surgical practice in Lowell, and called his seasoned attending physician. When I diplomatically approached the incident, the straight reply was "He shot himself!" We offered to have George come cross-border to recuperate, but an in-hospital pulmonary embolism took his life on November 19, 1965. Harold McGuire, the oldest son of Corbett and Marie on the neighboring farm, told Merlin and Eunice Fox that when he was quite young, George was kind in providing him with work and advice. Returning to Rossville, we and family brought George Rockwell Baylis to the Munro cemetery where, anonymous to all present, his namesake and my great uncle George Rockwell was interred almost 79 years before.

A notable change in our travel route through Penobscot and Aroostook counties occurred when the Bangor-Houlton section of I-95 opened to through traffic in 1967. It was cut through farmland, bogs, and rough country, and engineered for seasonal endurance. Although it eliminated our need to travel on Route 2A through the Haynesville Woods, we miss that backcountry trip.

We took Laurie Ann, Chip, Jean, and Peg to the 1967 Expo in Montreal. Chez le Roi restaurant, in the Old City, had walls of stone and a beamed ceiling. Waitresses wore vintage dress and served a Quebecois cuisine of meat pies, pea soup, and maple desserts. The candle lit and crowded cellar lounge made the clientele look like giants compared to tiny Peggy, looking upward, in the midst of it all. On a subsequent visit to Rossville, Peggy awoke early and offered to help out in the kitchen. A relative spoke up with "Ain't Peggy smart." There are still no flies on Peggy.

Our 1966 family Christmas present, Christine Ella, "Chris," was born prior to the holiday on December 14. She was another handsome blonde like her brother Larry! Our ninth, Paula Julie, "PJ," chose the warmth of July 17, 1968, to close the sixties decade of McGowan family growth.

CHAPTER THREE

TIMES, THEY ARE A'CHANGING

After Mother came home from Rossville in 1963, her mental capacity continued to deteriorate. She was admitted to D'Youville Manor Nursing Home where I was on the consulting staff. The care was excellent, and we could visit her often. The physical burden on the nursing staff became too difficult, and we transferred her to the Metropolitan State Hospital in Waltham, Massachusetts, for care and safe-keeping. We drove down with the children on weekends and would sometimes take her out for a ride. She didn't mind going back to the hospital.

Both our and the Moynihan families had grown to seven children each by 1964. Laurie and I and Bob and Joanne were going full speed with responsibility and whatever recreation we could manage. After Bob and I opened a satellite office in Nashua, New Hampshire, two interstate offices with hospital obligations kept us on the run.

Though I lost close contact with New Brunswick goings on after Ronald and George's passing, I never lost my passion for being in the out-of-doors, especially in Rossville. When I came across the St. John River Valley writings of Dr. George Frederick Clarke, they enabled me to revisit the places and people that I loved. Born in Woodstock, Dr. Clarke practiced dentistry, and was a keen out-doorsman, archeologist, conservationist, and historian who, as they say, "Wrote it all down." He preferred to have Indians from the Woodstock reservation as friends and companions when fishing or searching for artifacts. He wrote affectionately about Dr. Peter Paul, Noel Moulton, Noel and Peter Polchies, their families, and ways of life and death. "And of all Maliseets: quiet, dignified, intelligent and informative." He wrote of Noel Polchies, "Noel was a very dear friend of mine. He knew a great many quaint stories about his people, and the animals who inhabit the forest. He never boasted. He was truthful and courteous." Of Noel Moulton, "He was the most patient angler that I have ever known, and to watch him casting a line was a delight."

Dr. Clarke had an American-turned-Canadian, friend and author of the classic *The Bark and Skin Boats of North America*, named Tappan Adney. Both lived in Woodstock and spoke the Maliseet language. Unlike Dr. Fred, he had some idiosyncrasies, such as walking nude in his woods, which certainly captured a gossip's ear...or a "Tom's" eye. His tales are told in *The Travel Journals of Tappan Adney 1887–1890, Edited By C. Ted Behne*, 2010. The woods-skills and knowledge told of Adney's camping friends, Humbolt Sharp of Upper Woodstock and Maliseet companion, Peter Joseph, are make-do and get-it-done!

Dr. Clarke published *Six Salmon Rivers and Another* in 1960. Five, of the six rivers, are Miramichi, St. John, Restigouche, Kedgewick, Tobique, and Upsalquich. *Another*, is the river of contentment. My contact with the Atlantic silver salmon was confined to occasional summer fish peddlers, because the cost of fishing for the exciting "Leaper," was beyond my youthful non-resident reach in the cost of equipment, a guide, and a license. Of the Restigouche and his guide friends, David and Jock Ogilvy, he has full page photos of two salmon caught in Government Reserved Water No. 1 Pool. First is Jock holding a 38 pounder caught by lovely Marion McNair, daughter of the premier, and the second is David holding a 34 pound silver salmon caught by Dr. Clarke. Later in these tales, I'll bring you up to the Tobique north-country and reunite you with the Ogilvy father, Alex, and sons, outfitters.

Dr. Clarke was totally aware of his surroundings in each careful step when stalking woods or stream. His perception-to-pen talent enriched my knowledge of people, places, and history in the St. John River Valley. After reading the *Song of the Reel* in 1963, his observations and depth of description had me hooked.

Atlantic salmon and native wild brook trout are first cousins, and both survive in the settings of cold, clear, oxygenated water. The brook trout has a convoluted olive and black back for camouflage. Dr. Clarke describes the blue-grey flank as speckled with "golden and carmine side-moons," each red dot with a stunning blue-halo. On orange-to-white undersides, there are five carrot-colored fins, each with a white striped fore-edge. The species may be called brook, Eastern, speckled, or squaretail trout. In Rossville, it's plain "Trout." I was very happy with a kinfolk "License" to fish Trout Brook.

I knew that folks in the St. John River Valley above Fredericton were up in arms about a hydroelectric project that would create a dam at Macquatac in Kingsclear, and flood the lowlands as far up as Woodstock. I was hearing, reading, and becoming more concerned about what would happen to Rossville and Culliton. When the proposed project was in the making, Dr. Clarke, with disdain for dams and their social or environmental intrusion, was outspoken in behalf of ecological preservation. Fredericton native and historical author, Esther Clark Wright, published *The St. John River and Its Tributaries* in 1966. Sensitive to the impending impact on the province and affected population, she objectively detailed gains and losses. Need for an expanded source of electricity pressured the province, and the centralized St. John was a choice location. The opposition to displacement of about 1,000 upriver properties is described as drowning aboriginal sites and subsequent settlement achievements along a 60 mile head pond. Until then, the lands along the river had not been divested of their natural beauty.

Ardent antagonism to the Macquatac Project was fruitless, and the project moved forward. Lower Southampton and Culliton prepared for the radical change of clearing, relocation, and waterfront transformation. Some homes were moved in entirety by towing them across the river ice to the opposite shore. It was hard for me to imagine Nackawic butternut and fiddlehead flats submerged, St. John River islands vanished, graveyards moved, roadways but a memory, and hamlets with homesteads only history. Imagine the mixture of helplessness and hope that the parishioners of the Lower Southampton Anglican church had as it was being towed down the road in November, 1967 to its new location in Nackawic. The challenging river-rapids at Shogomoc and the scenic falls at Pokiok would be forever silent. The new Pokiok Bridge, just below the old Pokiok Falls, is attractive and necessary, but not as spectacular and natural as were the original cascades.

Forty-three years later in 2010, Joan Hatto Rae commented in a "Waterfalls of New Brunswick" blog archive: "Thank you for featuring Pokiok Falls. I grew up in Pokiok and the little village was so lovely and unique. It was heartbreaking to lose it to so called 'progress.' The village was completely devastated by the dam and everyone was supposed to move across the river to Nackawic but nobody moved. They all built or moved their houses up the road a bit and settled in. Now it has slowly regained a bit of its charm but it will never be the same for those of us who had the pleasure of crossing the old railway bridge and swimming in the old swimming hole out back of the falls. I thank you again."

My cross-border family burial grounds were moved from riverside in 1966, by funeral directors F.R. Flewelling and Son. It's right and proper that the cemetery foreman for relocation was Alec Ferguson, a true Scot of birth and burr, and a game warden who walked the Rossville Road when I was young. The Munro, Calder, and MacFarlane cemeteries, some dating back to the 1850s, were relocated and combined with the smaller existing Otis Cemetery in Nackawic. Like the Munros, the Calders emigrated from the Creich and Dornock area of Sutherlandshire in the Scottish Highlands. MacFarlanes originated from the western Scottish Highlands. The original Munro site, in Austin Munro's lower field, was one-quarter mile below the present flooded area near where the ball fields are today. The Munro section of the Otis Cemetery and its "Turf blankets," (coined from Maine friend, Capt. Elliot Billings, as grass Rest in Peace coverlets), and headstones became my rendezvous of memories.

Few remnants remain of the culture that my great grandparents, Annie Munro and George Baylis', brought from Scotland and England. Reminders of United Kingdom rule are York and Carleton Counties, Southampton and Queensbury parishes, King and Queen Streets in Fredericton and Woodstock, and images of the Monarch, Queen Elizabeth, in government and public places. "Grammie" and "Grampy" were carryover endearments.

With the Mactaquac HydroElectric Dam gates closing on November 6, 1967, some of those historical remnants were endangered. I worried about the fate of my old stomping grounds. My ingrained image of going to the store on graveled Rossville Road was walking past McGuire and Woodman farms, down Woodman Hill with William and Marie Davidson's house on the right. Guy and Daisy's drive was on the left. Next to them on the hill overlooking Trout Brook culvert, was Archie and Annie Morrison, with daughters Connie, Esther, and Maxine.

The rushing spring freshet on Trout Brook was huge, and the cement culvert beneath the road surface had to be wide and high. I remember seeing Roy St. Peter's old Ford hung up on the edge of the

DAVID DAVIS "NACKAWIC BEND" MAP - 1985

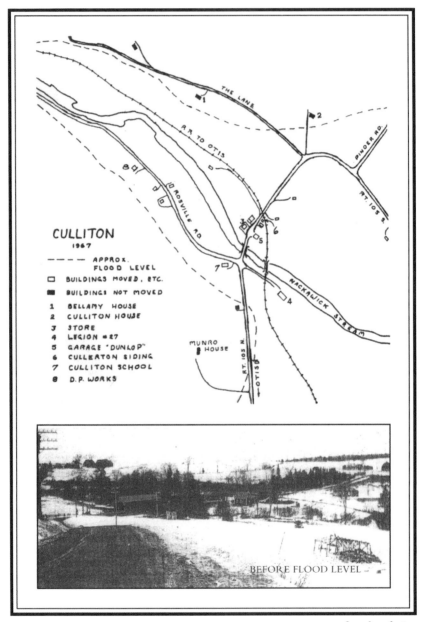

donahuedesign

ditch high above the brook. Roy, somewhat slumped in the driver seat, seemed unconcerned. There was no panic, because we had seen it before.

On the right below the culvert, Hedley and Elsie Mooers' small house sat in a gulley next to the brook. Their children, Earle and Jean, were younger than me. Rossville Road continued past the Bill and Nina Morrison farm family of 11 (Ola, Ruth, Joyce, Edith, Alton, Myrna, Avis, Peter, Violet, Robert, and Nina Anne), followed Nackawic Creek, and passed Myrl and Merilla Dunlop's house close to the Culliton School and covered bridge crossroads. The Nackawic CD of before and after flooding scenes, with hundreds of labeled black and white photos, and Marlowe M. Fox color slides, certainly refreshed my memory and will preserve Culliton's once high-spirited existence!

When the head pond rose to its capacity, that nostalgic Rossville stroll where the crossroads, bridge, schoolhouse, store, garage, railroad, and Royal Canadian Legion had always been located, *ceased to be*. Below and above the lake-like waters of the cove, the original width of the St. John river-bend had tripled and doubled. From Leona Munro's diary, 1966 and 1967 excerpts were:

July 25 CPR train made its last trip to Otis.
Aug. 30 A labourer was killed (crushed) at east end of Nackawic bridge.
Nov. 24 Dr. Bramstrup's house is being built at Otis.
Dec. 6 Started putting sewer pipes out along our line.
Dec. 22 Last Christmas program at Culliton School.
April 8 Earl Stairs closed his store on Culliton flat.
April 22 Lenwood McGuire burned his old buildings. Last of buildings to be burned on that road.
June 1 We went to the last graduation supper in old High School.
June 3 Earl and Marjorie Stairs have their [new] house wired and moved their chesterfield in today.
June 13 Old Rossville road closed to traffic. We have to go to Otis to get to Rossville now.
June 30 Last day at the old Culliton School, I have been packing books, etc. for the past week.
Aug. 12 We had supper at Legion Hall on Culliton Flat for the last time.

Sept. 27 They burned the old Culliton School.

Oct. 13 Last buildings were burned at Culliton Flat.

Oct. 28 Last wedding reception in Legion Hall on Culliton Flat.

Nov. 2 The army from Gagetown started to pack dynamite under old Pokiok bridge. All traffic is stopped. No children from the other side attended school.

Nov. 3 Old Pokiok Bridge across the St. John River blown up today.

Nov. 6 Mactaquac flooding started today. The school buses were allowed to cross the new bridge. The first traffic across on steel floor. Only school buses and mail trucks were allowed to cross.

Nov. 12 All islands and some of Bear Island under water.

Nov. 16 There is a foot of water over the Culliton Bridge. The buses came across this a.m. Road closed through Culliton today.

Nov. 26 I walked down the old road. Water is up over old school ground and 2/3 up Culliton [and Woodman] Hill.

Dec.1 River frozen over.

Thank God, my Baylis farm and those at the top of Rossville's Woodman Hill were spared from the rising waters!

When cousin Ella Stairs Briggs was appointed the Administrator of Uncle George Baylis' estate and effects on August 30, 1967, the 275 acres of Baylis farmland, deeded from 1883–1926, finally went before the courts. On October 8, 1968, a decree split the estate in five ways of "Undivided interest or moiety in the lands and premises" among Ella M. Briggs, Ella M. Baylis (Ronald's widow and guardian of their infant Brenda I. Baylis), Lucy McGowan, and nephews Earle and Alton McElwain.

Mother declined a one-fifth interest in the proposed sale. We appreciated the fact that she enjoyed being back on the farm with family and friends after Dad died. Ella Stairs Briggs and her family were especially kind while she was in Rossville. The remaining four grantees offered to give Laurie and me estate land on which we could move the workshop and convert it into a camp. My practice, family obligations, and the long travel distance from Massachusetts prohibited us from accepting. Mother's belongings were divided among family in New Brunswick. Other than photographs of Mother, my one remaining possession, frequently pointed out to our children, is her decorative piece of porcelain pottery.

Southampton Contractors Limited, the Corey family forestry partnership, purchased the estate, divided acres, and sold lots. David and Marilyn MacMillan bought the parcel (PID #75099093) that contained the house and barns in 1981 and have kept the property in first-rate condition.

A letter and photograph, dated April 18, 1969, were sent to me from David L. Myles, Research Historian for the Historical Resources Administration Mactaquac Program. The group collected photographic and other artifacts after properties were vacated in preparation for the flooding. Among glass plates found on the Guy Davidson property, a copied photo shows Mother, three sisters, her parents, and a horse in front of their home. He consulted Guy Davidson, who told him that Baylis farmhouse had burned. Guy was respected in the community, and his word and handshake were as good as gold. I was amazed, never knowing that a previous Baylis home existed. I showed the picture to Mother when she was quite senile, and she immediately remembered the horse's name. Afterward, I could not remember it, and still can't. I've unsuccessfully searched for the date and circumstance of the fire, but judging from the age of Mother and her sisters, the photo was probably taken around the summer of 1905.

CHAPTER FOUR

HOMESTEADING

April 1967, was a milepost in our whereabouts when Laurie and I purchased an 1892 home on ten acres of land at 55 High Street handy to the town center of Chelmsford, Massachusetts. It was perfect for privacy, convenience, and size. We hired Picard Construction Company from Lowell to completely renovate the home, and provide an amply lighted ground-level apartment facing the street, for aging Dr. and Mrs. Louis.

Dry-laid fieldstone walls bordered the front field and sides of the property. The back acreage was wooded almost down to seldom-used railroad tracks. Large sugar maples, that lined the long entrance driveway, gave us shade in summertime, colorful foliage in autumn, and sap when tapped in the spring. A massive copper beech tree reigned across the driveway in front of the house. In the midst of raising another generation, it was our "Family tree," and our kids climbed all over it. Grandpa Louis was the beech guardian and tree warden waving his cane at the imps on the limbs, telling them that they would break its branches! His physician's instinct for accident prevention was speaking, and he didn't want to see them fall.

While the High Street house was under construction, we were still living on Berkeley Drive. One day little Larry was playing with matches under our bed, and set the box spring on fire. He didn't tell anyone that a fire had started. Laurie smelled smoke, encountered intensive heat, and got everyone out. Luckily, the heat blistered door to three-year-old Beth's bedroom was closed. That was a hectic Halloween day. Neighbors, Sandy and Jerry Reed, took in ten-month-old Christine, and the rest of us moved into a motel for a few weeks. Fortunately, our Berkeley Drive home sold quickly as a "Fire Sale" before we moved to High Street in 1968.

Ella Briggs, in Canada, found Barbara Christie, the eldest of 16 children, to help Laurie in Chelmsford with our youngsters for a few

Our High Street Home, Chelmsford, MA, 1967

Renovated 55 High Street, 1975

summers. That first year, 1968, her parents, Gwen, Austin, and Barbara's grandmother, drove her down from New Brunswick. On the second summer, U.S. immigration denied her cross-border passage saying that she did not have working papers. I took a flight to Washington, D.C., and at Customs and Immigration, explained that she was with us for a vacation to help Laurie. That resolved the problem. Her dependability, mild manner, and kindness were excellent examples for our children. We stayed in touch throughout her University of New Brunswick degree in 1972 and marriage. A malignancy claimed her lovely life at age 44 in 1991. For over 30 years, we have traded Christmas cards with her mother, Gwen, the amazing grandmother of 35 and great grandmother of 46!

Though busy with two offices, raising a large family, and maintaining the High Street property, Laurie and I wanted a place where the family could get away together within a 100 mile radius of Chelmsford. We found a realtor in Ashland, New Hampshire, which sits dead center in the middle of the state. It was in the foothills of the White Mountain range above Lake Winnipesaukee and only 90 miles from home. The realtor, with snowshoes on standby, drove us up dirt Owl Brook Road to a small, old house on a hill on ten acres of pasture land. A Land Vest property, it was ours in February 1971 for $26,000! I knew the area from childhood visits to my grandfather McGowan's North Sandwich "Gray Gables" home in the shadow of Mt. Israel near Squam Lake.

From Little Squam Lake, the graveled road followed Owl Brook, forked left, and sloped upward. On the left, surrounded by pasture, our house was Cape style with a granite and stone foundation and pumpkin pine floors. We had a clear view across wooded hills and fields. A three-side pole shed almost full of hay bales, had enough room to stow our small motorboat, its trailer, and my Cub Cadet tractor. Fieldstone walls and some fencing surrounded the pasture. A large butternut tree stood beside the house. How the red squirrels carried so many butternuts into the attic and cellar we will never know. A small weathered sign on a tree named the place, "Whippoorwill." I remembered that the bird had whiskers to help it catch flies, but we never saw one. Its hyphenated whip-poor-will song at dusk was a pleasure on many occasions.

The area was perfect for all-season recreation. Neighbor Ray

Normandin, born on Martha's Vineyard, had a marina on Ashland River where we kept our boat in summer. Having gone across the Culliton covered bridge many times in New Brunswick, crossing one at the head of Little Squam Lake was fun. It was erected by two of the best New England covered bridge builders and restorers, Milton Graton and son Arnold. Their shop and yard was nearby.

We often ventured through the small canal at the other end of Little Squam into Big Squam Lake. We fished, watched loons, or went ashore on Church Island to view the pulpit and pews, under tall fir trees, where summer services were held on Sundays. Another favorite pastime was visiting Squam Lakes Science Center in Holderness. We walked the trails and saw birds and wildlife in a natural setting. The Ashland area was my hunting paradise in autumn. We snowmobiled on our pasture and the back roads in winter. Like Chip, at Holderness School, we skied at Waterville Valley and Tenney Mountain. Ashland was a perfect get-away for family and invited friends. I immediately knew that I had found another place of contentment within my northeast nesting ground.

Conveniently, Chip spent his junior and senior high school years at nearby Holderness School, graduating in 1977. Their academics, sports, Outward Bound trips, and ski privileges at Waterville Valley suited his style. Except when closed in winter, unpaved Sandwich Notch Road between the Valley and town of Sandwich was our favorite circuit through autumn foliage. There were no dwellings. At a roadside stream, we could swim in pools and slide over slippery rocks. Larry, Chip, and I camped at Hall Ponds and hunted the ridges and old apple orchards where bear clawed the bark and feasted on the fruit. Most memorable was a November 1979 hunt. Larry had taken a hunter safety course, and I gave him a .30-30 caliber Marlin rifle. Soon after we split up, the first shot ever fired from that carbine brought down an eight point, 210 pound buck!

The home was furnished with many pieces of collectible and useful antiques like a big cranberry scoop, Windsor chairs, a long harvest table, and corner pine cupboard. Natives, Howard and Libby Small and Howard's brother Orville, lived on the farm below us, and we became good friends. Howard had watched our house for the previous owner, from Massachusetts, who had his name etched on a granite slab. The gentleman didn't have the Small's respect, and Howard came up with a crowbar and quietly but decisively turned the previous family's granite inscription, as Howard said, "Into the ground." Speaking of burial, there was a small brick structure in the field across the road where a local lady was interred some years ago. We were told that her wish was not to be "Put in the ground."

The Small's farmhouse was like a museum with its stuffed owls, hand-hooked rugs, kerosene lamps, vintage upholstered furniture, rocking chair, family pictures, Libby's art-work, and collectibles connecting generations. It was a peaceful place to visit. She referred to their cattle as "Creatures." Small's warmth and that of their wood stove in fall, wintertime, and spring made us feel welcomed. In spring, they had us down to their sugar house by Owl Brook for sampling of taffy-like sugar-on-snow. They sold syrup and maple fudge made with their own butternuts at fairs for many years. Libby, in Grandma Moses' style, took to painting maple sugaring scenes on stoneware jugs. Not only did the landscape flow crisp and bright from her hand-strokes, but the depiction came directly from her bones. We bought one and treasure it.

Orville was very quiet, constantly doing chores. We were passing by one day when he was splitting wood in the pasture next to the road. Noticing a police car and fire truck at the farm, we stopped and asked him about the situation. He said "I guess something's going on up at the house" and returned to his labors!

Gravity-fed spring water to our house was kept running all winter to prevent a freeze, but the plastic pipe was so close to the surface of the pasture that the cattle's hooves kept breaking it. We corrected the problem by installing a deep pipe system. We had a stone mason, also a preacher, construct a fieldstone fireplace, and we installed a new septic system as another improvement. A farming neighbor, Mark Ober, kept cattle in our pasture, which in turn controlled brush overgrowth. In payment, he took care of a few of our beef cattle that we had slaughtered and packaged for the freezer.

Laurie's "Car" was a green twelve-passenger Dodge Maxivan. It had the capacity to carry all of our kids, dogs, and gear. Plus, it was equipped with a trailer towing power package. When we transported a snowmobile on the top of it, hoisted by block and tackle, the busload crew and Ski-Doo drew a lot of attention. The snowmobile came off on planks when we backed the van into a high Owl Brook Road snow-bank.

When we went to the Sunapee Craftsmen Fair, the ticket-taker asked if we were a camp! The Sandwich, N.H. Fair, traditionally held on October 12, was a fantastic one-day honest-to-god country fair. Amidst the aromas of fried bread and grinders, we watched horse pulling and animal judging, observed crafts and farm implements, and viewed awards for the best vegetables, pies, and preserves. There occasionally was snow on the ground. That family-filled van never made it to Canada, but the cross-border likeness in Ashland, New Hampshire and our ten acres in Chelmsford, was country living at its best!

Eight of our children were in Chelmsford public schools by 1972. Some became involved in town sports or dance instruction, but most of our recreation was at home or in Ashland. Though near downtown, my Fourth of July custom to fire a four shot volley with my old Winchester Model 97 12 gauge shotgun was apparently not a problem to anyone. The same was true, prior to deer hunting season, when safely sighting-in my .270 caliber Remington rifle. Our kids and the Kelly family next door were constantly back and forth across the stone wall between our properties. From our kitchen window, we had the pleasure of watching Prince, the Kelly's pastured pony. We had a 25 x 50 foot in-ground swimming pool installed for our kids and friends in 1973. It was officially opened when Uncle Jim McLaughlin pushed our dog off the edge. A diving board, slide, and barking dogs running

Family, Skidoo On Van, Ashland, N.H., 1977

around and into the pool made for lots of fun. It became a skating rink when frozen in winter.

Snowmobiling and skiing around the Ashland house on weekends meant tons of clothing piled in Laurie's laundry room on Sunday nights. By the end of February, we were tapping maple trees on High Street. Collecting sap in buckets, like weeding the garden in the summer, was not too popular a chore among the kids. Accumulated branches and split wood fired the evaporator that I set up in the pool house. Laurie finished off the evaporated syrup off in the kitchen as did Daisy Davidson, cross-border, in Rossville. Laurie used a candy thermometer to bring the batch to the critical 220 degrees F., poured it through a heavy white felt filter to separate the black nitre, and bottled it. By making, rather than buying, we enjoyed maple syrup more!

Two joyous occasions brought Laurie and me back to New Brunswick. In 1968, Joyce Briggs married Percy Jones at St. Ann Catholic Church on the Maliseet Reserve in Kingsclear. When Gwen Briggs married George Bradbury in 1972, we enjoyed the reception at the new Nackawic Royal Canadian Legion Hall where we were served by many women that we knew from around Rossville and Lower Southampton.

Sad farewells marked 1972 when Laurie's mother, Ella Louis, passed away in May. She had been so kind to me, had a strong faith, and was an extraordinary example of enduring pain and compromised mobility for many years. Then my mother, Lucy, died in September after prolonged nursing-home care and final hospitalization from what the old folks called "Hardening of the arteries." At Mother's wake, I remember an elderly gentleman telling me "To lose your father is difficult, but it is even harder to lose your mother." One consolation was that Laurie Ann, Chip, Jean, Peggy, Larry, Mary, Beth, Chris, and Paula knew them both.

CHAPTER FIVE
SENTIMENTAL SEVENTIES

Another healthy child, thank God! Katherine "Kate" Ellen's birth on April 24, 1973, was a celebration and joy. Her 15 and 14 year-old godparents were Laurie Ann and Chip. Five years behind Paula, diapers and baby bottles reappeared. Forever to be "The baby," she held her own among nine brothers and sisters. New Grandpa Larry Louis continued to live with us, mostly independent, in the downstairs apartment. Bats would occasionally swoop out of a kitchen fireplace and send everyone scampering. Grandpa was up for lunch from his downstairs apartment one afternoon, when one suddenly circled above the table. Not to be outdone by our youth and agility, he left the room in a rapid shuffle.

He enjoyed our friends, and they him. He was mobile enough to get out and around with friend, Bill Donahue, who he knew from annual St. Petersburg, Florida vacations. Dr. Louis came up to Ashland on occasion and appreciated the countryside. The small and crowded New Hampshire house was not easy for him, but he was a good sport. When younger, gardening fit his fancy. By the sweat of his brow, gladiolas, lilies, and roses graced Louis vases. He and I liked and respected one another and bonded easily. I never heard him use a cussword.

Confident in any setting, though not a social club member, Dr. Louis thrived on family, a few close friends, and treated thousands of patients with superior medical care. He educated us in the history of Boston Medicine having had pioneers like neurosurgeon Donald Munro, and cardiologist Samuel Levine, in his medical class at Harvard.

Among close friends, Dr. and Mrs. Harold Tingley were Newton neighbors. Dr. Tingley was a graduate of Harvard Dental School, and served with Dr. Varazstad Kazanjian in Dr. Harvey Cushing's Massachusetts General Hospital maxillofacial surgical unit in France during

World War I. He showed me a wire and wood apparatus that he and Dr. Kazanjian used on fractured facial bones. Dr. Kazanjian pioneered facial reconstruction, received an M.D. degree upon return, practiced in Boston, and authored classic texts on plastic and reconstructive surgery. Dr. Tingley became my friend, professional mentor, and got me a job at the Massachusetts Dental Society headquarters on Commonweath Avenue while I was a student. After my discharge from the Navy, Dr. Tingley helped me to apply for and become an oral surgery intern at Boston City Hospital in 1958.

Dr. Louis enjoyed good food, a cigar, a cocktail, and introduced me to the Manhattan. Only a few in our family over 50 dare to drink a "High-test" Manhattan! Even after Mrs. Louis' passing, we enjoyed his presence in personality and supportive medical advice. He quietly assessed our shortcomings, occasionally saying that we were "Burning the candle on both ends." It's not surprising that we quote his wise words to our children. At age 87, in June 1974, he died from prostatic cancer. Laurie and I try to take example from his advice, faith, and pursuit of education. Conscientious in saving, he was sensible in spending and charitable in sharing. Golden are his memories and his rings on my right and left hands. He was a father figure to me after Dad's death.

With Dr. Louis' passing and no siblings, Laurie and I, with our family of 10, stood solo. We strived not to be freewheeling in the sense of everyone going in different directions. As the children grew older, each had enough wiggle room to get out and engage in recreation. We sat as a family at mealtime, and it's been good for body and soul.

As newlyweds, Laurie and I never discussed not having children, because our lives among families had been happy. Like Laurie, who was adopted and "Brought home in a basket," I was accepted into circles of friends. The arrival of each child was celebrated with pride and joy. We always had young and old friends around for play, work, and special occasions. Our kids prepared school lunches and ran to catch the bus at the end of the driveway. I had 7:30 hospital surgeries and inpatient rounds to make prior to going to the office. Bob and I alternated nights and weekends on-call. At first, before we carried beepers (cell phones didn't exist), we might get home and immediately have to return to see another patient in the emergency room or ICU. Laurie and Joanne had the biggest day and night jobs of all, caring for the children and managing the household.

When Laurie and I were celebrating our 19th year since meeting, on New Year's Eve 1975, I received a call that friend and obstetrician, Hugh Mahoney, who delivered our last five children, was at St. John's Hospital in Lowell with a critical gunshot wound to the head. A gang from Troy, New Hampshire, on a botched theft, brutally shot and murdered Hugh, his wife, Ruth, and their 15 year-old son John. We can never forget the horror and injustice to innocent friends.

Laurie needed more than summer help to cope with our family requirements. As a result of asking patients in search of employment, I found Maria Kubit. Of Polish birth and a WWII concentration camp survivor, she married an American soldier and Lowell native, Walter Kubit. They had three lovely children and were active in Lowell's Polish community. Not only could Maria babysit and do housework, but she made herself available for lengthy stays when we traveled.

As a side note, I took care of Walter Kubit when he fell and fractured his jaw. Treatment and recovery were uneventful, but a year or so later, he developed an ulceration above a tonsil. Out of it came a piece of his broken lower denture that was not visible on x-ray and had imbedded itself in the tissues when he had the fall.

In 1974, with Maria's backup and the older four in their teens and at home, Laurie and I flew to Munich, Germany, rented a car, and drove down through the Bavarian and Austrian Alps to Rome. Remembering her 1950 trip with Dr. and Mrs. Louis, Laurie again saw the devastation of WWII bombing in a few buildings from our Munich hotel window. On a Sunday afternoon, we looked out upon a restaurant that local folks were using. It was truly German, and they did not speak English. My choice of what turned out to be rabbit was an omen of the exceptional days that were to follow. Among gigantic snowcapped mountains and green alpine valleys, most memorable were King Ludwig's castles and the small town of Oberammergau where the Passion Play of Christ's tempest has been performed by townspeople for three-and-a-half centuries. The Austrian passes and long tunnels cut through mountains were like those in Germany. From Bolzano, Italy, to Florence, we passed vineyard and olive tree landscapes around ancient village buildings of yellow-brown colored stucco masonry.

Duomo, the Basilica di Santa Maria del Flore, rose to greet us above Florence. Up close, we gazed in awe at its massive bronze sculpted main portals depicting the life of the Madonna. To Fiesole, with its shops and Roman ruins above Florence, we drove up a winding road lined with Cedars of Lebanon. At Cammillo restaurant in Florence, we sat beside the open kitchen, intrigued with its busy sights of culinary creation. The chefs, in turn, were enthralled with the American cigarettes that Laurie passed to them.

To actually and unbelievably arrive in Rome, was overwhelming. Standing at Michelangelo's sculpture of David was as impressive as gazing up at Lincoln enshrined in his Washington National Memorial. A travel hazard befell us upon departure. Our movie camera was stolen from baggage that we left in the hotel office while we were at lunch.

On a more recent trip to Europe, we spied a McCain Foods truck, and later learned that the company feeds six continents. Their international and Canadian corporate office remains in Florenceville, New Brunswick. Thus tagged "French Fry Capital of the World," it's a short distance above Woodstock on the St. John River. With a guide, Barney and I hunted partridge near Florenceville.

Overseas travel was fantastic, and Caribbean sunshine was heavenly in winter. But when returning from Europe, we were ecstatic to approach North America with Maritimes and Maine coastlines as welcome mats.

Near the end of the 1970s, the era of high school graduation parties and college acceptance congratulations was upon us. Laurie Ann entered Massachusetts College of Pharmacy's five-year program. Chip's choice was Providence College in Rhode Island. Jean chose Saint Elizabeth's Hospital in Boston, where she was born, to pursue an R.N. degree, and Peg ventured to the University of Vermont in Burlington for Dental Hygiene. Never stopping, we were like Willie Nelson's ballad, "On the Road Again," getting each adolescent established in a dorm or rental room. Their campus of choice remained within our Number One Northeast.

After the epic 1978 February blizzard, Route I-495 was impassable, but Jean and I donned our cross-country skis and travelled five miles from Chelmsford to Lowell to make rounds at St. John's Hospital.

Here's a quick switch from winter to summer. Laurie was familiar with Scituate's seashore, and renting a cottage on Cape Cod's warmer waters of for a week or two, fit our constraints of not travelling too far for a vacation. One rental was in Hyannis Port, down the street from the Kennedy compound. We recall seeing Edward Kennedy, Jr., standing on crutches, after he lost a leg to cancer, and seeing Pierre Salinger, the Kennedy/Johnson Press Secretary, strolling. Both seemed alone with their thoughts. Laurie went to Hyannis Marine Co. and bought a used 13 foot, nine inch Sunfish sailboat for family fun. They told her that the former owner was Jacqueline Kennedy. It's become a family heirloom and sails with the Mulkerns in Westford.

Our crowning glory was the 1979 purchase of an old home perfectly positioned on a Buzzard's Bay bluff at 28 Carey Lane, Falmouth, Massachusetts. Dr. and Mrs. Leroy M. Yale, Jr. built the c.1892 Shingle Style "Barnacle" as a retreat from their home and his practice on Madison Avenue in New York City. It was asymmetrical in form with numerous peaks, dormers, and porches. The home sat unoccupied after widowed Julia Cornwell, the only Yale daughter and last living child, died. Her heirs rented it to young scientists working at oceanographic institutions in Woods Hole. "Withering Heights," by locals' estimate, was deteriorating. The young singles' freewheeling life in a seven-bedroom spread on a private road came to an end, as did their birthday parties for dogs and other celebrations. Now we owned three houses!

That same year, the big Dodge van remained the workhorse for

Summer Fun c.1975, Canoe & Sunfish On Top

crew and cargo among Chelmsford, Ashland, and Quissett. Eventually, we gave it to Chip who sold it to someone in Mashpee on Cape Cod. Laurie deservedly upgraded, but downsized to a sleek, black Mazda RX-7. With that Wrankle rotary engine for power, she was a happy woman! We both relished the ride up I-89 to see Peg at the University of Vermont and visit with fellow Boston City Hospital resident Jack Farnham, who practiced oral surgery in Burlington, and his wife, Pat.

Our Buzzards Bay "Barnacle" had the appeal of ocean, western sunset, and most of all, rooms full of artifacts. A new roof, inside paint, and the joy of owning, made it ecstasy. Though not well insulated, we still were happy to be there in the heat of summer with open windows to catch the breeze or in frigid winter, when we could see our breath in the bedroom.

Our New Cape Cod Home, 1979

CHAPTER SIX
ENTERING THE EIGHTIES

I constantly compare Quissett Harbor to many in Maine, being deep, narrow mouthed, and sheltered. Families, originally from New England or New Jersey and New York, whose homes surrounded the harbor, took us under their wing. We were asked to join the Quissett Harbor House Land Trust whose mission was to preserve what once was an old hotel at the head of the harbor, its environs, and the "Knob," a granite and green wooded path peninsula at the harbor entrance, perfect for viewing sunsets.

For family cruising and fishing, we bought a classic Dyer 29 fiberglass boat that was being built by the Anchorage Company in Warren, Rhode Island. It had the downeast design appeal. In May 1980, we became members of the Quissett Yacht Club. Our "Lan Mara," Gaelic for "High Tide," joined a half-dozen Dyer 29s already on Quissett moorings. The soft chine hull was curved like that of a sailboat or canoe, and it had a heavy 160 hp. Perkins diesel engine driving the single shaft propeller. The Nick Potter design had the capacity to confront rough water, which we often did. Our family cruised and fished the waters around Falmouth and Martha's Vineyard. Lying southwest of Woods Hole, between Buzzards Bay and Vineyard Sound, are the narrow chain of Elizabeth Islands. We anchored and picnicked in harbors and coves along the 14 mile string of sparsely inhabited private islands with Cuttyhunk, the smallest Massachusetts Town of Gosnold, (year-round population 52) at the tip.

"Lan Mara's" raised cabin provided sufficient space and height for helmsman and guests. Large forward windshields and side glass panes afforded excellent visibility. The engine cover had a vinyl cushion, a back support section that could be raised, and was ideal for sleep or lounging. The open after-deck easily accommodated four fishermen. Below was a galley with stove, sink, refrigerator, and storage.

Opposite was an enclosed flush head. Forward below, was an anchor chain locker, capacity for two double bunks, and storage for the inflatable raft and life vests beneath the lower bunks. Radar, depth sounder, compass, foghorn and bell, searchlight, GPS, and VHS radio were handy and effective for navigation.

I once (truthfully more often), learned the hard way to always use and trust the compass. Departing easterly from Cuttyhunk Island one celebratory August evening with Jim and Peg McLaughlin, I mistook a land light for one on the Quissett shore. We safely, thank God, ended up across Buzzards Bay in Westport Harbor. The harbormaster came to our aid via CHF radio request. We called Chip to retrieve us while waiting in the Westport Police Station. Embarrassing? Yes!

A second steerage station was centered on the stern. The tiller could be disengaged from the helm cable for free rudder motion, and the clutch and throttle were mounted within easy reach. While fishing shoals and rips, or edging up to rocks, I had an almost 330 degree view of port-to-starboard and aft-wake waters. Very often, when I had two hands on the tiller and feet spread and braced on the rolling deck, I imagined cruising on a downeast course along the Maine coast. It never happened by sea, but fortunately hundreds of times by land.

In 1980, Laurie and I took advantage of attending an international surgical conference in Dublin, Ireland. This afforded the opportunity to explore my Irish heritage. From Shannon, Limerick, and Ennis to "Dublin's Fair City" for the meeting, we saw the Celtic monk's c.800 gospel manuscript, "Book of Kels," showcased at Trinity College. Also on exhibition, were absolutely fabulous, intricate and primeval goldworks retrieved from the depths of peat bogs. Not even stopping for an Irish Sweepstakes ticket, we headed north for Grandma McLaughlin McGowan's birthplace of Clonmanny, Donegal, on the North Sea. In bogs along the way, slabs of chocolate-colored peat were piled to dry-out for fireplace fuel. The undeveloped countryside and rocky coastline with forever breaking surf were proof to us that the West Coast was still wild.

We stopped at Galway City, "Where the Girls Are So Pretty," Sligo, and County Leitrim's Manor Hamilton of my paternal great grandparent's birth. Upon seeing McGowan and Hamilton carved on gravestones in the churchyard, I was spellbound remembering Thomas and Ellen's inscriptions back in Woburn. William Butler Yeats composed

"The Stolen Child" poem in 1886. We found, and stood in awe, at the Falls of Glencar, savoring excerpts engraved on a plaque.

> Where the wandering water gushes
> From the hills above Glen-Car,...
>
> Come away, O human child!...
> For the world's more full of weeping than you can understand.

From Bundoran, Donegal City, and Letterkenny up to Grandma McGowan's White Strand and Malin Head, I finally stood, in pilgrimage to her unspoken words through death, at age 94, about leaving home and family when 16 years old. Now that I think of it, Grandma had two sisters in Massachusetts. Aunt Magg Hamilton lived in Woburn, and I recall visiting her home on Arlington Road. Aunt Lizzie married a McLaughlin and lived in Boston. On the broad spread of sand and tidal inlets, Laurie and I watched horseback riders in the surf and a freckle-faced lad with red hair proudly posing with a small sea-trout. Above, and built long ago by peoples in servitude, were wide and high flat-stone walls dividing the grassy hillsides.

Also in 1980, Laurie Ann graduated from Mass. College of Pharmacy. The following year, Chip graduated from Providence College, Jean from St. Elizabeth's Hospital School of Nursing, and Mary and Larry from Chelmsford High School. In combined celebration, we had a backyard clambake by Woodman's of Essex and a funky four-man marching band to entertain our circle of friends. The leader was short, harmoniously theatrical, and wore a German helmet. June marked our 25th wedding anniversary, which we celebrated twice: at home with a Mass and party, and with family at our forever favorite Common Man restaurant in Ashland, N.H.

After two sporadic years of college, Larry decided to leave school and home, choosing wanderlust over the opportunity of a tuition-paid education. We guessed that he was not motivated and answered the recruiting slogan to "Join the Navy and See the World." Mary Ann entered Johnson and Wales Culinary Arts program in Providence. Beth chose the University of New Hampshire at Durham, and Chris was accepted at Simmons College in Boston.

From our coastal Quissett perch, we saw spectacular sunsets, witnessed wicked storms, and viewed sunny summer ripples or fields of sea ice. From the beach at the foot of our bluff, we could swim out to Minister's Rock, a property boundary mark. On our Dyer 29, we picnicked, fished, or set lobster traps. During summer vacation, Beth, Paula, and Kate worked for Bob Cook who was the food service manager at the Woods Hole Golf Club. Dr. An Wang, founder of Wang Laboratories in Lowell, told Beth to sign for his cocktails. I sat with him at a St. Johns Hospital benefit dinner and remember him wearing clean, white, low sneakers. Chris worked at the Landfall restaurant and also delivered fresh-grown foods for Peach Tree farm stand. Qualified in hospitality, as a student at Johnson and Wales University, Mary clerked at the Harborside Inn on Martha's Vineyard. She cleaned homes in Falmouth when off island. Chip worked with building contractor, Arthur Forziati, whose parent's house we once rented at Barlow's Landing in Bourne, Cape Cod. Arthur had been a teacher at Belmont Hill private school.

Prior to August, 1982, when Larry enlisted in the Navy, he was around home and socially toured Falmouth, day and night, on my Indian moped. He made a discovery above the garage that added to the antique fishing gear collectables found in what Dr. Yale labeled his "Shop." The dusty garage space had old boards, rolls of Belgian barbed wire, and an oblong wood-metal-and-leather travel chest. We opened the case to happily discover that it contained antique bamboo fishing rods, catgut leaders, a reel, lures, and a multitude of rod making materials. In fact, the Yale family left a wealth of things behind: books, pastels, etchings, film developing equipment, photos, house plans, tools, furniture, manuscripts, and turn of the century memorabilia that miraculously escaped distribution or sale. The "Things" of Dr. Yale relative to family, medical practice, and hobbies were ours, and we seized the opportunity to explore his life.

Lewis W. Francis, a Dr. and Mrs. Yale descendant in his late eighties, kindly mentored us as newcomers. He was sharp on foot, in mind, and was the wise steward of Carey Lane development. His Cheoy Lee sailboat was aptly named "Quickstep." When a child in Quissett, he told Laurie and me that his family called Dr. Leroy M. Yale, Jr., "Uncle Doctor." Lew referred to the boulder at the foot of our steps to the beach, as "Loaf of Bread Rock."

My family history of cardiovascular disease resurfaced at Quissett in July 1982. I developed neck and jaw pain while digging cedar post holes on our coastal bank to prevent further erosion. Dr. Kenneth Murphy, a cardiologist in Chelmsford (retired to Freeport, Maine), checked me out, which led to a coronary artery bypass at Tufts New England Medical Center. Early intervention was my savior, and Bob Moynihan was my thankful standby while I was laid up. Taking Dr. Louis' advice of "Don't burn the candle on both ends," we realized that we had to give up either our New Hampshire property or the Carey Lane home on Cape Cod. Our memorable home in Ashland was sold in October, 1983. We kept two acres in the event that we or our children might want to build on it, but we eventually sold that last acreage of our original purchase. Times vary; even the name of Owl Brook Road has been changed to Hicks Hill Road.

Though work, two houses, kids at home, and traipsing around the college circuit kept us busy, Laurie and I were in a better position to travel. That's because Dr. Jeffrey Stone, a Kansas City born oral and maxillofacial surgeon who had medical and dental degrees from Harvard Medical School and residency at Massachusetts General Hospital, joined Bob and me at Lowell Oral Surgery Associates. His state-of-the-art training in trauma, pathology, and reconstructive surgery, expanded the scope of our practice. It also afforded Bob and me more time off for family and leisure. Jeff's wife, Dotty, was the daughter of our family surgeon, Dr. Paul Burke.

Thus, we had the occasional opportunity to return to New Brunswick. After my cousin Ella Briggs lost husband Haldean to a heart attack in 1976, she married widower, Arnold E. Cronkhite. In 1985, Ella sent us a copy of *Nackawic Bend* that had just been published. Arnold is the young man with a dog in the 1935 haying scene on the cover. Over time, Laurie and I visited Arnold and Ella at their home on Otis Drive in Nackawic as often as we could. Ella was a fabulous cook, and Arnold was a great storyteller. They enjoyed camping trips to Prince Edward Island. We have photos of Arnold, with a partridge perched on his snowmobile. It regularly came out of the woods to see him for a few winters in a row.

Back home in Chelmsford, we sold High Street in October 1984, and downsized to smaller homes, still with trees and lawns, in neighboring Westford. In 1986, Laurie and I decided to demolish our 1892

*Arnold Cronkhite &
Pet Partridge*

*K.C. Irving Letter,
Oct. 23, 1986*

K. C. IRVING

P.O.Box HM 1701
Hamilton 5
Bermuda
October 23, 1986

Dear Dr. McGowan,

Thank you very much for your letter addressed to me at Saint John, forwarded to me at Bermuda, and due to my absence from Bermuda it has just now come to my attention.

I was delighted to hear what your building contractor thought of Irving lumber; I trust that you will be pleased with the results.

Thank you also for the photographs of yourself and daughter and for the invitation to call on you when in the Cape area. I do not travel as much as I did at one time, but if I am in that area it will give me much pleasure to say hello.

I know the Temperance Vale-Nackawick area very well; New Brunswick is a great province.

My very best wishes to you and your family for many years of happiness in your new home.

Sincerely,

Kenneth Irving

Dr. Charles E. McGowan
33 Depot Street
Westford, Massachusetts 01886

The New Barnacle, 1987

Barnacle In Winter

house on Cape Cod and build the home of our dreams. We found a magazine plan that suited the requirements for appearance and function on our seaside setting. Because the kitchen plan faced the street, we changed it to the back to be able to frequently enjoy the view, over the deck and lawn, of Buzzards Bay to the west. The builder's draftsman set the tone by suggesting that the layout should be "Pleasin' to the eye." It was just that, thanks to our design and the expert advice of foreman, Ray LaBonte.

I sent a letter to Kenneth Colin Irving, founder of New Brunswick's J.D. Irving, Ltd., with a photo of daughter Christine and me on a pile of Irving spruce framing lumber deemed high quality by our foreman. Spruce, from the woodlands of Mother's birthplace, prompted pride in our new home's bones. The New Brunswick farm boy, turned international entrepreneur, replied from his retirement home in Hamilton, Bermuda. We were flattered to receive a personal reply and impressed that he had not forgotten his roots. Mr. Irving passed away in 1992.

As a family project in the unfinished garage bays, we hand dipped the Canadian cedar siding shingles in stain, placed them on metal troughs to catch the run-off for reuse (a Rossville waste-not habit), and threw them, thoroughly stained, in piles, to dry.

One room in particular…all were ample, thoughtfully appointed, and bright…was an outstanding example of seafaring design. The exceptional woodwork of Ray LaBonte and his sidekick, Jeff, created the ship cabin den. It had full size glass sliders overlooking Buzzards Bay, and was between the sunken family room with a two story fieldstone fireplace and our master bedroom suite. Finished entirely in teak, each of many shoulder height custom panels on the side walls and beside each slider were perfectly set in surrounding joinery. They had matching panels on hidden-hinge door lockers on the back wall where I kept my secured sporting arms and gear. On each white side wall, above the paneling, two large brass portholes were interspersed with paintings, charts, and a small brass gimbaled oil lamp. Veneered teak doors to the bedroom and hallway had passageway inspired white louvre panels. On the overhead and faced with teak, six white beams arched the den, and had white tongue-and-groove finish boards between the beams. From the centered, square, teak-and-white simulated deck skylight, hung an antique oil ship-lamp that was

*Nautical Den in
The Barnacle.*

a gift of Dr. Arthur McGonagle. A Lowell friend who referred patients to me, Dr. W. Reid Pepin, steered us to a corporate gentleman in Wyoming, Pennsylvania who had a warehouse of nautical items purchased in bulk from Chinese shipbreakers. Laurie and I drove down, and bought an old ship's wheel, a binnacle compass with red and green iron correcting spheres, and a ships telegraph, each an antique and on a waist high pedestal. The brass telegraph has a face like a clock and a lever that rings a bell, conveying orders regarding the ship's motion to the engine room. As if on a ship, the wheel was centered to the sliders with the brass and glass binnacle to the right and the telegraph to the left, all positioned for the helmsman...Me! On the finished hardwood floor were Dr. and Mrs. Louis' Kerman Persian rug, oval mahogany desk, and Stickley chair with fabric cushions. An antique Windsor arm chair from our country home in New Hampshire was behind the desk. Memorabilia and books graced the locker shelf. Each and every teak surface had been meticulously sanded and oiled creating a soft warm patina that a shiny finish would smother. That room, and each in the "Barnacle," remains forever fixed in our visions.

As our practice continued to grow in Lowell and Nashua, Jeff Stone, Bob, and I needed more doctors, and we recruited two associates. After 31 years of practice, I announced that I was retiring and gave a one year notice. Bob followed, and Jeff Stone took the helm in July, 1992. We sold our Blanchard Farms condo in Westford and assumed permanent residence on Carey Lane in Falmouth.

By that time, seven children were married, and we had 12 grandchildren. Christine had wedding plans in September, Paula was at Rivier College in Nashua, New Hampshire, and Kate was enrolled at Providence College in Rhode Island.

Retirement also meant reality. As much as we loved and became attached to our Quissett home, maintenance costs and tax obligations were too expensive to justify a comfortable lifestyle for Laurie and me. In March 1994, it was sold to a quiet, lovely couple who were seeking a private spectacular ocean-front location. Both are economists of note and down-to-earth individuals who, we thought, would enjoy the heaven-sent vista and share it with their family as we did with ours. In a gesture to the home, we had "1892" engraved on a small granite boulder overlooking Buzzards Bay.

We transplanted to adjacent Racing Beach, with its protected woods and marsh land and across-the-bay sunsets. That home had comfort, charm, and view once on the one-floor living level. The stairs to get there from the garage were hard on Laurie. *Voila,* we found a Cape Cod style home in West Falmouth with easy access and one-floor living in a handy, pretty, private setting! Though it's home-base for all of our basic and medical needs, we never hesitate to pack up and head north!

PART THREE

IRONS IN THE FIRE

Laurie and I have never suffered from a lack of something to do.
We've thrived on diversified "Irons in the fire."
With regard to the eight irons (chapters) that follow,
we didn't latch onto one that was too hot to handle.

CHAPTER ONE
Sporting Camp Yarns

Each year, as soon as the green leaves turned to red and yellow, my instinct and affection for upland game hunting kicked in. I shot my first pheasant with a Sears 16 gauge single-shot shotgun on the western side of Woburn's Horn Pond Mountain when I was 16. I can still smell the powder smoke when I ejected the shell!

I had the annual pleasure of hunting ring-neck pheasants with Tim Toomey, a fellow classmate, intern, and oral surgeon. He first had a Brittany named "Rusty," and later, a German Shorthair, "Petra." We often met on Thanksgiving morning to hunt and then toast each other and the day, from his flask of bullion and sherry.

Tim had fond memories of deer hunting in Aroostook County with his father, a Cambridge police officer. My affinity for Maine was indisputable. Laurie and I stayed at the Camden Harbor Inn on a wedding anniversary and were wakened by the fire alarm in the middle of the night. As guests gathered in the lobby, we looked out the windows at a smoke like scene wafting around the eaves and floodlights; it was fog! No one was at the desk, we told guests that it was our anniversary, they brought us a beer, and the firemen arrived verifying that there was no fire. In 1980, we decided to go partridge hunting with Tim and his dog in the Camden area and made reservations again at the Camden Harbor Inn. Laurie and I stopped at L.L.Bean for my hunting license, and Tim drove up alone.

While waiting in the bar lounge for Tim and me to return from hunting, Laurie took in every conversation, and afterward, out-did our tales of a day in the field. Among regulars who met for a drink and a talk, was Harry Goodridge, the guardian and keeper of Andre the Seal, a 1961 Rockport-born harbor seal who had been abandoned by his mother. For 25 years in winter, Harry brought Andre to aquariums in Boston or Mystic, Connecticut. When Andre was released in the spring, he swam back to Rockport. Andre is forever in granite on Rockport harbor.

Tim's lovely fiancée, Mary Kennedy, a registered nurse, came up by bus a few days later for the weekend and was company for Laurie. I mourn Tim's passing in 2007, treasure our times together, and renew our friendship through Mary and their talented son, Tim III.

Don Martin, my high school classmate Nancy O'Rourke's husband from Winchester, shared his enthusiasm for game-bird hunting with me at the Norfolk Upland Game Club. I took a video of Don and his dog hunting pheasants. After Don died prematurely in 1984, I was able to pass the video on to his sons, Donny and Gary.

Chelmsford neighbor Gene St. Onge and I scoured the rural towns and fields around home for pheasant. Gene had successful deer hunts around our Ashland, New Hampshire home, where I can still vision and smell deer liver and onions cooking in his brother's camper.

I became more aware and intrigued with, New Brunswick's heavily populated white-tail deer and ruffed grouse game. Natives called the bird "Partridge," or "Birch partridge." Autumn L.L.Bean catalog covers and contents were seasonal calendars of desire to go north where their tested goods fit the need. Among other readings about northern wildlife and the hunt, I would take out my copy of Charles Leidl's *Hunting with Rifle and Pencil*, and absorb the fine illustrations. To make it even more New Brunswick, Liedl, an internationally known hunting and fishing illustrator, did the drawings in Dr. Clarke's *Jimmy-Why* books.

After that prelude with frost in the air and skitterings of snow on the ground, my thoughts changed directly to deer hunting. It was the time of the year when the smell of wood-smoke is most fragrant and, the smell of burning birch is a bonus.

Though I treasured our times in New Hampshire, my long-awaited desire to go on a Northern Maine hunting trip, and introduce Laurie to camp life, happened in 1982. I chose Camp Wapiti in Patten, Maine. Though snow blew through cracks in the cabin door, she stuffed them with paper towel as a make-do. I wandered the woods, and she traded stories and cigarettes with the kitchen crew who "Dished out the dirt." While at the camp, we travelled from Patten to meet Ella and Arnold Cronkhite for lunch at the original Ivey's restaurant on the Bangor Road in Houlton. In 1983, they came down to Chip and Joanna's May marriage in Cohasset, Massachusetts, and brought a brown quilt as a wedding gift.

The fall of 1983 marked the turning point when we started returning to Canada to be with our relatives and friends, deer hunt, and stay in sporting camps. "Sports" were Americans who came "Over the lines" to hunt and fish.

My first New Brunswick hunt was at the Governor's Table Camp on the Southwest Miramichi in Juniper, run by Hugh "Hoot" and Charlene Smith. A stop at the Bangor Mall was necessary to buy Laurie a port-a-potty because the cabin didn't have a toilet (like the upstairs bedroom in our apartment as newlyweds). The camp was otherwise comfortable and the food good. One other older couple from somewhere in the South were non-hunting guests. He was an out-of-doors columnist who returned repeatedly to fish for salmon and trout when in season. Laurie remembers driving Charlene in to the small village of Stanley to do errands. During the drive, in spite of her diabetes, Charlene happily consumed her cache of sweets.

As a non-resident, I was required to have a licensed guide. At first, my young guide chose to cruise the roads and clear-cuts from a truck. After that, I decided to hunt in the woods on foot. Laurie was in her element in camp kitchens, helping out, drinking coffee (and cocktails at night), smoking cigarettes, and trading hometown tales. The kitchen crew told her about a childlike and harmless local lad who exposed himself at a school-bus stop, received some good country-doctor advice, and avoided further trouble. He worked at chores around the camp and, to us, was funny and friendly.

Forty-six years before in 1937, there was an outfitter listing in *Fish and Hunt in New Brunswick* that told a story about the area and the times. "George W. Crossman. Sporting camps located at Half-moon Cove, Juniper Brook, and Louis Falls on Southwest Miramichi. Salmon and trout fishing. Deer and bear hunting. Also partridge shooting. Rates, $2.00 to $6.00 per day. P.O. address, Deersdale, York County, New Brunswick. R. R. station, Half-Moon." Without *any* exaggeration from long ago, I know that the provincial government and tourist boards were avid promoters of the superb camping, fishing, golf, and hunting resource with maps, brochures, and booklets. Among the numerous, an 11 page, small newspaper version,

*1932 Tourist
Booklet*

TOURIST EDITION, *Fish and Game News Bulletin, 1936,* featured
"Fredericton The Capital City," a "mileage to Fredericton" map with
Boston as 461, and ads galore such as "Oland's Red Ball Brewery"
to "Aula Tourist Cabins: Price overnight, Adults $1.00 and Children
50 cents," to "James S. Neill & Sons, Sportsmen's Headquarters since
1838, Hardy Fishing Tackle 'The Best,' Genuine Hudson's Bay Blankets and Coats," to "Palmers Moose Head Brand Footwear," to "Colwell & Jennings, Extra Large Stock of English China: Wedgewood,
Spode, Paragon, and Royal Albert." Under a column "Shoot Skeet," I
found out that "The first Skeet Club in Canada was started in St. Stephen with Fredericton installing the second club shortly thereafter."

In 1984, before November deer hunting in Canada, I bought a second hand .308 Winchester Arms rifle at Kittery Trading Post in Maine. Its fast action for a second shot (first should be enough) clinched the purchase.

In 1984, we found Alex and Vicki Oland Mills, Old River Lodge on the famous Miramichi River at Blissfield, New Brunswick, somewhat in the middle of the province. We learned that Vickis' family, the Olands, had been brewers of Moosehead beer in Saint John since 1867. The camp porch overlooked the famous Atlantic salmon stream, and Alex was active in efforts to restore and preserve its fishery. Marty Stewart, from nearby Taymouth, was my guide. He won a local Best Guide contest in paddling and poling a canoe, fire-building, a kettle boil, and axe competition. He told me that the prize was a trip to the Caribbean, and I couldn't picture Marty under palm trees! Marty descended from Scots of the 42nd Highland Regiment that came to Canada to protect the border at the end of the American War of Independence. They were granted land above Tay Creek, and men in Marty's wedding party wore traditional kilts. Bride and groom left to honeymoon in Venezuela!

In 1985, Cousin Joyce Jones, and husband Percy, with friends Merlin and Eunice Fox, purchased an old log camp at Riley Brook on the Tobique River, a tributary of the upper St. John. I'm told that the Tobique (TOE-bick) is named after a Maliseet tribal chief, Noel Tobec. Others say it's of French derivation, but the best description is "Happy Water." Invited to stay there and hunt in 1986, Laurie and I drove about 145 miles up from Rossville. Famous for its hunting and fishing grounds, bigwig sportsmen from the U.S., travelled to that remote region in late 1800s and early 1900s. They were put up in small camps like Percy's as buckboard stop-overs between train connections and deep woods camps in the Serpentine, Long, and Trousers Lake area, an 18 mile tote road portage. When in his 90s, our old friend in Quissett, Lew Francis, acknowledged a trip into that wilderness from his home in Brooklyn Heights when he was a young man.

Our seven-day stay was filled with memorable incidents. While hunting, I experienced a terrifying encounter of trees, otherwise straight and strong, randomly crashing in high winds. Whether or not it was an old-fashioned nor'easter or an isolated twister, I got out of there quick! Another day, when I aimed at a running buck, the trigger pull was silent because I didn't snap the firing-pin slide all the way into the chamber on my new-to-me .308 rifle. We heard coyotes howl up on the distant ridge toward dusk. Laurie and I drove 25 miles to Plaster Rock (named such from old-time gypsum mining) to listen to Eunice and Merlin's son, Mike's band. We expected to hear country, but it was rock. We expected applause, but the custom, amazingly, was silent approval. I came upon what might be the explanation for no applause in that Plaster Rock hall. You never know where tradition might surface even though the participants don't know why. It seems that solo singing was popular in the old lumber camps, and when that happened, everyone in the appreciative audience kept quiet. An impressive ending to the show, was driven snow pounding at our windshield, all the way back to Riley Brook.

My guide, Jim Richardson, brought me to the famous Miller family canoe shop in Nictau, upriver from Riley Brook, at the Forks in the Tobique. It had been operating since 1925. They had early pictures of baseball greats, including Babe Ruth who had stayed at the Miller boarding house hotel in 1925 while on a hunting trip. Others known to fish on the Tobique were John D. Rockerfeller and Mr. L. L. Bean. Third-generation Bill gave me a tour of the shop. Friend Mary Buckley from back home in Woods Hole told me that she was a nurse with Bill's great Aunt Mary, who she came to visit yearly since 1947. Mary

Jones Camp At Riley Brook, Guide Jim, New Saab, 1985

and husband Ken had a Miller canoe, so there was at least one down on Cape Cod, far from the Tobique! Bill knew the Buckley's when he worked in Woods Hole, 1970–1972, as an electrical engineer at the Steamship Authority…small, small world. He claimed the "Nobska," that did Nantucket runs, as his favorite.

We sat spellbound around the Jones' hot wood stove one night with Percy and Joyce and Merlin and Eunice, when Ranger Frank "Junior" Hathaway came for a visit and told us about chasing poachers. Those deer thieves came down from a northern county, shot through peep slots in the plywood structure on their pickup truck, and were hard to pin down. Junior never took off his heavy coat and warden's beaver fur hat since they insulated him both from cold air outside and, to us, extreme heat near the stove!

That late autumn was cold and snowy. Laurie and I were parked in line at the Riley Brook store waiting to use the outdoor public phone to call home, since there was none at the camp (no cell phones then, either). Suddenly, a truck came in behind us too fast and skidded into our new Saab's trunk. The driver came forward and spoke with a decided but excitable accent. We thought that he might be one of the upper county poachers described by the ranger. Wrong! The driver was an American hunter from Massachusetts who had borrowed his friend's truck that day. Moreover and surprisingly, the deceptive stressful accent was a true Irish brogue. The fortunate outcome insurance-wise, was the fact that, though practically at the end of the world in Riley Brook, the damaged vehicles both had Massachusetts license plate registrations!

In August 1986, Ella Briggs Cronkhite unexpectedly passed away in Halifax from complications of open heart surgery. Laurie, Paula, Kate, and I came up to her funeral and burial at Temperance Vale. There's a story in *Nackawic Bend* that refers to a previous heart problem, her quilting talent, and her popularity in the community. Mrs. Perley (Willa) Bradley said: "Right now [Jan.'84] six women are finishing a quilt for Ella Cronkhite who just had a heart attack after she put the quilt on."

Returning to the Old River Lodge in late November, we anticipated a snowfall for good tracking. It eventually snowed about 18 inches in a week. After wading through deep drifts one day, Marty Stewart and I finally quit. One hunting party didn't return to camp, but Laurie fortunately overheard them say where they were going. Thus, they were consequently found stuck in snow and rescued. The fact that their guide was also a preacher, may have helped. Though our brand-new Isuzu Trooper had a four-wheel drive, it was no match for the snow conditions. The Mills finally brought a road grader in to clear the way out to the main road. We, with other sports in a big camper, got out to make our way home before Thanksgiving.

There was heavy snow again in 1987. With Marty guiding, we went to his family farm in Taymouth. Getting out of the car in the barnyard, I went to load my rifle before entering the woods and discovered that I had the wrong ammunition! We found the right caliber in a store, came back, and proceeded to hunt. Upon entering the woods, a buck heard us, gusted a cautionary snort, and we never saw him. When approaching the top of a ridge, two does exploded in front of us out of their blanket of new-fallen snow.

Returning to Riley brook in 1988, we brought son Chip, his wife, Joanna, their two-year-old, Charlie, and our daughter Kate to stay at Junior Hathaway's hunting camp. They were the first of our kids to come with us to a hunting camp. As we travelled north and stopped in Camden, Maine, Joanna was impressed with the windjammer schooners dockside in winter-wrap. We sat beside the restaurant fireplace for drinks and dinner. All of that scenery and setting did not prepare Joanna for the camp life that she was about to experience. When we arrived at the Riley Brook camp, and she saw the partitions open at floor and ceiling, it was quite a shock for a city girl. She was a bit more at home again when another Canadian hunter arrived with a box full of oysters from the Bay of Chaleur. Kate, who at 13 had begged us to take her, was getting homesick and weepy. A mood remedy kicked-in when Laurie and she were driving our Saab on a snowy woods road, and a doe jumped out barely clearing the hood.

I had no worries about Chip enjoying the experience. Hunting close to the camp road, he unexpectedly met a big buck eye to eye. With scope sighting at such close range, the 30.06 missed its mark, and the buck said farewell.

I first met Willard Way of Shogomoc Sporting Camps on Charlie Lake, New Brunswick, at a 1989 Worcester, Massachusetts Sportsmen's Show. Guide Leonard Gordon from Nackawic came with him. I approached Willard and immediately shocked him by mentioning the name of an Allandale neighbor, Bobby Lowe. Bobby, you remember, was the trapper and guide that I had met through Uncle George Baylis in 1945. Willard said travels to the shows and stays in the city were a big outlay for the outfitters. One hundred years before, loggers from the North Woods, had a different expense when in the city. In Bangor on short stays to and from the logging camps, the cost was the Devil's Half Acre "Spree" that liquored-up thirsty throats, and watered down savings!

I booked a November hunt at Willard's Charlie Lake camps, not far from my family across the St. John River in Lower Southampton. Upon arrival, we soon learned that we were acquainted with people and places that the Ways, their kitchen staff, and guides knew. We were accepted as Valley folks. Having cooked for and fed 12 of us at home, Laurie was comfortable in the hunting camp surroundings, and everyone was comfortable with Laurie. That was the beginning of our friendship with the Ways.

Willard had been a supervisor at the Sabian Cymbal plant in the nearby village of Meductic. Sabian owner Bob Zildjian, and his wife

Mark, Muriel, and Willard Way Mark, Muriel, and Willard Way

Willi, were neighbors of the Ways at Charlie Lake. In 1946, after serving overseas, Bob had come up to hunt at Willard's folks' farmhouse. Fondness for the Ways, and the strong work ethic of their community, led to Bob to locate a factory in New Brunswick after he and his brother, Armand, split their father's suburban Boston cymbal business. As Zildjian refers to "Cymbal" in Armenian, Bob's company became "Sabian," derived from the first two letters of "Sally, Billy, and Andy" Zildjian names. Among drummers and cymbalists, "Sabian" and "Zildjian" are world famous names.

In that 1989 first visit, we were comfortable in one of the original cabins. I have a picture of Laurie, relaxed in camp clothes, and jolly, rotund camp cook, Francis Morrisette in his white apron. On our next booking, the Ways gave us a handy first-floor bedroom and bath in the new main lodge. It had varnished hand-hewn beds and tables, game mounts on white pine polyurethane finished walls, and a wonderful view of Charlie Lake. We could watch otters or beaver swimming, and view the opposite shoreline, hoping that a moose might be feeding in shallow lake water. The large cathedral-ceiling common area, next to our room, had long supporting overhead log beams, a fieldstone fireplace retained from the old lodge, lounge chairs, and lengthy dining tables. While I was hunting, it was a convenient place for Laurie to connect with the camp women or sit at her sewing machine. Among stuffed species of fur, fish, and feathered game, a massive moosehead-and-antler-mount presided over all.

Hunters had coffee and homemade donuts with the guides before daybreak to give us a jump-start before going out to the stands or trails. Mid-morning, a full breakfast was cooked-up by the kitchen crew, and the sports and guides traded stories.

My preference was hunting alone and moving slowly. If my mind wandered, a partridge flushing, red squirrel scolding, or a branch snapping was a wake-up holler. With a new sparkling snowfall underfoot and rising sun at my back, I spotted a doe lying down, with big ears on alert, unaware that I was watching her, because the morning glare was directly in her eyes. It was a privileged sight for several minutes. That image and a "Bucks only" game-law prevented me from shooting. On another hunt, sunlight reflected on a movement several hundred yards across a gulley in a clear-cut. It was a large feeding buck, and his back was to me. My open-sight, very long distance,

*Our First Cabin at
Shogomoc Camps*

Francis Morrisette & Laurie

shot disturbed his feeding and he was gone. In the Way's 5,000-acre spread, including Crown Land, I was hunting in a section called "Burnt Camp." Stalking slowly, I heard a flapping sound. Thinking that it might be a startled partridge or a raven rising from a treetop, I saw, in a few more steps, a cow moose flicking her ears. The wind was in my favor, and she was not spooked. I was on high alert, wondering if a calf might be around to protect, or a bull to charge at me. Anyone who has seen the height at which a moose can stand, breaking substantial small tree tops or high alder branches for food, respects their size and strength. Big tooth marks and hanging strips of bark confirm their enormous appetites and lower jaw power. As I watched her for about ten minutes (behind a sizable tree for insurance), she proceeded to scratch her neck with a back hoof. What a weird sight! I carefully walked away and spied her watching me, non-hostile, from a rise above. Who found the encounter most interesting, me or the moose?

The 1990 hunting season at Charlie Lake began with bad news. Muriel Way called us to say that Willard had died of a sudden heart attack. It happened in the lodge, but the guests could not revive him. We were still more than willing to return, since Muriel was carrying on with son Mark and his wife, Joan. Mark was born with hemophilia, home schooled when young, and coped with the hemorrhagic consequence of his blood's inability to clot normally. He graduated from the University of New Brunswick and worked the sporting camp and woods operations with Willard. Though transfusions of an anti-hemophilic blood factor helped to control coagulation, his knees were severely arthritic from bleeding into the joints. Everyone pitched in to help Muriel make it through the season. She was a very strong woman, and we got to know her quite well. She knew my cousin Ella and was a friend of Ruth Winona Grant, the historian who wrote *Now and Then, A history of the Southampton area along the Saint John River* in 1967.

In 1991 we asked daughter Mary and husband, Matt Mulkern, to come up to Old River Lodge on the Miramichi, share in hunting camp life, and celebrate her November 7th 28th birthday. We hunted by canoe on the Cains River, a productive native trout stream in spring and summer. Alex Mills, his lawyer friend from Fredericton, Wink Forbes, and Marty Stewart trucked the canoes in to guide us. I think that it was Keith Wilson from the Wilson camps who helped to transport the three canoes. It was snowing and cold when we paddled through pools, poled through eddies, and got out to push the canoes over shallow bars.

When paddling is not possible or practical, New Brunswick guides use "Set-poles" to skillfully maneuver flat-bottom canoes up, down, and across streams. Like the longer pike pole that's used to move and guide floating logs, a set or "setting" pole is about ten-foot long and two inches in diameter. Some are iron shod for rocky bottoms. Dead black spruce, stunted with tight, slow-growth rings, is the best shaft for light weight and strength. If one of those guides or bateau boaters saw what I saw for sale on eBay, it would blow their boots off! It was a *two-piece*, modified *seven-foot*, oak or ash setting pole with *brass* fittings. Do you suppose that it belonged to a guy who got tired of poking someone with a *ten-foot-pole*?

As we drifted, an owl followed overhead for a while, and we observed six or so partridges sitting in a tree. Our only trophy was shed antlers found when we landed to hunt along the river flats. Reward, was lunch, with tea brewed over a campfire that warmed us, our eyes, and our hearts. Laurie remembered following Vicki, in the Mills' creaky camp van that had bad brakes, over bumpy woods roads to bring us out from where the Cains River met the Miramichi.

When in the camp, we enjoyed visiting with Joyce, the cook, and with the guides. We'll never forget Vicki leading her pony into the lodge. Laurie's love was their blue-ticked white female English setter, who lounged at her side, returning the affection. A guide told us about a gentleman who brought a client to Alex' law office in a trailer behind the Lodge. In his urge to pee while waiting, he went into the bushes. While exposed, a bee stung his "Business." Rapid retreat!

In 1992, New Brunswick beckoned as usual. With Willard gone, but Muriel, Mark, and Joan preserving Shogomoc Camp tradition, we returned with old friend, Dr. John Reichheld, and second wife Pat. They enjoyed the accommodations and mingled easily with the guides and other sports. John and Pat were very impressed with a visit to Cousin Joyce and Percy Jones' new home at their Pinder Stables Farm in Temperance Vale. Percy, an electrician by trade, and Joyce owned an apartment building complex in Fredericton and used their good taste and construction knowledge to build this up-to-date, large residence. Local couples have had wedding photos taken in the house and on the grounds.

We came to know, rely on, and enjoy the company of Melbourne Way, who knew the property and Crown Land in downright detail like his brother Willard. Mel left the farm to join the RCAF and flew with the RAF on many missions in WWII. Afterward, he became a nuclear plant engineer living across the USA. In retirement years, he was an energetic camp handyman, advisor to hunters, and talented breakfast cook, who helped Muriel tremendously after Willard's passing. He kept the family homestead and land on the Charlie Lake Road and returned annually, as does his son, Stewart, from Georgia. Mel's stories, local or global, were historical gems.

Muriel gave us copies of tales about Charlie Fleming the Pirate coming upriver to hide and settle down, thus giving the lake its name. She also told us that Allandale guide and trapper, Bobby Lowe, was so agile that he could jump over a rail fence while wearing snowshoes. She gave me Willard's copy of "Hunter Bill," composed about Bobby, by his friend and old songwriter Weymon A. Thornton of Upper Kingsclear. Tales of Robert Vernon "Bobby" Lowe keep reappearing in Allandale country where he lived for 60 years.

CHAPTER TWO
TROPHY HUNTING

I was not the only family member to bring trophies back to Massachusetts in our memorable years at sporting camps. Laurie brought heirloom New Brunswick quilts home to spruce up our bedrooms and keep us warm. Finding those fine hand-sewn, sometimes sewing-circle (a volunteer cluster of women) made coverlets, meant searching. While I was in the woods, she was tracking down tips from camp folks and relatives in search of quilters.

Lottie Mae Steeves was the first quilter who Laurie discovered. She lived in Hartland on a hill above its celebrated "Longest Covered Bridge in the World." We had Lottie's historical and pictorial City of Saint John Bicentennial Quilt, hand appliquéd and hand quilted, one year after New Brunswick's 1984 Bicentennial Celebration. When Laurie purchased it on November 21, 1985, Lottie told her that a Mrs. McCain (Mrs. Marion "Billie" McNair McCain of the corporate frozen food processing family) requested another quilt like it. As a sponsor and supporter of Atlantic Canadian Art, Mrs. McCain's duplicate went to Saint John, was dismantled, and each panel framed for museum exhibition…so we were told.

The museum quality intact quilt has 20 front panels and a solid fabric backing with fine stitching throughout. The internal batting is not thick, but dense, and evenly distributed. Within borders, from top to bottom, are five rows of four blocks. Each tableau block and the borders are appliquéd.

Row by row starting uppermost, two corner blocks read 200 YEARS. Centered blocks are the New Brunswick Coat of Arms (granted by Queen Elizabeth II) and the Saint John Bicentennial Design of Fundy Gulls with arched dates of 1785–1985.

In the next row, are the War of 1812's Carleton Martello Tower and cannon, United Empire Loyalists arriving with a baby, trunk, and

Lottie Steeves Bicentennial Quilt, 1984

musket in 1783, a pioneer wife carrying a pail in front of a homestead with stumpage, and a farmer tilling the ground with a pair of yoked oxen.

The third row symbolic panels begin with burning buildings in the disastrous 1877, "Black Wednesday," city fire. Next panel is 1791 Partridge Island Lighthouse in Saint John Harbour and a 1927 Celtic Cross Monument to 600 Irish (of 1,000 plus, multi-ethnic) immigrants who died there in the 1847 typhus epidemic. To the right, is a depiction of the Statue of Sir Leonard Tilley (1818–1890), Father of the Canadian Confederation. The last panel in that row is a portrayal of an itinerant preacher on horseback holding a bible and greeting a farmer who is standing between stumps and holding an axe.

The next four panels below show the Dr. James Patrick Collins Celtic Cross Monument beside the Three Sisters Saint John Harbour navigational lamps; St. Andrew and St. David Anglican Church in Saint John; Three Saint John Loyalist gravestones: Dr. Azor and Gloriannah Betts, Mrs. Freelove (and her only son), wife of Capt. Thomas Elms, and Robert Wood; and fourth in this row, a two-team stagecoach transporting a couple and their belongings.

The last bottom row blocks are Barbour's General Store and Little Red Schoolhouse; "General Smyth," the first St. John River Steamboat; "HMS Bream," a War of 1812 Naval three master flying the flags of St. George and Canadian Red Ensign; and, Fort Howe with cannon, 1777, commemorating the siege of Saint John.

Sometimes with the help of local quilter Bonnie Billings, Lottie produced beautifully made full and crib size quilt patterns. We have Lottie's Dresden Plate pattern in queen size from 1986 when Laurie also bought a child's quilt, fabric Christmas tree skirt, and a doordraft stop. Daughter-in-law Joanna went with Laurie to Lottie's home and purchased a baby quilt, in 1988, for her soon-to-be-born nephew.

Laurie bought a ten panel quilt depicting the flower of each Canadian province from Lottie in 1989. The border is patterned with colorful maple leafs. It's been handed down to our daughter, Paula, in York, Maine.

I was delighted to discover via the internet that Lottie's daughter Jo-Anne and husband, Peter Craig, have the Christmas Crab Quiltery in Woodstock. Their website "Quilting and Me" had a tribute to Lottie and related quilting or knitting carried on by Jo-Anne and her sisters,

*Lottie & Quilt
At Show*

Janet, Sheila, and Charlene. Last year, we brought Lottie's quilts to
Jo-Anne's shop and heard that Lottie died a dozen years prior. She
respectfully recalled that Lottie, as a single mother, found a source of
income in her talents by working out of her own home. Jo-Anne told
Laurie and me that her mother referred to the blocks on the 1989 provincial flower quilt as "Floral emblems," and that our 1985 quilt had
won a blue ribbon at the Saint John Bicentennial Quilt Show.

I didn't know Lottie, but Laurie remembers her pleasant personality, and that she was healthy looking and well groomed. I do know
that her maiden name was Thomas, and that she claimed Sir Leonard Tilley, whose statue she appliquéd on the Bicentennial quilt, as an
ancestor. Though that quilted artifact of New Brunswick history was
passed down to our daughter Mary Ann Mulkern, Laurie, Mary, and
I decided to donate it to the Carleton County Historical Society in
Woodstock.

We searched for a certified appraiser, and Betsey Telford-Good-
win in York, Maine, had the credentials. Her associate, Lisa, told me
that it hand-washed well and was strong and sturdy. Hopefully, Jo-
Anne Craig may do the small amount of re-stitching required. The
current appraisal affirms the market value to be 12 times the purchase
price, and the replacement cost is over 22 times the purchase price!

Those thousands of dollars can't hold a candle to the number of Lottie's hand stitches in this quilt.

Kellie Blue-McQuade, Exectutive Director of CCHS, sent us a note that the quilt arrived safely and its gift was greatly appreciated. We hope to see it on display and learn more about Lottie.

Laurie remembers Mrs. Nelson Lyons of Doaktown as another quilter and craft source that she discovered when we stayed at the Mills Old River Lodge in 1984 and 1986. We sought the quilter's name by calling the Doaktown Library. I spoke to Manager Belva Brown who had been on staff at the Atlantic Salmon Museum where we donated Dr. Leroy M. Yale's vintage salmon fishing artifacts 27 years ago! Belva's e-mail verifies that recall: "I remember Mrs. Helen Lyons well. She quilted with my grandmother at the Anglican Church Hall for years. Her husband Nelson helped her quilt on her projects. The dear lady passed away many years ago. They lived on South Road beside Russell and Swim's Mill, now owned by the Irving family. Her sister-in-law, Mary Lyons, is still living should you want any additional information."

Another quilt of emerald green and dark blue colors was pieced by Laurie when we booked hunting accommodations at Camp Wapiti, Patten, Maine. It was finished by Temperance Vale church ladies in 1982, courtesy of cousins Joyce and Gwen. Chip and Joanna McGowan have it in their home.

Fine hand-stitched heirloom quilts of the countryside go hand-in-hand with living on a farm. In Laurie's search and findings, we've learned about sewing skills and historical patterns, enjoyed their practical beauty, and passed quilts down to our children. The fact that our Lottie Steeves' City of Saint John Bicentennial unique work of art is back home in Carleton County, at Woodstock's Connell House, is rewarding.

The next time you see a vintage or modern quilt, appreciate its craftsmanship, design, and gist. If you're *really* fortunate, experience a quilt's between-the-covers warmth and well-being.

CHAPTER THREE
SHIFTING BASE CAMPS

Muriel and Joan Way bore a heavy load in 1993 when Mark succumbed to complications from hepatitis C, transmitted through contaminated anti-hemophilic transfusions. Returning to Shogomoc Sporting Camps in November 1994, we admired Muriel and Joan's strength in coping with business and property responsibilities. We looked forward to being with them, their guides, hunters, and Melbourne Way. Among the "sports" who returned each year, we got to know Arnie, an optometrist from Florida; Dave, a drapery designer from Massachusetts who installed palace tapestries for oil-rich Arabs; Jack, a state police officer; Dick, a golf club owner; Jimmy, a grading contractor; and Dube, a canoe builder and avid hunter who somehow seemed to overcome very bad eyesight when getting around in the woods.

Bill Hawkins, from Nackawic was my regular guide. We both knew many folks in the area, and our companionship was as good as the hunt. A WWII veteran, who took up forestry after getting out of the army, his woods wisdom and tales suited me fine. I guess that you could rightly call him a local historian. Not surprisingly, Bill and Laurie hit it off well. We were treated as family by the Ways and the guides.

Whether with coffee, ashtray, conversation, or chattering sewing machine, Laurie was willing to get up and help out in any way. She went to Fredericton for blood sausage for hunter Jimmy Gallant from Hanover, Massachusetts. Like a hungry French Canadian, I joined Jimmy at the breakfast table, and we ate "Boudin Noir" sausage to our heart's content. There were no other takers!

Our daughter Paula, and husband Chris Kondos, joined us at the Way camps in November, 1994 to experience the spectrum of sporting camp life that we relished. Paula was not afraid to go out alone to hunt deer and bear. We road-hunted partridge in an unusual burst of warm weather, and Chris, an expert shot, downed a few. It may have been on that trip when someone local said "You shoot a pa'tridge on the ground and a ruffed grouse (same thing) in the air!"

Paula and Chris fortunately got to meet Bill Ingraham, because they knew that the Ingraham's were always good to me, and that I was proud to know them. We have a photo of Bill at the Pinder Koze Corner Special Care Home. At age 91, he was alert, happy, and optimistic. Three of Bill's expressions, when asserting a story, were "I'll tell you, mister man," "Boys, you-know-now," or "Sweet precious." Many years earlier, when I asked him to pose for a picture in his dooryard, he quickly agreed but said that he first wanted to go in the house for his hunting cap and teeth. With Bill's passing, the 1995 Ingraham homestead sale was very sad for the family and for me.

In 1995, with Laurie and me, John and Pat Reichheld made their second trip up to Charlie Lake. John and I got brand new pairs of rubber boots that Willard had never worn. We never presumed that we could walk in Willard's shoes.

Since John was not familiar with the lay of the land, I put him in a tree stand, on a stump, or in an old barn loft that overlooked Mel's upper fields. He read financial reports, snoozed, and occasionally thought how unproductive hunting could be! One day, not too far from the camp, we split up, and I stalked along an old tote road. Suddenly, there was a bear in front of me. I raised my rifle, centered the sight on black fur behind a front leg, and my .270 caliber round struck home. The bear turned and ran into the brush. I put another bullet in the chamber, went into the bush, and found my lifeless game. John heard me fire from a distance and said that I calmly walked up to him saying "I just shot a bear." It has forever satisfied my quest for bear hunting, but not bear sighting. The hunt was fair and square; bear are entitled to more decency and fair play than by baiting. It's been said (prob'ly by flatlanders) that nobody eats bear…twice. Cook it like a pot roast, and they'll come back for seconds!

The camp had a green 8N Ford tractor with canvas scabbards for guns and a three-point hitch platform for hauling game out of the bush. I had an old Ford tractor back home, and easily drove back to the camp with my bear. An aggressive camp sport shot a deer right after I got the bear. He couldn't stand the heat of competition, and wanted to show off his trophy. Hoisted in the game shed, it came down twice because his rope and tackle were too fragile. As the sports and kitchen crowd, who gathered to watch the antics, got bigger, he got more excited, telling the guides what to do and jumping around and the like. Somehow on the third try, the single hanging light-bulb got tangled, blew out, and darkened the last act of the comedy until someone found a flashlight! To me, that shed forever represented a classic theater production of what a screenwriter might call "The Deer Scales." I, in fact, am that playwright.

Prior to crossing the border into the U.S., we and the Reich-helds stayed in St. Andrews, Canada's oldest seaside resort town. On Remembrance Day, uniformed members of the Canadian Forces, and RCMP constables in scarlet dress, honored those who served and sac-rificed their lives overseas. We saluted, with the same solemn intent as our Canadian allies and neighbors.

With packages of butchered bear meat in a cooler and salted bear-skin with head intact, we found a taxidermist in Bar Harbor, Maine. I had a bear rug in mind. John was concerned that a barred tooth bear-mount would panic our grandchildren. In the end, I gave the rug to our Falmouth Rod and Gun Club.

Our 1997 and 1998 returns to the Ways camp were as comfortable as ever. Muriel gave us the courtesy of having my cousins come over to visit, and she and they knew many people and places in common. Sheila, from Laurie's wartime childhood days, and husband, Bob Hut-ton, came up to Charlie Lake from Fredericton. A Nackawic pulp mill worker arrived after supper, one evening, with an assortment of hunt-ing knives. The steel blades, with handles crafted from antlers, were super sharp, polished, and salvaged from the mill's shredder parts. I bought one out of admiration, for a family pass-down, and not need.

The camp canoe shelter was next to the cool shed where game was hung, weighed, and dressed (my "Deer Scales" theater). Willard used to guide for salmon fishing, as well as hunting, and had a camp on the Miramichi River. Among many canoes on racks, some had a flat stern with an outboard motor mount. Another was a 20 foot "Freighter" with a wide beam that could carry a heavy load. I spied a restored green 15 foot, fifty-pound, canvas-over-wood "Bobs Special" canoe, c.1956, made in the Chestnut family Fredericton factory that existed between 1905 and 1979. They supplied the famous Canadian north-land Hudson's Bay Company with all types of Chestnuts for their outpost use. A Chestnut company slogan was "New Brunswick is where the good canoe cedar grows." This canoe that I purchased was not like any other, since its bottom had been torn out by a salmon-sniffing bear. Joan Way had taken over some of the camp's ownership and business, and I couldn't resist buying it from her in 1998. On the way home, we purchased Christmas gift toboggans for each of our ten kids at L.L.Bean, and stowed as many as we could under the canoe on the roof of the Saab sedan.

The following spring, with fly rods and the Chestnut canoe, Chip and I chased brook trout in Sky Pond, New Hampshire, close to our Ashland home. Cellar storage wasn't fair to the canoe's history, and I donated it to the Falmouth Rod and Gun Club for display. It hangs happy above the bar, surrounded by game memorabilia, and inspires members to tell true and tall tales.

When it was quiet around the camp, Muriel would invite us to her living quarters next to the lodge. She devoted more time to reminiscing, because she appreciated our River Valley family connections. She told us that she grew up in Temple, where the Shogomoc Stream flows into the St. John, started nursing school, but left because of illness. She said that, after marriage while living at Willard's folk's farm, they established a home and sporting camp on the shores of Charlie Lake in 1946. Including Crown Land, they had ownership access to 5,000 acres of forest, perfect for logging and hunting. As more hunters came, they gradually added five sleeping camps and two cottages, modernizing the accommodations. Over the years, descriptive names were given to hunting areas: "Sugar Shack," "Bear Baths," "Burned Camp," "Joan's Fields," "Moose Call," and "Burnt Car." A long-time hunter named John from Connecticut had a favorite stand on a massive boulder halfway up a beechnut ridge above the lake. He had a bronze plaque cast honoring Willard and installed it on "Johnny's Rock." To commemorate Shogomoc Camp's 50 year founding at Charlie Lake, I carved a wall plaque, inscribed a tribute, and depicted a green fir tree on a blue lake-shore. It pleased the Ways.

Mildred spoke affectionately of old Indian friends from the Fredericton area, who had the aboriginal privilege to hunt anywhere and would courteously tell the Ways that they were going into the area. In return, they had free access through the gate, and everyone got along well. I came upon one of their very primitive deserted hovels deep in the woods. Remnants of an old mattress, bits of tar-paper, and rusting tin cans littered the spot. She said one tribal member recently drove in to show her the biggest moose that she had ever seen, taken somewhere in the Charlie Lake back country.

Age slowly caught up with Muriel, assisted living was necessary, and our stopovers became memories. On one of the last visits, Muriel gave me Willard's New Brunswick Guide badge, which, someday, I intend to give to an archive. Since her passing at age 84 in June, 2000, Joan Grant Way, Mark's widow, of Canterbury Grant ancestry, has bravely kept the Shogomoc Sporting Camp tradition and forest management business going, with the help of her brother Larry Grant and his wife, Beth, with their little Mark. We visit Willard, Muriel, and Mark at rest in the Ritchie Extension Cemetery, think of them often, and value our times with them.

October bird hunting replaced November deer tracking, and allowed time for research at the Provincial Archives in Fredericton. We began to stay down river near Fredericton at the Holiday Inn, in Kingsclear beside the Mactaquac Dam. It was pet friendly to our "Barney," and became our handy "Base camp" from 2000–2008. At dinner in 2005, a couple noted our age and slower pace, and introduced themselves, asking if we needed any help. Bob and Karen Atwin were gracious. Karen, a university counselor, gave Laurie a beaded neck pouch, and a silver bracelet inscribed with a bear, for healing and relief from her painful arthritis. Bob, First Nation Maliseet, Chief at the Kingsclear reserve, and subsequently executive director of First Nation Education Initiative, Inc., gave me a gift of insight into the respect that a native hunter has for God-given game.

On the next day, Bob showed me two magnificent bull-moose shot by native hunters. He explained that prayer offerings were said over the wild creatures in thanksgiving and reverence. Food from the hunt was divided among tribal members, especially the elderly and needy.

Bob arranged a bird hunt for me and Barney with guide, Danny Villeneuve. We had a glorious day with Dan to guide me, and his dog North to show Barney, what partridge and woodcock hunting is all about.

Over the years, while staying in Kingsclear, we've attended St. Ann Catholic Church on the First Nation Reserve. Beaded and feathered religious artifacts on the walls and altar bespoke of generational worship of the Great Spirit. Among Maliseet parishioners were children, young parents (who articulated the psalm readings very well), and the aged, who humbly sat in the back pews. I admired their devotion and humility. The graveyard was testimony to tribal names of long standing. We sadly read that St. Ann burned to the ground on Sunday, December 11, 2011.

On our way home through Maine in 2005, we stopped at Al and Patty Estes Three Rivers Wingshooting Preserve in Milo. Barney's freshman expertise was tested after the handler set a quail in the thicket and asked novice Barney to "Find the birdie." A released game bird conveniently flew up and sat on the ATV tire next to us, and we have a picture of Barney, merely sniffing, and unfazed by its presence! While Barney is one of the best-looking Brittany's that you have ever seen, his pointing talent went ker-plunk! To carry the adventure one step further, Barney Boy stepped on a console switch of our '91 Saab and locked me out. Laurie, once more, saved the day by having an extra key.

During our 2009 and 2010 stays in Fredericton, Larry Ford hosted hunts on his Barony farm, above the St. John head pond, and at his family's camp in Allandale. The only trace of St. Dominic Catholic Church in Allandale, as on my dedication page photo, was a few remnants of the graveyard.

Barney on Point, Milo, Maine, 2009

Being with Larry sustained the flavor and companionship of partridge hunting and just plain walking in the woods and on tote roads. When we took a break, Larry lit a lunch (noontime dinner) fire, boiled a kettle for tea, and handed out sandwiches and sweets. Awful good! Barney slept a little, but he begged a lot. Larry's friend-in-a-flask named "Fireball," treated us to a taste of northern comfort. Over the years, Larry bagged some trophy bucks not too far from his house and sent me pictures of some of those taken. There's been clear-cut lumbering in that once successful "Honey hole" of mixed growth where wildlife seek sustenance. He turned to hunting with a camera, and recently sent me a note: "I shot 3 bucks, 5 does, and 5 moose." With bad winter weather and heavy snowfall in three days, he's fed 24 deer in back of his house. When he wasn't watching the deer during the day, they were unaware of his trail camera count at night!

Every sporting trip lingers vividly, when fondly recalled or retold. Canadian outfitters, and the American sports who return to the camps, constitute cross-border ambassadors. Laurie and I recall registered New Brunswick guides as friends: Hoot Smith, Juniper; Marty Stewart, Taymouth; Percy Jones and Jim Richardson, Riley Brook; Bill Hawkins and Larry Grant, Charlie Lake; Danny Villeneau through Bob Atwin of Kingsclear First Nation Maliseets; and Larry Ford on the Barony.

We missed 2011 because Laurie had a much-needed and very successful hip replacement at New England Baptist Hospital in Boston.

My "Hunts" resumed in 2012 on the University of New Brunswick campus at Harriet Irving Library and the Provincial Archives, searching for cross-border manuscript information.

When upriver to visit Cousin Alton and once again driving on Rossville Road, I naturally saw the present landscape. But I also saw mirages of old familiar farms. Baylis growing fields "Across the road" are still cultivated. Absent are three roadside elms, shown in photos of Ronald and dog in 1925, my spaniel Skippy in 1939, a farm view in 1950, and background for Uncle George standing on a ten-foot snow-bank in March, 1963. Catching a glimpse of what was once the Baylis farm, I had the same heart-stopping, home-again feeling.

CHAPTER FOUR

MENU OF MEMORIES

These 82 years of back-and-forth whereabouts make a delicious menu of reminders.

When driving on Massachusetts I-495, or on the I-95 Maine Turnpike and New Hampshire Blue Star Turnpike, I feast on sighting New Brunswick license plates, whether tourist or trucker. Dr. Bill Deighan from Bangor told me that the yellow, black lettered Sunbury Transport trucks were locally called "Bumble-bees." Here's another anecdote. If early settlers had their way, Bangor would have been called Sunbury. Their envoy preacher to Boston was humming the hymn "Bangor" when the recording clerk asked for the name of the community. The parson misunderstood and responded with the name of the hymn.

When in Harpswell on mid-coast Maine, we buy wild, low bush Maine blueberries at the Vegetable Corner store or at roadside stands. They either go right into a pie, muffins, pancakes, or are frozen. After all, blueberry pie is Maine's designated dessert! Mary Egan, Jean and Jim's neighbor, sends husband Phil over with a big pan of the best-of-the-best blueberry cake that we devour from breakfast through late-night snack.

We consider Jasper Wyman's Washington County wild berry packets at our Falmouth Windfall Market, to be the equivalent of frozen gold, available in any season. We have McCain frozen appetizers, pizza, vegetables, desserts, and potato products in most markets. Maritime Canada lobster, crabmeat, mussels, and sardines are year-round favorites. Cans of Portland's baked beans catch my eye on store shelves (bought or not), and I try to buy Maine or P.E.I. grown potatoes. Laurie loves Gifford's Ice Cream from Skowhegan, to which she adds chocolate or caramel sauce and sprinkles. Among hungry-for-summer Canadians in our Falmouth, Cape Cod, tourist-town, most are from Quebec or Ontario and a few are from the Maritimes. Canadian runners, like ours, eat up the chance to compete in our 12,800 participant August road race.

At low tide, clams are king in Harpswell when Jim Burbine and Chip McGowan dig steamers, little necks, and quahogs. If you pronounce them "**KWA**-hogs" rather than "COE-hawgs," you're not from New England! Anyone's not a true New Englander if they say "SCAA-lops" instead of "SCAU-lops"... Amen. Chip and Jim concoct "Chowdah," "Stuffer's," and "Casino" which we gobble to our heart's content. When Sheriff George Bradbury (no relation to George Bradbury in New Brunswick), asked for my license while clam digging with Jim, my only credentials were a balding scalp and white hair. I took my hat off to prove it. He let me go with only a warning.

The aroma or sight of balsam whets my appetite for Christmas spirit or a walk in the woods. Early in December, it's not unusual to see trucks from the Maritimes heading south with loads of Christmas trees. In the frosty days of November when I was hunting cross-border, bundled holiday balsams would be stacked in fields ready for shipment to the States.

When I see New Brunswick's, J.D. Irving Ltd. service stations as far down as Massachusetts, and their ocean tanker terminals in Bangor, Portland, and Portsmouth, N.H. harbors, I lunch on scenes of the old days in Culliton and the two Irving gas pumps in front of Stanley Stairs general store.

I can't dine in this menu of memories, without mentioning the accompaniment of favorite music. While driving, if the silence is too boring or the radio-news too blaring, CDs of Atlantic Canada or Maine songs and instrumentals pleasure my palate.

There's an item on this menu that often states the cost as "Market Price." An explanation will take up the rest of this chapter. I'm referring to *LOBSTER*. I'll let you look at its handler's ways and means, and then boil-up the creature for you to eat right in the rough! What's cookin' in the lobster business right now, is neither a boil nor a broil, but a "Roil" or stir-up. Understand this: a lobsterman who has his own boat, gear, and license is accountable to himself for dealings, profit, loss, and upkeep. Even the weather, good or bad, is his alone to enjoy or obey. This roil that I'm talkin' about is a wage-earner stir-up before lobsters reach the stove.

Though Canada and U.S. trade is acknowledged as strongest in the world, issues of inequity arise when making a living becomes a predicament. Maine and New Brunswick currently share such an abundant lobster resource, that prices are being driven down. As the pendulum swings from paucity to plenty with an over-supply, and an inflated cost of doing business, worker wage suffers.

The combined annual harvest is approaching a record 300,000,000 pounds destined for a global market. With supply and demand both satisfied, the live and frozen industry grew to provide more jobs for captains and stern-men on the waters and middlemen in distribution and processing. For many years we saw no conflict with Shediac, New Brunswick trucks delivering live lobsters to Boston's waterfront.

Another fly in lobstering ointment, can be the difference in the open season between Maine and the Maritimes. As *bad* luck would have it last year, 2012, for the Canadian lobstermen, the Maine guys had an early and plentiful soft-shell catch. Anyway, Mainers unloaded their excess catch, said to be a lot of "Canners" barely legal-size, on the Maritime processors and drove the dock price down for Canadian lobstermen. When Maine trucks went cross-border with the surplus catch to New Brunswick, trouble started.

Turmoil escalated as Mainers, with only three processing plants in the state, sent lobsters to New Brunswick's twelve at $2.50 to $3.00 a pound. Not able to do business at those prices, New Brunswick lobstermen blockaded Maine trucks from the plants to bring provincial prices back to practical. A delegation of Canadian lobstermen threw traps into the reception area of the Federal Minister of Fisheries at Fredericton to protest U.S. lobster trucking cross-border.

To reverse provincial processing plant shutdowns, a subsidy agreement shared by Canada's Maritime Fisherman's Union and processors, increased the pound price paid to their lobstermen to a sustainable $3.00 and $3.50. With the dollar fortunately close to par, cross-border collaboration eventually worked out the differences. The August 12, 2012 *Boston Sunday Globe* Editorial, "Pulling back the claws," hit the nail on the head: "Look for a common approach to safeguarding an iconic regional industry." Canadian processors may follow McCain Foods example and open facilities in the Pine Tree State; who knows?

Other factors can affect catch and price. Scientific tracking reveals

Mother's Day Menu,
St. Stephen, N.B.,1963

that Gulf of Maine water temperatures are rising little by little, thus causing lobsters to move inshore to molt earlier than usual. Since cod, by God, have decreased in numbers, there are fewer of them to eat the young lobsters. If more lobstermen decide to fish the slower winter months in deeper waters, that could push the price of winter lobsters down.

Last August (2012), we bought 16 lobsters off the dock for a family boil in Harpswell for $3.50 a pound. A tip was genuinely appreciated, the margin of profit being barely sustainable. I must stop for a moment and share lobster ads found in the *Portland Press Herald* for July 27, 1940: "Two Lights Pound, 4 for $1.00" and "Willard's Pound, South Portland, 5 for $1.10." Another price reflection cross-border in St. Stephen, N.B., shows a Mother's Day meal in an ad dated May 11, 1963.

A fanciful and indirect effort to protect the shellfish resource was introduced in Maine's 1939 legislative session. Intent on protecting the traditional clam chowder recipe, the bill proposed that it would be "Illegal to put tomato in it." As a New Englander, I'd second that sacrilege!

Mainers figured out that improved methods of processing lobster were needed, and that marketing had to be modernized. There are startups in which trap-to-company wharfs, Maine only certified catches, and new processing plants, are trying to help sustain livelihood in the lobster business. Though large regional co-ops can influence harvesting, marketing, and legislative challenges more than one man operations, there exists a grass roots component of Maine fishermen families and friends who put a shoulder to the wheel in ideas and actions that can both protect the fishery and give fishermen the opportunity to make ends meet.

In the November 2012 *Harpswell Anchor* newspaper, reporter Kara Douglas interviewed Monique Coombs, lobsterman Herman's wife. She is championing an awareness of catch-to-consumption in the "Food system." Whether from dock to pot, pound to processor, or plane to Pasadena, strategies for freshness in transportation and handling is the passion and pursuit which Monique delivers to the seafood and fishing industry. Credit also goes to Cozy Harbor Seafood in Portland and Shucks Maine Lobster in Richmond. Shucks went to the 2013 European Seafood Show in Brussels, Belgium, in April to exhibit and market their innovative lobster processing system.

To offset an estimated 80% that are processed, a "Buy 'em Live and Eat 'em Whole" emphasis would bring more profit to local pounds and reinforce Maine as the source.

When I see very low lobster prices advertised on signs along the Portland waterfront, or at any downeast wharf, there's a seasonal reason and a statistical reason. Early season (late May into June) "New shell" or "Shedders" have soft shells after a recent molt and don't necessarily carry the same price per pound as the older "Hardshell." The statistical reason is reflected in the Maine Department of Marine Resources 2012 harvest report of the catch or "Landings." It predicted 123.3 million pounds with a value of $331 million (less than 2011 of $334.7 million). By-the-way, the 2012 record weight for a Maine-caught lobster was 29 pounds. That's the good news. The bad news, known best to lobstermen, is that prices were lowest since 1994…and still are in 2013.

There's a shrewd and strong factor that runs the lobster industry, and that's secrecy. According to experience, I've caught 'em here on the Cape, I've bought 'em all over Downeast, and 'et 'em in both places while absorbing what I see, hear, and read about the industry. With a lobsterman's loyalties, his territorial respect, and the middle-man factor, it's not what's said and posted that really drives price and wage through good times and bad, it's the man-to-man and day-to-day understated dealings that drive "Market Price" on the menu.

CHAPTER FIVE
REWARDING RETURNS

It wouldn't be fair to describe returns to New Brunswick without telling the tale of our 1996 pilgrimage to ancestral Scotland. Ordinance Survey maps are a must; the Landranger series is by district and the Sheet maps are by town. My purposeful destination was the parish of Creich, the home of my maternal Munro ancestors, in the most northern Highland county of Sutherland. After staring at their Otis Cemetery markers for years with "Sutherlanshire" dimly inscribed in marble, I was returning for sure!

Our May Day flight on Iceland Air from Boston had a brief stopover at Keflavik Airport near Reykjavik prior to our morning arrival in Glasgow. We took a train to Edinburgh, on the Firth (Bay) of Forth, and registered at the Sheraton Grand Hotel for a two-night stay. On the next day, we took a happy and historic "Hired livery" tour of Edinburgh Castle and notable city sights. In the evening, we attended the elegant "Taste of Scotland" dinner-with-wine show at Prestonfield House Stables, where Laurie and I delighted in traditional pipe and dance performances. While waiting for our driver, we said hello to a "Proper" couple, unsmiling and very well clothed, who chose to ignore us...or was it our euphoria that offended them? Maybe they thought that we were boisterous Americans like the peacocks who paraded and squawked around the portico as we left.

From the grand old city, with nine days of booked accommodations ahead, we picked up a reserved rental car and motored north past Perth. I stopped at James Crockart & Son in Blairgowrie to buy knee-high Le Chameau rubber boots. The olive-green "Chasseur" beauties can't be beat for construction and calf fit. The proprietor, Mr. Jamieson, said that Italian sportsmen with fistfuls of lira stopped for their outfitting wants on their way home from shooting or fishing preserves. A93 became mountainous through Cairngorns National

Park forest and turned east to follow the River Dee past Balmoral Castle where the Royal Family had their "Northwoods Camp." Winding north on A939, the "Old Military Road," I thought of the Military Road between Macwahoc and Houlton in Maine.

The drive among heathery hills, trout streams, and small villages was easy and comfortable all the way to the River Spey and its "Whisky Trail." It was our intention to straightaway tour and taste. Highlights were a stop at Glenfiddich Distillery at Dufftown and, on a Sunday with permission to enter the grounds, viewed Macallan's Easter Elchies estate house that we had only seen as a logo on a bonnie bottle. The name of the adjacent town, Craigellachie, is as pretty and mellow as the Highland Single Malt Macallan Scotch whisky… trust me! Twice, thrice, or more distilled, 'Tis truly the water of life. On a graveled side-road, we came upon Highland cattle in a pasture. They're massive gentle creatures, with long brown silky appearing coats that, falling between their horns, almost cover their eyes.

Up through Elgin, we doubled back along Mornay Firth toward Inverness (Do you feel car-sick?). At Nairn, we stopped where "Bonny Prince Charlie" Stuart and his Highlanders fought and lost at the Battle of Culloden to the government loyalists in 1746. We're not historical event buffs, but the heather-clad plains and depictions of the clash were impressive.

Arriving in Inverness, we were in the Highlands at last! To celebrate, we bought plaid tam o'shanters (Scot "Tams" or caps) at the Clan Tartan Centre. For the past 17 years, the scarlet pompom and red wig tams have colorfully crowned us and our lads and lasses for laughs and photos. Of Highland dress, I knew of the kilt but not the sporran. It's a leather or fur belt-pouch worn in front and is often decorated with tassels. I walked away with more respect for the Highland dress ensemble and its ceremonial presence on pipers at funerals or weddings. Leaving James Pringle Weavers, we crossed the square and went on a tour of the mill, operating since 1790, giving us insight into the art of mechanized weaving. The Glendruidh House Hotel was our lodging for the night.

At Pringles, I learned that the Munro and Murray clan mottos were "Dread God" and "Quite Ready." Each made me more eager to get on A9, cross Cromarty Firth Bridge, and continue northeast to Tain of the Murrays. Laurie and I had a delightful lunch at Morangie

House Hotel. The semicircular dining room had a broad view of Dornoch Firth, the next bay above Cromarty. Highland Scots identify according to region. The same is true of their single-malt whiskies that emanate from local grown barley, a clear-water spring, and an oaken-cask distillery. We raised our glass of Glenmorangie Single Malt Scotch, poured neat, and saluted Mary Murray as "Lovely," and George Munro as "Hardy."

Crossing over the modern 2929 foot-long firth bridge into Dornoch, we toured the city center and saw the centuries old Cathedral and Castle. Since I don't play golf, the world sixth-best-rated Royal Dornoch Golf Club "Links" didn't interest me as much as getting to Creich.

After driving three miles west of Dornoch on A9(T), I was actually there at Creich, my ancestral destination! It gave me the same feeling as with each crossing over the St. John River from Pokiok to the Munro lands at Lower Southampton. Creich Parish, on the north shore of the firth, is a 30 mile long, two-to-ten-mile wide rural region. It's comprised of woods and low uplands in contrast to "Munros," a term that Scots commonly use to describe Scottish peaks over 3,000 feet, I accepted the lofty reference as a compliment to the Munro name.

The lay of the land was just like the St. John River Valley, and the still firth waters like Culliton Cove at Nackawic. Along the way, Spinningdale and Little Creich appeared remarkably similar to my visions of Rossville and Culliton. There were flats on the firth like those where Nackawic Stream flowed into the St. John prior to the 1967 flooding.

The first traditional ancestor in the Highland Chief line was Donald Munro. The descendancy Chief of the Munros of Swordale was Hugh Munro, 9th Baron of Foulis. Our Lower Southampton branch came from that ancestry. Munro and Calder neighbors in Creich emigrated together, settled near each other, and were often related through marriage.

We explored back roads and country lanes. In the Swordale (of Nordic derivation) area next to Bonar Bridge, we came upon an ancient cemetery in a field. It overlooked a veritable St. John River Valley scene of hills, woods, and farmland. As I walked among many unreadable and tilted stones, a few marked Munro divulged that I was on the same sacred soil referred to on my great grandfather John's stone in Otis Cemetery as "Born in Sutherlandshire Scotland 1831."

Continuing north on A836 through Lairg and past Loch Shin, we arrived at the *extremely* remote hamlet of Altnaharra in the midst of the Highlands. We stayed two nights at the Altnaharra Hotel, a 150-year-old sheep drover inn. Hosts Anne and Daniel Tuscher were hospitable innkeepers, and the inn's ancient ambience was welcoming. There was a local logging operation that we could relate to those in Maine and New Brunswick. Altnaharra was a rare unspoiled angling retreat. Before leaving home, I eagerly packed fishing gear, never having cast a salmon fly on North American waters! While I was fishing, Laurie watched shepherdess "Crissie" and her dog round up a ewe that was having difficulty with birthing. Laurie said all went well, and could hardly wait to tell me about that sighting and the pet sheep that came trotting past her in the hotel hallway. Whether fishing, golfing, or gawking, wear thorn-proof pants if moving through the Highland "Golden" gorse!

From there, we drove up to the North Sea. Turning west at Tongue on A938, we saw large salmon-rearing farms in the bays. Past Durness, we saw the road sign "Cape Wrath," and knew that it had a shipwreck history. Sheep were everywhere. Laurie had to get out of the car once to shoo away a ewe and her twins who assumed that the middle of the road was theirs. Our rental Hyundai was very reliable. The curvy and craggy roads were single lane with periodic turn-off spots that were absolutely necessary when automobiles met from opposing directions.

Heading southwest along the rugged coast, we arrived at Inver Lodge Hotel that overlooked Lochinver Bay. The Outer Hebrides Isle of Lewis, on the western horizon, was a four-hour ferry trip from the mainland. From our window, Laurie tossed apples on the grass, and a stag came to gobble them. We could see a large fishing fleet in the harbor and RNLI (Royal Lifeboat National Institution) orange-topped vessels on ready alert for search and rescue. We met a friendly couple in the lounge who told us a lot about Scotland. Turns out, he was the Police Commissioner for Edinburgh.

South on A835, we stopped at Ullapool on Loch Broom and saw Highland Stoneware in the making. Laurie was introduced to the potter's wheel, glazes, and kiln firing at MassArt and has favored that craft ever since. Shipping boxes on the shelves were marked L.L.Bean.

That brought us right back to home ground! We bought freehand painted bowls, plates, and a lamp (heavy!). The Scottish glazed stoneware scenes of salmon, seacoast, and flowers have continued to grace our home through many moves.

Driving, *always on the left*, down the coast, we crossed over the new bridge onto the Isle of Skye. When we came upon a replica of a crofter's cottage, my Scot and Irish ancestral homes became a reality. Laurie and I stayed at Cuillin Hills Hotel overlooking Portree Bay with the jagged Cuillin mountain range on the horizon. Leaving Skye, it was a unique experience to travel to mainland Mallaig by Highland Isles car-ferry. We saw a German film crew boarding a small ferry to an outer island. On the dock, a man showed us his mixed catch of fish that whet our appetite for a fresh seafood lunch. That we had, at a local harborside restaurant, accompanied by friendly conversation with those seated around us. Most, I recall, were on holiday.

Driving east to Fort William, where Lochs Linnhe and Eil converge (went to a map for spelling; pronunciation is up for grabs), we bought another suitcase to accommodate our must-haves. It was awesome to see the statue of Clan Chief Donald Cameron, tall and strong, in Highland regalia. I thought of Fredericton, New Brunswick, where Poet Bobby Burn's statue has stood for 100 years beside the St. John River.

On A828 and B85 to Oban (of the single malt whisky), our next stop for two nights was Annie Paul's Taychreggan Inn at Kilchreggan by Taynuilt on Loch Awe. That's another colorful mouthful of the "Burr!" The names became as familiar to us as Maine's Millinocket and New Brunswick's Miramichi. The inn had a Royal Automobile Club three-star rated cuisine, and we found the wild smoked salmon exquisite. Incidentally, one of the chefs that we met at Altnaharra, deep in the Highlands, was in the traditional kilted wedding party of a chef here at Taychreggan. While I was out fishing with a "Ghillie" (guide in New Brunswick or Maine), Laurie (always with attention to detail!) spoke of a local lady in a white blouse and plaid skirt who came to lunch specifically for the locally cured salmon. They served my trout at dinner, and I devoured it as if it was a skillet-fried speckled beauty from Trout Brook in Rossville.

En route to Glasgow along the "Bonnie Banks O' Loch Lomond," our fortunate finale was Gleddoch House, a country estate hotel and golf course at Langbank, a Glasgow suburb on the south bank of the River Clyde. Parked beside the entrance was a gray "Land Rover" type of Mercedes Benz, a model I've never forgotten. Reception graciously upgraded our room to one above the foyer that looked out on the Clyde Firth and Dumbarton Castle on the opposite bank. Massive oil rigs were being towed out to the North Atlantic from Port Glasgow. Rhododendrons were in bloom and the groomed links were apple green. Lodging, lunch, drinks, dinner on arrival, and breakfast were all superior and priced very reasonably. Prior to our May 13th departure, it was a relaxing stop-over before leaving Scotland.

The Scottish Highlands trip gave me a better concept of the Munro migration to New Brunswick, of similar latitude. The Highland coastline and rugged interior had fields sloping to the sea or streams, similar to New Brunswick's terrain. The Highland Council, one of 32, has the largest area of 10,000 square miles with a 2010 population of 222,000. New Brunswick, in comparison, is almost three times as large with three times the population. Highlanders brag Ben Nevis, at 4,576 feet, as the highest peak in the British Isles, and New Brunswickers claim 2,690-foot Mt. Carleton as the highest mountain in Atlantic Canada. As my mind migrated back to Rossville, I remembered that Nackawic hosts the "World's Largest Axe!"

Glasgow International Airport, from whence our land trip began, was a short driving distance from Gleddoch House on the Motorway. Isles of Lewis and Harris, uppermost in a 130-mile coastal island chain, were soon under our wings as we left the Scottish mainland. Close to my heart, and in my closet, hang (Isle of) Harris Tweed jackets of pure Scottish wool. Clo Mor, "The big cloth," is still hand-woven by crofters like those of old. They're "Warped" (arranged) to duplicate countryside hues: yellow for the sands, fern-green for the hills, brown for the Moor, and many more. From the Outer Hebrides, we flew back across the Atlantic with a better understanding of my thoughts when over the Maritimes and Maine. We will have to wait a year, but there will be a national referendum about whether to separate from the United Kingdom and become an independent Scotland.

Beamed up by Highland spirit, I could return to New Brunswick with the intention of some tale telling. Now, I'll get back to the details of our trips to and from New Brunswick. Laurie adopted my cross-border attachment to family, friends, forest, and farm. Since we met

61 years ago, I've learned to share her affection for sandy or rugged seashores, scents of salt water, and foods out of the sea. As a result, I treasure memories of fishing offshore from Plum Island from a Merrimac River marina in Newburyport, Massachusetts, and lobstering in our diesel Dyer-29 on Cape Cod.

I must say that Laurie *did* have a longstanding Downeast link in West Southport, Maine. Ever since we met, I recall that she looked forward to a Christmas card from Mary McDonald Lakeman. When Laurie was a tot in Newton Center, Mary and Peggy McDonald, neighborhood teenagers, babysat her, pushing a carriage up and down Center Street between Newton Highlands and Crystal Lake. Laurie's father was their doctor and delivered the youngest, Rosalie (now Killion, who remains one of our best friends on Cape Cod). Mary married Weldon Lakeman, a merchant mariner, and they moved to West Southport and raised a family.

Mary and Laurie exchanged Christmas cards and notes over the years. Those led us to visit the Lakemans. Weldon showed me the lay of the land, while Laurie and Mary gabbed. Grass never grew under Mary's feet, and she ran a tourist overnight-cabin business. Cards continued, but we didn't see Mary for a few years until after Weldon died. By then, she was living in Boothbay, our visits were more frequent, and we renewed memories over dinner and drinks. I had the privilege of sitting between two great gals with gray hair, one the baby and one the sitter. Hail to Mary's fun-loving soul! On a top shelf in our family room, a peaceful life-size ceramic dove watches over us. It was a gift from Mary Lakeman. Like those relaxing visits to Boothbay on our trips north, we've acquired a taste for traditional stop-offs.

In Portsmouth, New Hampshire, 165 miles from home, Motel 6 accommodates us and welcomes Barney. He is a master of putting his front paws up on the reception desk while wagging his tail. Jim and Peg McLaughlin, live in Exeter, N.H., and our Paula and daughters, Lily and Ruby, have a home in York, Maine. Portsmouth is perfect for visiting, shopping, and dining. We go to BJ's Wholesale for goods and low-priced gas, Dick's Sporting Goods for skeet-shooting ammunition, or over the Piscataqua Bridge to Kittery Trading Post and the outlets. Excellent eateries are Black Trumpet (a mushroom) on Ceres Street at the old waterfront, and Anneka Jans restaurant opposite the Naval Shipyard gate in Kittery. Joanne Moynihan, my partner Bob's wife, has a harbor-view home on Kittery Point, and we try to visit her every so often. We frequently travel on two-lane old Route 1, which was the only main highway before I-95 existed. Weaving from inland to shore and back, it's full of memories, good food, and spots to rest.

Reconnecting with I-95, we head north toward Portland. Exiting onto I-295 above Scarborough, we watch for air traffic in and out of the International Jetport. Maine Medical Center is perched high atop Portland's Western Prom. As a premature newborn, Paula's Lily had superb care in the neonatal unit. We're longtime members of the Portland Museum of Art, anticipate each new exhibit, and always find gifts, books, and note-cards in its store.

Passing the container terminal where tour ships to and from Nova Scotia also dock, we approach the Old Port district in downtown Portland. On waterfront Commercial Street, there's always something to do and see in all seasons. At J's Oyster, I make a lunch ritual of Allagash White draft ale with a baker's dozen (13) of oysters on the half shell. Laurie has hers with Dewars Scotch whisky. We call her favorite cocktail a "DOTR," Dewars On The Rocks! We've been going to J's long enough to know that the end row and corner bar-stool seats are usually occupied by regulars. With Laurie on a walker, everyone from waitress to patron makes an effort to help us to a table.

It's odd, in tourist season, to see giant cruise ships berthed at the upper waterfront deep water docks, and crowds filling the streets. It seems as if a high-rise apartment building or two has come up out of the sea. I look forward to attending the Portland Yacht Services annual Maine Boat Builders Show on Fore Street each March, to admire the fine craftsmanship or practical gear that make the show genuine Downeast. Fred Forsley, owner of the Shipyard Brewery, is a nephew of Dr. Dick Forsley, a Lowell surgeon who I first met in 1961. A visit with Fred, tour of his brewery, or purchase of gifts for family has become a routine.

While leaving Portland on I-295, I respond to the Baxter Boulevard exit sign in the same way that I did in the '30s and '40s. Uttering "Baxter Boulevard" has always been my pleasure, and learning about Percival Baxter's link with Baxter State Park and Mt. Katahdin has been another boost. He may have been perceived as the privileged son of Portland's mayor, and later became governor, but he was not a wimp in business, charity, or open-air sport. It took me a long time for me to know him better. After 40 years, I opened my eyes to *Greatest Mountain: Katahdin's Wilderness, Exerpts from the writings of Percival Proctor Baxter*. It only took me a few hours of reading to fully comprehend his foresight, dedication, and generosity in acquiring vast tracts of privately owned land. The mountain and the man have perpetual prominence at the very top of Maine.

The Eastern Promenade extension of Fore Street has replaced the Baxter Boulevard route of my youth. The road and walkways portray a panoramic view of the Portland waterfront, Casco Bay islands, and entrance to Back Cove. Jam-packed summer mooring fields below are testimony to the popularity of boating. Water edge Narrow Gauge Scenic Railway, thrills passengers via steam-power locomotive and passenger cars. The promenade attracts strollers, dog-walkers, cyclists, frisbee fans, and gazers, who park along the way. Sun-seekers bask randomly on grass or blankets. I note that it is well used for fresh-air fitness and sledding during the winter.

The part of the promenade that I like best is Loring Memorial Park at the northern hairpin turn. The circular parking turn-off is a memorial to Major Charles J. Loring of USAF Korean War sacrificial and Medal of Honor fame. Between the granite curbed and cobblestoned mid-circle lie random groups of raw-cut granite boulders set amid trees and plantings. Two ten- foot granite posts vertically read "Remembering." Four lesser granite pillars on the lawn are engraved in sequence with "Heart, Presence, Integrity, Spirit." The helmet and goggle image of Major Loring on a bronze plaque, is a handsome homage.

Laurie can sit in the car, view the Loring Memorial, and look down at the highway where Tukey's Bridge connects the neighborhoods of Munjoy Hill and East Deering. When I walk Barney with the wind out of the north, I can smell those B & M beans baking and watch steam rising from the factory stacks.

On I-295 north again via a hair-raising lane loss and left merge into heavy traffic, I drive to the upper Yarmouth exit. At the Delorme Map Store on the right, I double back to Route 88, pass over the familiar old cement Royal River Bridge, and we're at the Royal River Grillhouse on Lower Falls Landing. Depending upon the season, I park among vacant boat stands or shrink-wrapped boats that make our Saab wagon appear pint-size. We prefer to sit in the ship-shape bar area to scan the bar crowd and talk with the wait staff.

After good food, drink, and conversation, we're back up on Freeport's narrow Route 1 to a Barney-friendly room at the Best Western Freeport Inn. Having stayed there for 40 or more years, we're at home with delicious and healthy breakfast at the Café. While waiting for the order with a cup of coffee, I try to sit where I can watch the kitchen, take in the sight and smell of food being served, gaze at the prints and originals of Downeast scenes on the walls, and read the Forecaster. First stop in downtown Freeport has always been at L.L.Bean. I occasionally recognize relics of days gone by like the Dutch Village overnight cabins and Maine Idyll Motor Court cottages (still in operation since the 1930s) visible between Route 1 and I-295 two miles north of downtown Freeport.

When north near Brunswick, Laurie and I are acquainted with the area through many years of Mid Coast travel. At Bowdoin College campus in Brunswick, we drive onto Harpswell peninsula's ocean-end Routes 123 or 124. Along each road's dip and twist, the extensive 216 miles of waterfront is periodically hidden from view by woods, farms, and small villages. Now get this! The Burbine and McGowan homes in Harpswell, are *precisely* 250 miles halfway between my territorial focal points of Cape Cod and Nackawic! From Falmouth, Massachusetts to Harpswell, Maine, the direct line distance, mostly over water, is only 145 miles. That is why sailing northeast from Massachusetts, is referred to as going Downeast.

Prior to discovering Harpswell, we went to the Boothbay Harbor Fishermen's Festival at the end of April with our Burbine family and Jim's mother, Barbara. From an upper deck at the Tugboat Inn, we've watched the waterfront competition. There's always a booming fisherman's voice on the loudspeaker. He knows every event and every competitor. Foot races over a line of floating lobster traps promptly put most contestants in the water. Upon a signal, in another event, captain and stern-man run down the ramp to their lobster boat, juice it up, go out into the harbor, set a line of traps, and come back into the dock so fast that everyone holds their breath hoping that they can stop! Each run is timed, and the winner reigns for another year. On Sunday, being solemn (the guys and gals have hangovers), a crowd from there and from away gather at Gray's Wharf waterfront restaurant. No one under 18 can attend, though the drinking age is

21. Stories are told, mostly about one another. It's a fun afternoon of "BEE-ah" and bull.

Laurie and I enjoy seeing purple, pink, and cream spiked lupine blooming along Maine country roads and fields in June. It's always reminder of salvaging and saving lupine seeds in Newfoundland with hopes of growing them at home. In August 1998, Jim and Jean Burbine arranged for Laurie and me, their seven year-old daughter Jackie, and Jim's mother, Barbara, to fly on Air Canada to Newfoundland, rent a van, and tour the province. Among the many harbors, history of the devastated cod fishery was ever present. I had heard Stan Rogers sing "Make and Break Harbor," and was humbled to be on that rugged coast among resilient, fun-loving "Newfies."

We got baptized or "Screeched-in" to the "Newfie" culture by kissing the cod, taking a "Whack" of Screech rum, and singing Newfoundland's traditional "I'se da b'ye dat builds da boat and I'se da b'ye dat sails her. I'se da b'ye dat catches da fish and brings 'em home to Liza." The song took, but the lupine seeds didn't. While on a bird watching boat, one native Newfie, a puffin, must have resented my Yankee presence and bombed me with you know what!

At Harbour Grace, "The Spirit of Harbour Grace," a DC-3 caught my eye: 'twas another like that of my 1947 Christmas flight to Presque Isle! Retired and restored, the workhorse was powered by dependable Pratt and Whitney engines and had a history as long as your arm. Douglas Aircraft Company in California made it in 1943 for the Army Air Corps, and they were called C-47s. After WWII service in North Africa, it flew for U.S. Resort Airlines, Quebec Air, and finally Air Labrador, transporting mail and cargo between Newfoundland and Goose Bay until 1988.

While touring Long Point Lighthouse in Twillingate, we by-chance ran into Bessie (Ingraham) and Ivan Bradley. Instead of standing in Ingraham's Rossville, New Brunswick dooryard not far from Trout Brook, here we were overlooking "Iceberg Alley" and whale waters!

Here we are once more, as I describe trips up coastal Route One on the way to Bangor. We leave the coastline above Belfast and Searsport, pass through Bucksport, take 1A, and stop at the Best Western White House Inn south of downtown Bangor. It provides good lodging, breakfast, and an opportunity to look around the city. The updated inn overlooks Dysart's Truck Stop & Restaurant where there are comings and goings 24/7. Tractor-trailers from every state in the Union and each eastern Canadian province pass through daily. Walking Barney along the parking areas gives me a good chance to survey an 18 wheeler's origin. Confirmed by a White House Inn desk clerk, some long-distance truckers register overnight for a rest, shower, and breakfast all included in the room rate. We've been served supper next to the antique pickup truck inside "Dysaat's" restaurant. After filling the gas tank at the Bangor Mall, it's a divided highway drive up I-95.

At the Orono exit, we recall Christine's University of Maine years from 1987 to 1989. I also remember passing through the campus with my parents in 1939. In 1949, I considered the wildlife management program as my alternative to attending Tufts College. There has been a Canadian-American Center on the campus since about 1965, and it offers undergraduate and graduate programs. It's a natural, because Maine is enfolded by New Brunswick and Quebec, and almost half of Maine's residents have Canadian roots. The Fogler Library has a Canadian Studies Office where reference material can be accessed.

When with Christine in Orono, we visited the old and acclaimed Shaw and Tenney paddle and oar shop (still there) on Water Street. They made the two-piece, takedown oars for our 1980 Dyer Duck inflatable boat, but no longer manufactured them. Pat's Pizza, trendy with the college crowd, has been popular since 1931. At Governor's Restaurant in Old Town, we couldn't help watching a school-bus load of teenagers and their chaperones gobble mountainous desserts after eating bright-red hotdog "Snappers" with a "Charge" of baked beans.

We also became familiar with the Orono Fire Department. After the first year in a dorm, Chris lived in a house downtown with a crew of classmates. An electrical extension cord chafed under one guy's bedframe, and just about burned the house down. After Christine relocated, the first house had a second fire that finished it off. Calling the fire department about details for an insurance claim, I started to identify the situation when a curt voice cut in with "I know. It's the only house in town that's burned twice!"

In a December 1989 ceremony with balsam fir trees on the stage, Chris graduated with a blizzard raging outside. The minister for benediction and the speaker from Portland couldn't negotiate the stormy roads. "Weather" or not, she got the degree. A career in graphic design probably began when she opted to spend time in the college art department. When Paul and Chris were dating, they had long drives between Orono and Massachusetts. After graduation, Christine did graphics for a Boston architectural firm, and then for State Street Global Advisors. She now carries on independently while managing her household of husband, Paul, and three children. She contributed to this book's graphics.

Between each I-95 exit in Penobscot and Aroostook (aka "The County") Counties, towns and unorganized townships or plantations have colorful names. Recalling them in sequence up or back ain't easy! Roadside markers like Alton Bog, Argyle, and Edinburgh or Hersey-town [T2-R6], Benedicta, Crystal, and Smyrna, along the double-barrel highway attract my curiosity more than Watch Out for Moose signs. By the way, should anyone drive through the Alton Bog that flat, primeval expanse above Bangor, in a severe lightning storm, it's possible that they might witness a geyser. Between WWI and WWII, the Army tested and set-off explosives around the bog, and it's said that some might not have been detonated!

We have our own landmarks to talk about while driving. Passing the Lincoln exit, we recall taking Route 6 East many times for 60 miles to reach the St. Croix River border stations between Vanceboro and St.Croix, New Brunswick. With long ups, downs, and crests, we've suddenly come upon moose crossing the road at dusk. Laurie prefers I-95 at that time of day!

I urge those who regularly "Go north" on the Lincoln to Houlton section of I-95, to try its predecessor Route 2-A, between Macwahoc Plantation and Houlton. It's my oft-mentioned Military Road, and it's still a '30s and '40s experience in those haunting Haynesville Woods. Cole's Express trucks led the way when the state didn't plow snow on that stretch in the 1920s. Allie Cole Land Transportation Museum in Bangor acquired those plows that both opened the road and delivered freight. A popular country hit in 1965 was Dick Curless' "A Tomb-stone Every Mile," preserving road hazards and ghosts in song. Truckers and others tell of the woman in white who appears in the middle of the road, climbs in when they stop, and just as quickly, disappears. She is the ghost of a new bride killed when her imbibing husband lost control of their car and smashed into the timbered thicket

Well above Lincoln on I-95, there is a bountiful and beautiful stand of white birch, some call it "Paper-birch," in the median strip. The sight is brief but breathtaking. The Mt. Katahdin vista turn-off, mile-marker 252 North in Benedicta, is a scenic stop for us and a rest stop for Barney. Then, we cruise northward with "Ktaadn" to my left, and play David Mallett's "The Fable True" CD album. Dave recites excerpts from *The Maine Woods* tidings of Henry David Thoreau alongside guitar, fiddle, and bass background music. It's a double David treat.

The Herseytown TWP (Township) marker always makes me think of my Hersey neighbors who came from Maine. They were generous folks who welcomed me and other neighborhood children into their Winchester and New Boston, New Hampshire, homes. I kept each of their Christmas card family portraits from the early 1940s, and long after. I sent all the cards that I had saved, with Mrs. Hersey's remarks, to her children last year. The Herseys summered on Shin Pond, northwest of Patten, Maine, where son, Elliott, and daughters Althea, Alison, and Stephanie still gather with their families. Elliott, I discovered, has recorded the Hersey pedigree, and many must be Mainers. I get occasional updates on the clan through correspondence with Althea or directly from their relative Ed Rogers, who owns J.R. Maxwell restaurant in Bath where our family likes to feast.

We favor two lunch stops in Maine that have good home cookin'. Norma's Restaurant is in York, and the Brookside Inn Restaurant is on I-95, exit 291, at Smyrna Mills, south of Houlton. Our longtime favorite in New Brunswick, is the Moonlight Inn between Fredericton and Woodstock on old Route 2 River Road, at Dumfries.

Take exit 7 on I-95, and Norma's is on Route 1 near the Stonewall Kitchen complex, which is also worth a stop-and-purchase. I almost always order Norma's tasty Western sandwich on white bread, and a piece of lemon meringue pie. They were Dad's favorites.

While in Smyrna, the Pioneer Place general store is a wonderful Amish experience and general-store supply of country necessities. Hanging lamps and a manual cash register indicate that electricity is not used. Young boys wearing long-sleeve shirts, and blue pants with suspenders, stock the store. I bought Laurie a paring knife with a handle that suited her arthritic grip. I walked out with an Amish wide-brimmed straw hat. Their homes, barns, fields, and pastured livestock are kept spick-and-span.

The Moonlight Inn and Motel was by-passed when the new Trans-Canada Highway was constructed. It's been there along the St. John from as far back as I can remember. The friendly service and quality of food even now attract the local population. It's been a magnificent place for us to meet relatives for lunch and enjoy a drink or a glass of wine (once available in government-only stores).

On Saturday mornings in Fredericton, New Brunswick, we go to the Boyce Farmer's Market. It's been operating since 1951, and has as many as 250 vendors from along the St. John River Heritage Corridor. We've enjoyed the crowds, diverse local and ethnic cooking odors, fresh produce, arts, and crafts. I've yet to taste a better brook trout pate` than that bought for our cocktail crackers. I especially recall home-knit winter hats that we bought as Christmas presents for our grandchildren.

With each trip to New Brunswick, border crossing remains personally porous. I relished reading Jacques Poitras' 2011 *Imaginary Line, Life on an unfinished border.* No better up-to-date tales exist than in his zig-zag routes of travel inquiry along the entire 318 mile New Brunswick-Maine border. He unveils past and present cross-border government policy and its impact on social tradition and trade. Other than being a writer, he's a correspondent for CBC News, covering New Brunswick and border events.

Each New England state and Atlantic province, along with Quebec, are unique by hand-hammered history and together represent northeast mainland and maritime ties. We frequently hear and read about incidents that effect border life and crossing. Economic confrontations occur occasionally, as with the lobster fishery and processing disputes. The most publicized, and the most horrific in our time, was the 9/11, 2001 terrorist attack on the United States. Its repercussions on border crossing have been extensive and mandatory.

Though sometimes delayed with protocol when Laurie and I cross the border into Canada, we understand the stringent requirements and restrictions. In reward, cousins Joyce Jones and Gwen Bradbury (excellent cooks by talent and heritage) give us put-up preserves to take home. Joyce, Gwen, and Weldon Briggs still remark on "Aunt Lucy's beautiful cooking." They talk about Mother's tomato soup cake with cream cheese frosting recipe from the *Victory Cook Book.* It's a family favorite that Laurie shared with our Woods Hole Museum cook book, *Woods Hole Cooks It Up.*

JELLY ROLL

3 eggs (beaten); 1 cup white sugar; 3 tbsps. sweet milk; 1 cup flour (scant); 2 tsps. Acadia baking powder; ⅛ tsp. salt; 1 tsp. vanilla or lemon flavoring.

Sift baking powder with the flour. Mix and pour in a long, shallow pan (batter about ¼ inch deep). Bake 12 minutes in a moderately slow oven.

Turn onto a cloth, spread with softened jelly or lemon filling and roll quickly, wrap in a cloth to keep in shape.

—Mrs. Albert H. Tompkins
—Mrs. J. K. Glass

TOWN TALK CAKE

1 cup sugar; ½ cup butter; ¼ cup buttermilk; 1 egg; 1½ cups flour; 1 tsp. soda; 4 tbsps. cocoa (heaping); ¼ tsp. soda, cook in ¾ cup boiling water.

Cook in moderate oven.

Method: Cream butter and sugar, then add egg, then buttermilk, vanilla, salt, put 1 tsp. soda in flour, also cocoa. Cook ¼ tsp. soda in ¾ cup boiling water and add lastly.

—Jean Stephenson

SANDWICH CAKE

½ cup butter; 1 cup sugar; 2 eggs; ½ tsp. soda; 1 tsp. cream of tartar; ¼ cup milk; 1½ cups flour; vanilla.

Put in pan; then put first, one cup dates cut fine; second, 1 cup nut meats cut fine; third, 1 egg white beaten stiff; fourth, 1 cup brown sugar, over all.

Cook in very slow oven.

—Mrs. John Anderson

TOMATO SOUP CAKE

1 cup sugar; ½ cup butter or shortening; 1 can tomato soup; 2 tsps. cinnamon; 1 tsp. soda; ½ tsp. cloves; 1 cup raisins; ½ cup nut meats; 1½ cups flour; salt.

Mix in order given, sift soda with flour.

Bake at 350 for 30 min. —Mrs. Perley Smith

DAYTON CAKE

1 cup butter; 2 cups sugar; 4 eggs; ¾ cup milk; 3½ cups flour; 1 tsp. cream of tartar; 1 tsp. soda; 1 cup walnut meats; 1 cup raisins; 1 nutmeg.

Cream butter and sugar well, add well beaten eggs, sift flour and cream of tartar and soda twice, and add alternating with the milk. Put nuts and raisins through meat chopper and mix in last with nutmeg.

Bake in a slow oven.

—Mrs. Thomas Gallagher

BANANA WALNUT CAKE

1½ cups sugar; ½ cup shortening; 2 eggs well beaten; 2 cups flour; pinch of salt; 1 tsp. soda; ⅔ cup sour milk; 1 cup banana pulp (takes 2 bananas); vanilla; 1 cup chopped nuts.

Method: Cream shortening; add sugar and blend well; add 2 beaten eggs, vanilla; dissolve soda in sour milk and add to mixture; put salt in flour and add.

Last of all add banana pulp and nut meats. Bake in moderate oven.

—Mrs. George W. Campbell, Jr.
—Mrs. W. I. Jones

SUNSHINE CAKE

Whites of 5 eggs, beat light, add ½ cup of sugar; 1 tsp. vanilla; ¼ tsp. cream of tartar. Yolks of 5 eggs, beat light, add ½ cup sugar, pinch of salt.

Put yolks in whites, then blend in one cup of sifted flour, sifted 5 times.

—Agnes Wasson

SUNSHINE CAKE

6 egg whites, 6 egg yolks; 1½ cups white sugar; ¼ tsp. lemon and orange extract; 1½ cups pastry flour, sifted twice before measuring; 1 tsp. cream of tartar; ⅓ tsp. soda; 2 tbsps. cold water.

Method: Beat whites till stiff; fold in sugar gradually, then yolks of eggs beaten till lemon color. Add flavoring and water. Fold in flour with cream of tartar and soda. Bake in moderate oven in tube pan. Use any plain icing.

—Mrs. Wm. A. Martin

COLD WATER POUND CAKE

1½ cups white sugar; 1 cup butter; 3 cups pastry flour; 3 eggs; ¾ cup cold water; 1 tsp. cream of tartar sifted with flour; ½ tsp. soda dissolved in cold water; 2 tsps. lemon extract.

Cream butter and sugar, add beaten eggs; flour and water alternately. Bake in moderate oven 1½ hours.

—Mrs. Elizabeth T. Smith

DEVIL FOOD CAKE

2 cups Swans Down cake flour; 1 tsp. soda; ½ cup butter; 1½ cups brown sugar; 2 eggs; 3 squares chocolate; 1 cup milk; 1 tsp. vanilla; pinch of salt.

Cream butter; add sugar gradually. Beat after each egg is added; sift soda with flour and add melted chocolate, vanilla, salt and milk.

—Mrs. William McCormack
—Mrs. Frank Tompkin

Tomato Soup Cake Recipe From Mother's 1942 Cook Book

Harold McGuire, who lived across Rossville Road from the Baylis farm as a child, recently told Joyce Jones that he saw me "making false teeth" on the Baylis wood stove! I recall the instance, about 1961, when I began specialty training in surgery but wanted to do a bit of "Kitchen dentistry" for Mother. Having brought all the necessary lab material to New Brunswick, I put two bronze denture curing flasks in boiling water. As far as I was concerned, there was no law in Rossville about practicing without a Canadian license! I hope my denture recipe turned out as good as Mother's cake!

A few years ago, Gwen Bradbury had a family gathering at her home in Upper Kingsclear, and I was able to reconnect with my first cousin, Brenda Baylis Nicholson and husband, Curtis, who live nearby. Brenda is a retired Visiting Nurse, Curtis an engineer, and they have two children, Gregory and Lynn. Curtis came from Temple, upriver, where the Harold Davidson and Willard Way families lived and died.

Last year, I drove upriver from Fredericton, twice to see my only other Canadian first cousin, 85 year-old Alton McElwain and wife, Verna, who are retired to Hartfield, the next hamlet above Rossville. Many years ago, they crossed the border to Caribou where Alton found a job, and they raised sons David and Robert. We talked about old times and deer hunting. Over the years, Alton sent me letters and photos that helped to provide information for these tales. I took a close-up photo of Alton and me. It might be scary to our grandchildren, but it was heartwarming to us.

Whether at Gwen Bradbury's in Kingsclear, with Joyce and Percy in Temperance Vale or Riley Brook, or at a restaurant in Fredericton, a family sit-down supper is always a happy event. Laurie and I are the oldest of three generations of cousins enjoying one another's company at the table. Humorous stories abound! One tells of a local lad who was questioned by the RCMP about arson. His response was "Arson who?" We joke about friend Gene, in Riley Brook, whose shed "Lounge," with TV and beer, is as relaxing as those in the city, and local news is always a topic. Since beer is the preferred beverage, the owner sees to the recycling, because he has dump connections.

New Brunswick wit, said typical of the 1800s Province Men working in the Maine lumber camps, was carried over to the operating room at Lowell General Hospital in Massachusetts. The surgical supervisor, Elaine Chase Ryan, from Hartland, and I often traded provincial particulars. When I mentioned the birthplace of a New Brunswick acquaintance, which will remain anonymous, she said: "-----'s like lemon pie, there is no upper crust."

CHAPTER SIX
FREEPORT AND BEANS AGAIN

L.L.Bean at Freeport, Mid-1960s

The "Upper crust" of Freeport, Maine is one of personal achievement and outdoor popularity. When "L.L.Bean" is voiced, or its catalogs are cast over the face of the earth, folks nod in familiarity. If you want to join in with the locals, just call the company "Beans."

In the early 1940s, Bean was a visible Freeport Village surname on the town list: "Charles W. on Pownal Road, Guy (Postmaster) and Mary at 6 Morse, L.L.Bean mnfrs leather & canvas specialties 59 Main, Leon L and Claire Freeport Realty Co 2 Holbrook, Lester C and Hazel 5 Morse, Ortha R 81 Main." By the mid-1960s, L.L.Bean expanded into the demolished Oxnard Block, next door on Main Street as pictured on a postcard. In the June 1, 1981 issue of *Harvard Business Review*, a case study profiled L.L.Bean growth. Though

Boston is Beantown and Portland bakes beans, whether from away or in Cumberland County, no one mentions Freeport without voicing "Beans." That out-of-doors supplier, founded by Mr. Bean in 1912, has become a central green space surrounded by the L.L. retail complex. It's a mecca for millions. It's a caregiver's pride.

Over the years, I've donated accumulated Bean gear to their archives. Ruth Porter and Debra McCormack are dedicated archival caregivers of the collection housed in a 2005 addition to the former L. L. Bean home on Holbrook Street with a plan for historical renovation in progress. Laurie and I bequeathed a giant long handled camp fry pan and cover, an ash pack basket with canvas cover, rawhide-and-ash Bean snowshoes and harness, and a Swiss Army knife sheath with a brass snap marked Bean. We also donated an October 13, 1941 *Life* magazine article: "Maine's Bean Outfits Sportsmen Everywhere," and April 1955 and March 1970 issues of *Down East* magazine, which featured L.L.Bean advancement and growth. With Beans being as much about Maine as about merchandise, the pleasures of my 1951 and 1952 Katahdin climbs rest in donated memorabilia: an Appalachian Mountain Club guidebook with data and maps, my two hand-made wood back racks with knapsacks, hand written notes of plans, provisions, itinerary, perspectives, and photos.

On my den shelf, below a 100th anniversary Bean canoe paddle, I have a 14 book collection that tells the "Whole nine yards" of Mr. Leon Leonwood Bean and the L.L.Bean Company. Among the factual, anecdotal, and chronological depictions, I can open any page in any book and find reminiscent reading.

Two books "From the horse's mouth," duplicate his talent of approaching customers in simple and direct terms. The first book is Mr. Bean's bible to us old-timers, the 1942 brick-red cover *Hunting-Fishing and Camping*. Proof of popularity is that the Dingley Press, a first-floor renter (1942–1972) in the L.L.Bean Warren Block, had run off 104,000 copies in 14 printings by 1956. The next insider book is *My Story: The Autobiography of a Down-East Merchant*, 1962. The last sentence of the foreword is proof that he saw youths' safe haven in natural settings. "Since the great outdoors is also a big help in keeping boys and girls out of trouble, I wish to dedicate this book to the Teen-agers of America." What a generational gem!

In kin-following-suit, daughter Barbara Gorman's son Leon wrote

L.L.Bean, The Making of an American Icon, Leon Gorman, Chairman, former President, and Grandson of L. L. Bean. I feel that Leon Arthur Gorman is the gold standard of hard earned succession. How proud L. L. would be to see the *100ᵗʰAnniversary Edition of Hunting Fishing and Camping with Updates by Great Grandson Bill Gorman.* Bill strides right alongside Mr. Bean, page by page, adding his own comment. Both are speaking at their best. In chapter 43: Baxter State Park, page 103, I found a photo of Pinnacle Rock on Dudley Trail, Mt. Katahdin. It caught my eye quick, but the guy on the pointy end was not me on Index Rock (same as Pinnacle) in 1951. I've never seen a more striking black and white map of Maine's counties, towns, townships, and plantations than on both the original and the anniversary *Hunting Fishing and Camping* end pages, entitled "1941 Deer Kill in Each Town" and "2010 Deer Harvest by Town in Maine." Let alone all the places, name all the counties, and I'll buy you a beer!

In 1981, Bill Riviere with the staff of L.L.Bean, and L.L.Bean, Inc., published *The L.L.Bean Guide to the Outdoors.* The Maine woods and river cover painting was by superior out-of-doors artist and columnist, Tom Hennessey. It showed a canvas canoe on shore, a fly-fisherman playing a leaping-salmon, and a guide with ready net. I immediately opened the book. On inspection of the first sheet 1922 Maine Hunting Shoe ads, and "Contents" page, I shut the book and immediately took it to the cash register. From Leon A. Gorman's introduction all the way through 11 chapters of woods wisdom, the purchase was a worthy investment. It brought me back to my Katahdin climbs, and served as a checklist for those which might follow, actual or imaginary.

M. R. "Monty" Montgomery, the *Boston Globe* outdoor columnist, broke the Bean Pond ice in 1984, jumped in solo, and wrote *In Search of L.L.Bean.* His is a tale of transitions in family management, marketing technology, and customer profile.

L.L.Bean Fly-Fishing Handbook by Dave Whitlock, 1984, satisfies the thirst of experienced or novice fly-fishers. The full color leaping brookie on the cover, by artist Francis Golden, is awesome. It's a 112 page company edition based on Bean Fly Fishing School methods with Dave as both the writer and the instructor.

In 1983, L.L.Bean, Inc., Angus Cameron, and Judith Jones served-up *The L.L.Bean Game & Fish Cookbook.* Leon Gorman did the prep.

Mr. Bean, his buddies, and friends of the outdoor culinary clan supplied the recipes. Many recipes are Downeast, and testing is worth a try!

The *Game & Fish* cookbook was so well-received that Corporate Bean enlisted wife and husband, Judith and Evan Jones to prepare *The L.L.Bean Book of New New England Cookery* in 1987 on the company's 75[th]anniversary. From "Appetizers" to last chapter "Drinks, Relishes, and Sauces," the food choices from home and from away are Yankee by tradition.

Leon Gorman had an inspiration that the company should publish "A Company Scrapbook." The first edition, supervised by William David Barry and Bruce Kennett, came to fruition in 1987. Titled, *L.L.Bean, Inc., Outdoor Sporting Specialties*, it's presented in decade-by-decade chapters from "L. L.'s Oxford County Boyhood" through "The Eighties." They contain features from various sources that embrace Beans. Some are local from the *Portland Press Herald* and others from as far away as the *Dallas Morning News.*

Carlene Griffin, a Bean employee for 45 years, literally and figuratively sat prominent among L. L. himself, Leon Gorman, corporate L.L.Bean, and generations of workers. Carlene's entertaining, *"Spillin' the Beans, Behind The Scenes at L. L. Bean*, 1992, balances Mr. Bean's *My Story*, in company and customer perception. One of her anecdotes quoted "Kip" Goldrup, whose folks were among the early workers: "Boy, I'll tell you, you get me thinking about those old days and you can be sure Mr. Bean had quite a team going for him. Everybody liked everybody else, and we put out the best work a human being is capable of."

There's a 90th Anniversary, 2002, *L.L.Bean, Inc. Second Edition* published by Beans, and once again, is directed and updated by William David Barry and Bruce Kennett. John Gould, a 60 year "Country correspondent" columnist for the *Christian Science Monitor*, composed the insider introduction. He came to Freeport at age eight in 1916, and bears out what Freeport was like when Mr. Bean came into the picture. This edition, like the first, has gathered stories and photographs arranged by decade and numerous contributions by family members, employees, and source groups. The book has been a primer for me. I learned that Leon Gorman, instilled with company creed, joined resistance to the Lincoln-Dickey dam's proposed intrusion on the Upper St. John River Allagash watershed. His opposition was successful.

A 2011 *L. L. Bean, The Man and His Company, THE COMPLETE STORY by James L. Witherell*, has almost as many pages as *New England Cookery*, but more than any other Beans book in my collection. Witherall's tales, and downright *details*, begin with Mr. Bean's birth, and end with L.L.Bean, Inc., keeping up with the cutting-edge marketplace. The anecdotal and actual held my attention throughout Jim's breadth of research.

Guaranteed to Last, L.L.Bean's Century of Outfitting America by Jim Gorman (no relation) in 2012, with a foreword by Leon Gorman, is a contemporary acknowledgment of the L.L.Bean commitment to the outdoors and customer satisfaction. The hard cover tote-bag fabric is forest-green and white. To boot (no pun), the clever cover has stitching, an attached L.L.Bean clothing label, and a window that frames a colorful 1950s family camping scene on the front leaf. *Everything*, in the book's time-line, is about Mr. Bean, corporate L.L.Bean, and America's major events. Depicted employees, on the job hourly for one whole day, constitute an important ingredient in the iconic company pie. If I walked around the Freeport retail store, with this book in hand, tracing similar goods from bygone ads, a curious cluster might be seen, looking over the shoulder of an old time Bean customer.

I must interject by saying that I research and collect New Brunswick travel pamphlets and maps. Among my earliest is *The Tourist's and Sportsman's Paradise*, published in 1913, one year after Mr. Bean started his business. Since the 1890s, word was getting out around among the rich and famous and the adventurous and eager that hunting moose, deer, bear, and partridge, and fishing for salmon and trout, were at their best barely across the eastern border of Maine. The province prodigiously printed it as "The Land of Cool Breezes and Enchanting Scenery," and "Canada's Unspoiled Province." That sporting and vacation paradise was within reach of Americans by the same sea, rail, and road routes that Atlantic Canadians came down to seek economic opportunities in the northeast. To this day, the provincial government has never failed to publicize profusely, but by gosh, the sporting resource and its outfitter accommodations still provide the mainstay of satisfaction and desire to return.

At the same time in 1913, the Bangor and Aroostook Railroad Publicity Department was publishing *In the Maine Woods*, about

Northern Maine sporting attractions, for a mailing charge of "Fifteen cents in stamps." My six by nine inch 1930 copy cost ten cents in stamps back then and contained 169 pages. I go into these details, because it's history! It opens to an 18x26 inch *very detailed* foldout map that can take up sizeable time in search and recognition, as can the storytelling that follows. There are tales, treks, maps of all kinds, photos galore, hotel and outlying sporting camp locations, and travel data. Many Maine business ads came from as far south as the canoe company classifieds in Old Town and Waterville, and Portland's T. B. Davis Arms Co. (who also sold blasting powder, dynamite…for loggers, I guess). Not one L.L.Bean ad by gosh! Word of mouth about Freeport's Main Street kingpin must have been enough. Do you suppose Mr. Bean had an *In the Maine Woods* copy in his desk drawer to check on any competition? By 1941, the same 15 cents in stamps got you 127 pages of greetings, 16 chapters of stories, two pages of fish and game laws, ten pages (In small, small print) of Sportsman's Directory, and the rest in any ads that might make your northern Maine experience comfortable,…by the B&A R.R. of course! My 1952 magazine copy has 79 pages of the same, but for 25 cents mailing. Ample photographs leave nothing to the imagination. Chapters invite ladies and cameras. "The Deacon Seat" chapter of very, very tall tales told from a long camp bench has few equals. You might say that the many professional athlete, manager, and writer photos taken while hunting or fishing the Great North Woods are of the sports celebrity sort. All of that Northern Maine B&A publicity to sportsmen and vacationists "From away" continued up to 1957. You can bet your boots that it was to Beans benefit!

A tradition by road has been an L.L.Bean sportsmen's stop-over on their way to, or returning from, northern Maine or New Brunswick. "Vacationland" has appeared on Maine license plates since 1936, and neighboring New Brunswick had plates with "Picture Province" from 1959–1972. Now, the wildlife and conservation logos on plates satisfy locals and catch the eye of "Wannabees."

I've occasionally thought about starting a collection of catalogs, but numerous covers in books on Beans have served me well. There's a fine display of catalog covers in the Freeport store between the Big Bean Boot entrance and the Hunting and Fishing section (it may have moved). I'm like a kid staring, moving from cover to cover, and joyfully finding the 1930s to the 1980s covers that match the timeframe of many of my *Cross-Border Tales*. It's just another reason to return to the Beans sanctuary. One of Mr. Bean's retail terms, "Blucher," seems to belong to him and him alone. I refuse to look Blucher up in a dictionary. It's the catalog word that he's put next to "Men's and Women's Handsewn Moccasin." Beans Blucher Moccasin sold for $2.95 in 1936 and $48.00 in 1987, postpaid.

Reminders of vintage Bean goods and the era that they represent are scattered throughout the retail space. Small glassed-in dioramas on rough board pedestals mix hunting, fishing, and camping relics, the precursors of what we buy today. Enlarged sepia reproductions of catalog pages, images of L. L. himself, and old employees working at their trades adorn the walls. Wildlife taxidermy is always watching us. Beans décor does, *and definitely does not*, change!

Over time, I've had to get used to Beans acquisition of properties, and whole buildings dedicated to departments. Even in one building, some aisle goods can change and be up or down a level from a previous visit. If a bit confused, I stop at the information desk just to talk about whatever comes into my mind about Beans of yore. Then, I head for the real whereabouts of Mr. Bean's out-of-doors. Yep, I walk over to the pool under the main staircase, and instinctively search the spring-clear rippled waters for native brook trout. Often hard to detect against the pebbled rocky bottom, I look for the fanning forefin white stripes. There's always the reward of finding and watching the beauties glide around, not endangered by my old alder pole's line, hook, and worm.

With each return, I reassuringly see walls, counters, and racks filled with Bean goods and gear backed by guidance from employees who know their stuff. Yours truly often has a story-trading-clerk-customer dialogue that extends even to the cash register as I repeat again and again: "I remember the image of Mr. Bean at the top of the showroom stairs." I can't describe his facial features, but I *know* that I saw him there! When placing telephone orders, I ask where the agent is located. A "Maine" response leads to a current weather inquiry, basically the comfort of keeping in touch.

Two winters ago, I was nonchalantly standing in Beans Freeport lobby with "One arm as long as the other" (as Maine storyteller John McDonald would say). Dressed in a red-plaid mackinaw, hunter orange cap, forest green wool pants, and Bean boots, I must have looked local. A couple approached, asking if I'd pose for a picture with their daughter. Having eight female offspring, I couldn't refuse, but in all honesty said, "I'm old, but I don't work here." It was a pleasure and a compliment since they were from Brazil. But then…they might have looked upon a birch tree with a sap spile and hanging bucket as authentic!

Here's a good story, not about Beans, but about folks "From away." At a northeast surgical meeting at the Colony Hotel in Kennebunkport, Marshall Dodge of "Bert and I" recording fame was the after-dinner speaker. Though he mastered Downeast diction and wry humor, half of the audience who lived south of the "Boston States" didn't know what the hell he was talking about!

Aside from tales gleaned while hanging around Beans, I have personal papers of L.L.Bean importance. One is a January 5, 1994, reply from Leon A. Gorman after I sent him a photo of our Brittany Barney on a Bean dog bed. It was gratifying to know that such a busy corporate president would respond personally, stating:

> Thanks for the delightful photo of Barney. There is an object lesson for all humankind: that we should relax a little. It looks inviting.
>
> I am glad you enjoy your visits to Freeport, and I appreciate your compliment about our representation of Maine. We work hard to maintain a flavor of Maine in many things we do, and it's rewarding to hear comments like yours.
>
> Thanks again for the photo. I hope you will visit us again soon.
>
> Yours truly, Leon A. Gorman

After participating in a Bean Discovery Wingshooting program, I sent Leon Gorman a letter of appreciation, and he responded:

> November 17, 1997
>
> Dear Dr. McGowan,
>
> Thank you for taking the time to commend our company and employees. I'm delighted you enjoyed our Wingshooting Outdoor Discovery Program, and that Sim Savage, Keith

MacDonald, and George Philip upheld L.L.Bean tradition of excellence.

Over the years, we've worked hard to create a resource for people with a genuine interest and love of the outdoors. It's rewarding when customers let me know that our efforts have been successful. I've passed your comments along to Sim, Keith, and George, as well as their supervisor. I know they'll be as pleased as I am at your recognition of their value to our organization.

Thank you for sharing your experience with me. All of us here at L.L.Bean look forward to being of service to you and your family again soon.

Yours truly,
Leon A. Gorman

PS: Thanks, also, for including your wonderful short story, 'The Deer Scales.' I enjoyed it tremendously.

That deer hunting story was the same tale I've told about shooting the bear, when I stayed at the Way's Shogomoc Camps at Charlie Lake, New Brunswick, and the hunter that wasn't about to be outdone.

Mr. Gorman, not surprisingly and in his consistent and courteous manner, returned a personal thank you note to me once more on December 22, 1998, when I praised my shopping and shooting school experiences. Leon Arthur Gorman is the key player who energized the family business into a business family by always practicing an unpretentious consideration for fellow folk: employee, customer, or corporate. I think that he was reared right and stuck to it.

Since first meeting Laurie and her parents, I've kept an aspect of Mr. Bean's private life in mind, never making much of it, but never forgetting it. As I've said, my mother-in-law, Ella Rushforth Louis, was a nurse in training at Carney Hospital, the first Catholic hospital in New England, at Telegraph Hill in South Boston. She knew that one of her classmates married L. L. Bean after caring for someone in his family.

Not until recent years of reading his autobiography and other books about him, did I discover that Bertha Davis Porter Bean, his wife and mother of Carl, Warren, and Barbara, died in 1939. In *My Story*, there is a 1939 group picture of Leon Bean at age 67, and his four brothers. Henry was 78, Otho 75, Ervin 62, and Guy 62. Their only sister, Inez (Cummings) had died 20 years prior. In the same year, Mr. Bean came to Boston (maybe Mass. Eye and Ear Hospital) for a series of eye operations and a prosthetic replacement after he lost the vision in his left eye. Claire L. Boudreau from Belmont, Massachusetts, was his private-duty nurse. Private duty nurses gave patients special and singular attention, even though staff nurses delivered the customary care.

Leon, 67, and Claire, 47 (last birthday age by marriage certificate), were married in both Watertown, Massachusetts (Sacred Heart Parish on Mount Auburn Street), and Freeport, Maine, on July 27, 1940, my ninth birthday. On that particular Saturday, I was probably on summer vacation at my grandmother's farm in Rossville, and my uncles were busy with getting in the hay crop.

Claire came to live in the Bean home in Freeport Village on Holbrook Street just a few blocks down from the store. From home-base Freeport, the Beans chased salmon and trout cross-border in summer and salt-water Florida game fish in winter. They also had places to relax away from Freeport on Crystal Lake in Dry Mills above Gray and cottages at Belgrade Lakes, west of Augusta and Waterville, in Maine.

Mr. Bean's *My Story* has seven pictures of Claire: alone with a trophy eight-foot sailfish, one with her mother at Palm Beach in 1941, and five of Leon and Claire together (he was eight inches over Claire's five-foot-four). They had a winter home at Miami Shores before relocating to Pompano Beach above Fort Lauderdale. Claire appeared as small, very trim, had dark hair, and wore glasses in each picture. The photo sites were either in Florida, displaying salt water trophies, or on the Tobique at Plaster Rock, New Brunswick, with a salmon catch. By L. L.'s telling, they fished the Tobique River every year from 1940 through 1957. He must have sensed that the salmon run was endangered when the hydroelectric dam at Tobique Narrows was built in 1953. Whenever Claire went with Mr. Bean to fish the Tobique, I suspect that she recalled her first New Brunswick border crossing in 1914. Among photographs that he chose for *My Story*, are pictures with L. L., Claire, and salmon on the Tobique. Another was with son-in-law Jack Gorman in June of 1945 with a catch of trout and salmon. In the background, the log camps appear like those of Gulquac Lodge as seen in travel brochures.

Long beyond the Bean's and Jack Gorman's imaginings and 36 years later, Bud Leavitt, the *Bangor Daily News* "Outdoors" columnist put L. L.'s grandson and Jack's son, Leon A., on the Tobique. On July 29, 1981, Bud wrote that "Leon Gorman, the L.L.Bean wagonmaster, had a crew of employees in tow field-testing new salmon fishing equipment." I guess 'twas a Bean clan generational return to the Tobique.

Back to February 14, 1941 and Mr. Bean's *Hunting-Fishing and Camping* third edition, "Salt Water Fishing" chapter. In the photo of Claire with an eight foot sailfish catch, look closely, and you'll see her mother and L. L. smiling in the background at Palm Beach. I remember smiling when I caught a big wahoo out of Ft. Lauderdale on a ballyhoo rig! Fishing wasn't the only thing on L. L.'s winter agenda in Florida. Carlene Griffin said that he would send oranges and grapefruit up to his workers in Freeport.

That did it! I've been following Mr. Bean, one way or another, for 75 years. Here they were on the Tobique in New Brunswick where Laurie and I, 30 years later stayed at Riley Brook while on hunting trips. The Beans were members of Gulquac Lodge, a fishing club that was north of Plaster Rock at Oxbow, and below Riley Brook. Located at the end of a road (by GeoNB Topo, Ogilvy Rd. at Oxbow on Rte. 385), three miles from the main road, the lodge was named after Gulquac Stream that entered the fir treed opposite bank of the Tobique's oxbow shaped lower loop. That portion of the Tobique is in Lorne Parish, Victoria County, about halfway down on the 90 mile river course as it flows southwesterly to meet the St. John.

William Victor "Bill" Miller III, the famous canoe crafter at Nictau above Riley Brook, told me about his personal connection with the lodge and Mr. Bean. Bill sent me a 1915 picture of the Gulquac Lodge with a Model T Ford beside it. Also called the Ogilvy Camp, it was built by Alexander Ogilvy and his Scottish born sons, Hendry (correct spelling, a family name), Jock (John), and David, and operated until about 1945. They had an ad as early as 1913. Author Dr. George Frederick Clarke first stayed and angled there through the 1920s and into the Great Depression years, before following David and Jock to their "Larry's Gulch" camp on the Restigouche. Linguist that he was, Dr. Clarke phonetically captured the Scot in Jock using "Na doot, Doct-orr" for "No doubt, Doctor." Harry Chestnut of the Fredericton Chestnut Canoe factory fame stayed at Gulquac, fished in a Vic Miller canoe with Jock Ogilvy, copied its flat bottom and bow-wider-than-stern lines, and marketed it as the Chestnut Ogilvy. By Bill, "My grandfather did not get any credit for it, but he claims that they didn't get it quite right." The Ogilvys had three miles of riparian rights (exclusive use of the waters for fishing by property owners) adjacent to the lodge, "from about a mile above Big Gulquac stream, to 'The Priest's Rock' below Little Gulquac," wrote Dr. Clarke. Set back and facing the river, the lodge was an elegant square two story home with roofed front porches on both levels, cedar-shingled, and had white trim. On its left were barns and service buildings, and to the right among fir trees, were log camps as seen in 1931 provincial promotional pictures. According to the 1937 N.B. Tourist Travel booklet listing of guides and outfitters, the Ogilvy brothers, Jock and David, operated 16 camps in various salmon rivers including, home camp, Gulquac Lodge…"Rates from $2.50 per day up."

Pardon this diversion, but Tobique research brought out a yarn worth telling. An 1891 *The Canadian Guide-book* for tourists and

We offer to sportsmen and tourists the best big game hunting to be found in the Province of New Brunswick, where the forest primeval is still unmarred by the logger's axe, and the lordly moose, king of all animals, roams as yet unmolested. Moose, caribou and deer plentiful; bears a few; partridge abundant. Good canoeing on beautiful lakes and streams. Trout fishing unsurpassed; Togue fishing good. We possess excellent Atlantic salmon fishing on the Tobique River, with good lodge accommodation for ladies and gentlemen. Grand opportunities for game photography. Prices reasonable. Service first class. Further information on request. Write or telegraph, OGILVY BROS., Oxbow, Victoria Co., N. B.

Ogilvy Bros. Ad in N.B. Tourists & Sportsman's Paradise, 1913

sportsmen in Eastern Canada, included "Up the Tobique by Canoe." The same Victorian formality that I've read in other books prevailed, in that the author did not use the names of his companions but repeatedly called them the "Artist" or the "Ecclesiastic," and that puffery bored me. Then I came upon the word, "Slitheroo." I grabbed it, because it turned out to be a tar and grease-boiled-down ointment to ward off "Sand flies, the insidious and all-pervasive bite-um-no-see-um, and fine Tobique variety of the mosquito." It wasn't an L.L.Bean fly-dope, but its unique identity emerged as clear and crisp as if Mr. Bean himself coined it.

From the 1890s on, the Tobique wilderness area camps, clubs, and lodges were becoming increasingly famous where only fish and game were dressed for dinner. The 1900s attracted big business, political, theater, and professional sports names such as Abercrombie, Rockerfeller, Stimpson, Roosevelt (Teddy's son Archie), Barrymore (John), and the great Babe Ruth.

By the time that the Beans first stayed at Gulquac, the Ogilvys' advertised "a number of comfortable cottages for guests," "We furnish camp accommodations, board, guides, and canoes at a fixed charge per day," and "Good accommodations for ladies at all camps." While David and Jock focused on their more northern salmon fishing camps, Hendry ran Gulquac until the early 1940s when the Fraser forestry company bought the lodge for their customers' hunting and fishing use into the 1950s. Bill's maternal grandparents, Mr. and Mrs. John Clarke, assumed its management under lease when John Clarke had retired as a Fraser woods-boss. Well-off American Sports from across the country like Mr. Bean, Jack Hawkes from National Cash Register, and Percy Glenn of Hollywood sound production got together as members of the Gulquac Lodge, and the Clarkes ran it. Mr. Clarke died in 1960, and Mrs. Clarke retired in 1965. Bill could have had the job and ownership of the lodge property, but the U.S. Navy and Vietnam had other plans for him from 1963—1967 paying only 72 dollars per month at first. During the 1950s at Gulquac, when young Bill was eight or ten years old, he was practicing canoe poling. Down at the dock wishing to go fishing, Mr. Bean called out "Master Miller, would you be so kind to bring me my canoe?" and Bill came to shore. Come to find out, he was in L. L.'s canoe, but the embarrassment was overcome by Mr. Bean's thanking him "for giving it up!" Bill never really gave it up, because "It's where I got all my experience in handling a canoe at a very young age too!"

Bill tells a lodge tale that happened a bit later but probably never ceased to circulate. Seems that the California gentleman who owned the radio and TV sound company for *The Jack Benny Show*, *Lucy*, and *Dick Van Dyke Show* among others, and his wife were guests. A guide needed a ride home about four miles from the lodge, and the wife (an insane driver) gave him a wicked scare. Safe at home, he thanked her for the "Two drives." "Two drives?" she said. He said "My *first* and my *last!*"

I could go on and on about Bill Miller's Tobique tales of family, history, and canoe crafting. Concisely, the Saint John *Telegraph-Journal* of June 23, 2007 "Salon" edtion did a great job, with reporting by contributing editor and photographer Marty Klinkenberg who interviewed Bill. One of Bill's photos shows two guides and five 1925 major league baseball players, all in *suits and ties* (contrary to the backcountry setting!), posing in front of the Miller House Hotel: "St. Louis Brown's pitcher Joe Bush, New York Yankees slugger Babe Ruth, Washington Senators catcher Muddy Ruel, Yankees catcher Benny Bengough, and Chicago White Sox infielder Eddie Collins." L. L. Bean loved baseball and would have jumped into that lineup in a moment's notice!

Knowing that Gulquac Lodge and the Tobique were among L.

Bill Miller on the Tobique at Nictau, 2007

L. and Claire's favorite trout and salmon retreats, those downhome anecdotes were added incentives for me to take the Bean bait.

When L. L.'s remaining brother Otho died at 85 in 1952, Claire, Carl and Warren's families, along with Barbara and Jack Gorman and their children remained as close family. On the last page of Mr. Beans *My Story,* there is a picture of Leon A. Gorman, his older brother, John T. Gorman, Jr., and Warren and Carl Bean at a Directors meeting on August 23, 1961 with Mr. Bean and Shailer Hayes.

Way before my time, but coincidental with my northern Maine travels, Mr. Bean had a hunting camp in Haynesville, Aroostook County, from 1911 into the 1920s, and maybe later. It's about 25 miles south of Houlton and ten miles from the Canadian border. Both he and I would call Route 2A "The Houlton Road, The Military Road," or "The Haynesville Woods." Haynesville settlement, a clearing, surrounded by fir trees, had a few homes and small store with a gas pump at the fork of the east and west branches of the Mattawamkeag River.

After hunting on Valentine Ridge (west of the upper Danforth Road and the Mattawamkeag River), and three-and-a-half miles from camp, L. L. lost the trail. By compass, he walked west, and by luck heard the blast of a saw mill whistle on the road to his camp. He finally got back a half-hour after dark.

As Laurie and I followed the paths of L. L. Bean in the Haynesville

Five Major League Baseball Hunters at Nictau, 1925

Woods and Leon and Claire Bean's good times on the Tobique, our bond with the Bean legacy has intensified. Without siblings, we reach out to those who we like. We circulate the Bean bliss among our family by gift and word.

L.L.Bean means a lot to me through conversation, use of gear, catalog browsing, archival visits, or plainly when cruising through the Freeport store. As sentimental and satisfying as that cruising is, I respect the behind the scenes management that makes Beans the best. As sharp lobster industry strategy effects catch and price figures, Bean managers fuel the company's service and fiscal engines with *disciplined devotion and depth*!

CHAPTER SEVEN

More Beans, Please

Let's have another serving of L. L. Bean, the man and founder. There's a certain complexity and air of mystery about the private lives of Leon and Claire Bean. L. L.'s background, by his own account and those of his biographers, has been an open book. Claire's has not. Remembering my mother-in-law's mention, 60 years ago, of knowing a nurse for an ill member of the Bean family, I discovered that the nurse and second Mrs. L. L. Bean was Claire L. Boudreau. I had a gut feeling that she had things in common with my cross-border family, and I was right. She was part of the same Maritime migration to Massachusetts as was my mother, but from Acadian Nova Scotia and three years older. Thus, I had the irresistible urge to poke my curious nose into her ancestry.

I've always been quite comfortable among French Canadian folk. A Boudreau household (no relation to Claire) backed up to my Lake Avenue home in Woburn. There were grandparents, a son Henry who was Dad's age, and grandkids my age. Grandfather Charlie, born in Nova Scotia, sharpened neighborhood skates in his shop and was a talented skater. Charlie Boudreau glided around Horn Pond on metal skate bottoms that clamped to the sole of his heavy leather boots. I had a similar clinch-key pair before I had laced shoe-skates. He told me that the snapping turtles in Horn Pond were so big that one stuck its head out of the water when he was fishing and "Barked like a dog!"

In my college years, with friends, I traveled to the Canadian Clubs in Waltham and Brookline to enjoy square dancing and Cape Breton music. A few of my dental school classmates had Acadian or Quebecoise surnames: Allaire, Babineau, Boisvert, Delisle, Desmarais, Perron, and Vermette. Not only did I have Greek, Irish, Italian, Jewish, Polish, Portuguese, and Yankee patients in Lowell and in Nashua, New Hampshire, the Merrimack River mills drew many French Canadians to the Valley, and thankfully to my practice. I was on the surgical staff of St. Joseph's Hospitals in Lowell and Nashua that were administered by French Canadian Orders of Nursing Sisters.

Fellow surgical resident at Boston City Hospital, Roger Larrivee, came from Westbrook, Maine, had a full French speaking education prior to graduate school, and practiced in Manchester, New Hampshire. He married red-headed Catherine Foley from Munjoy Hill in Portland. Now deceased, they were our lifelong friends and hosted many St. Patrick's Day corn beef and cabbage dinners. Before Roger died on Christmas Eve 2005, he and a Haitian nurse sang Christmas carols in French.

I'm a bit of a Francophile, and "Je parle francais, un peu." We miss Village St. Jean Hotel and the Charnaud family on St. Barthelemy, French West Indies, where we vacationed for so many years among islanders and their Caribbean grandeur. Getting around the island is too difficult for us at present.

Saturday night on Cape Cod usually finds us at the same table (next to the bar scene) at Restaurant Bleu in Mashpee Commons. Maître d' Jaafar from Morocco and the wait and bar staff have become our friends in service and in fact. Among a variety of presentations, Chef-owner Fred Feufeu and sous chef Benoit create "Bacalao" (cod fish chowder), poached foie gras "Au Torchon" with warm truffle honey peaches, goat cheese salad with beets, grass-fed rib-eye steak "Marchand de Vin," potatoes au gratin, bordelaise sauce, and grilled asparagus.

I'm ready and rarin' to go with cross-border tales, and must get back to Clara Boudreau, Claire L. Boudreau, Claire Lavinia Bean, and Mrs. L. L. Bean who all are the same person. Claire's early life goads me to start telling it in my best Canadian French, but I'll back down. Surmising from what I've learned about her verve and vigor, I'll bet that Claire would take me down a notch or two on no short notice, and then pin my ears back! Neither would I call her a "Bluenose." She might take offence before I meekly told her that cold seasons made Nova Scotian noses blue.

She was born Clara Boudreau on February 15, 1894, to William C. and Mary Victoria (David) Boudreau at Port Felix, Whitehead, Guysborough County, Nova Scotia. Whitehead peninsula juts out into the open Atlantic south of the channel that separates Cape Breton Island from mainland Nova Scotia.

Though this tale is meant to be all about Claire, there's a 1901 census register that describes the Boudreau family. As my Baylis family name had various spellings, so did the "Boudro" family in Guysborough, Nova Scotia. It listed "William C. 34 Fisherman, Mary 30, Evangeline 10, Clara L. 8, Mary L. [Louise] 2, Sophia [Rita] 10/12." The 1911 census had a "Boudro" listing of "William C. Light House Keeper, Mary, Clara, Louise, and 'Retta' [Rita]." In addition, there was "Theresa 8, Alphonse 6, Daniel 5, Sylvester [Alfred] 4, and Reginauld [William Joseph]." With Evangeline out on her own, there were still eight children at home.

Boudreau family life in the fishing and farming community of Port Felix involved church affiliation at Saint Joseph's parish in Port Felix East and diligent parochial schooling for the children. Fishing the Atlantic and shipping off to near and distant ports were acceptable norms. At the beginning of the 1900s, there were still lots of sailing vessels carrying lumber to ports down along the Atlantic coast. Tracking the paths of Boudreau parents and nine children in a page or so hasn't been easy to follow, but the particulars mark a cross-border, 1900s era of Maritime migration to Massachusetts. Family was fundamental, and the Boudreaus remained close forever.

Nearby New England had better economic opportunities, sometimes similar trades, prior family member emigration, and methods of travel to relocate. Liverpool, Halifax, and Yarmouth were popular migration ports to the States. Passenger lists of steamships and border crossing manifests revealed a steady stream of out-migration comparable to the rushing tumble of the log drives. For many who wished to go by rail, Mulgrave on the Canso channel was the Canadian Pacific Rail (CPR) junction for eastern Nova Scotia and Cape Breton Island.

Let's get back to Clara (Claire) and the tale that I've set out to tell about her coming to Boston. Her first border crossing was in September 1914, to attend Carney Hospital Training School for Nurses in South Boston.

She must have been a spunky 20-year-old to travel alone from Port Felix to the CPR at Mulgrave, then to McAdam Junction, New Brunswick, the cross-border rail filter for all four Atlantic Provinces, and pass inspection by U.S. Customs and Immigration officers at Vanceboro, Maine. I read that, during the 1920s migration from the

Maritimes, it was not unusual to feed 2,000 cross-border passengers on 16 trains a day at McAdam Station.

It was another 400 miles, via Maine Central and the Boston and Maine Railroad, for Claire to arrive at Boston. To intensify the excitement of transit, the First World War had just begun. Citizens and immigrants alike became more aware of a world much larger than their North America. Short-form manifests by U.S. border inspectors, detailed a passenger's travel and personal profile. Claire's revealed that she was 5 feet 4 inches tall, with dark complexion and hair, brown eyes, and weighed 114 pounds. Her sisters, Louise and Rita, were also small and had the same hair and eye color, complexion, and similar weight. I note on manifest documents, and later on naturalization papers, that all had beautiful handwriting, a credit to their Port Felix schooling. I'm certain that Claire soon saw that daily life in rural Port Felix was quite different in the City of Boston.

In 1918, sailing from the Port of Halifax, Louise and four other 20 year olds from Nova Scotia, were escorted by registered nurse Carolina Sampson to nursing school at Boston Free Hospital for Women in Brookline. Rita didn't arrive for nurse training at the Boston Free Hospital until 1922. The Free Hospital later merged with the Boston Lying-in Hospital to become Brigham and Women's Hospital.

Everyone, especially those in healthcare and funeral fields knew the devastation and death of millions from the global Spanish influenza virus pandemic that lasted from 1918 until 1920. Hospitals, where Claire, Louise, and my in-laws Dr. and Mrs. Louis worked, were beyond capacity, and the government set up tent cities. The heaviest death toll mysteriously hit those in their late 20s (There were no vaccines, antiviral drugs, or antibiotics that could stave off bacterial pneumonia).

In 1919, motivated I suppose by dreams and pressure to find work, the William Boudreau family moved from Port Felix to Halifax, residing first on Almon Street and then on Edinburgh Street. According to census, William worked as a "Labourer." With Evangeline, Clara (Claire), Louise, and Rita already stateside in Massachusetts, eventual migration to the Boston area must have been William and Mary Victoria's goal.

After graduating from Carney Hospital c.1920, Claire boarded for two years at the Boston Nurse's Club and Registry at 839 Boylston

Street opposite Boston Common. Louise lived there in 1922, and she and Claire moved to 24 Ivy Street in Brookline. Claire filed "First Papers" or Intentions for Naturalization to become a U.S. citizen. When Rita graduated, the three occasionally roomed together or separately but always favored the Brighton-Allston section of Boston.

Alphonsus, 17 and the oldest son, a five-foot-seven lad weighing 125 pounds, sailed from Halifax, with his 21 year old sister Theresa, in December, 1922 on the Dominion Line's "White Star." He was bound for Holyoke, Massachusetts declaring that his father, William C., roomed at 11 Main Street. Theresa's manifest destination was Clara's (Claire), 24 Ivy Street address in Brookline.

Frugally, they all traveled in E Class on steamers. William C., Mary, and sons Sylvester (Alfred) and Reginald came next on the Boston & Yarmouth Steam Ship Company's "Prince George" from Nova Scotia on May 12, 1923. They gave Claire's Brookline address as a destination. They moved to 12 Saunders Street in Brighton, a multi-family home similar to all that they rented thereafter. Large apartment buildings and multi-family "Three Deckers," in most of Boston's 23 neighborhoods, served as boarding houses for many immigrants.

Folks from Nova Scotia often stayed with the Boudreau family as boarders. When a family member or boarder was out of work or ill, the rest supported them. One lodger was 56 year old Uncle Daniel Boudreau from Port Felix, a master mariner who had lived in Salem working at his trade from 1893 to 1907. On a 1923 port arrival document, he gave "6 Colan St."(perhaps Colborne Road), Brighton, as the residence of "nurse, Miss Claire Boudreau" for an intended visit of six months. His January, 1924 naturalization application address was 504 Green Street in Cambridge (maybe with Evangeline Boudreau?). He stayed single, became naturalized, and from then on was a "Live-in uncle" wherever the Boudreaus went!

On November 20, 1926, William C. Boudreau, age 53 (by death certificate), died from lobar pneumonia. He was waked at home on Saunders Street, had Requiem services at St. Columbkille Church in Brighton, and was buried at St. Joseph's Cemetery in West Roxbury.

That left Mary Victoria as head of the household. In her 1928 petition for U.S. naturalization, she referred to her four daughter's location as: "Evangeline…Cambridge, Claire…Boston, Louise…Needham, Rita…Brighton." By 1929, Mary Victoria and son Daniel had moved to 297 Faneuil Street, Brighton. From there, they moved again to 22 Royal Street in adjacent Allston joined by nurse, Claire, ware-houseman, Alphonse, and leather sorter, Alfred.

In 1923, Louise Marie married Charles Y. Bleakney, a builder and trucking express owner from Petticodiac, New Brunswick, and they lived in Needham. In 1928, Theresa Angelica, a bookkeeper, married Joseph R. Lucy, an assistant chemist and later a guard at the Suffolk County House of Correction on Deer Island. At first, they lived in the Commonwealth Avenue section of Allston. By 1930 census, Rita Sophie remained single and was an attendant at Boston State Hospital.

In 1933, Claire, matriarch Mary Victoria, Daniel, Alfred, Regi-nald, and Uncle Dan relocated to 22 Exeter Street in Belmont, Mas-sachusetts. In the 1940 federal census, Theresa and Joseph Lucy with daughters Jeanne Therese, born in 1930, and Paula Ann born in 1938, lived with the Boudreaus in Belmont.

Mary Victoria, Claire Lavinia, Louise, Rita, Therese Angelica, Alphonse, Alfred, and Reginald became United States citizens. In WWII, Alfred served in the U.S. Army and Reginald in the U.S. Navy. Alphonse, Daniel, Alfred, and Reginald apparently did not marry.

It continues to amaze me that in the relatively small Brighton-Allston area of Boston, my family connections, as well as those of Claire Lavinia Bean and her Boudreau family, are remarkably coinci-dental. Laurie's father, Dr. Laurence J. Louis, practiced general surgery at St. Elizabeth's Hospital for 40 years. Our five older children were born there, daughter Jean graduated from its School of Nursing, and my Murphy cousins Ruth, Norma, and Frank Jr. lived with Aunt Ruth and Uncle Frank on the hill above Oak Square. Lo and behold, I dis-covered that John Gould, of Maine literary fame, was born in Brigh-ton in 1908! John, in fact, knew more about Maine than most natives.

After Claire and Leon were married in 1940, Mary Victoria would spend a few months with them when they wintered in Florida. There's a handsome picture of Claire and her mother in a wicker bicycle-wheel pushchair at "The Patio" in Palm Beach. Both were dressed "To the nines," wearing fashionable hats of the day. I'd seen pictures of my mother-in-law Ella Louis, (Claire's classmate), smartly outfitted like Mrs. Boudreau.

Mary Victoria, Alfred, Alphonse, Daniel, and Reginald still lived on Exeter Street in Belmont in 1955; the old term, "Bachelors Hall," comes to mind! At age 89 on May 20, 1958, Mary Victoria passed away at home in Belmont from heart failure. Her funeral Mass was held at Sacred Heart Church in nearby Watertown. The burial was at St. Joseph Cemetery in West Roxbury where husband William was laid to rest 32 years before.

It's been said that Claire Bean's care and companionship helped Mr. Bean to live as long as he did. When 94 in 1967, he died in Pompano Beach, Florida, and his remains were brought back to Freeport to be interred in the Webster Cemetery. Claire became a member of the Company Board, and Leon Gorman wrote that he and she had a good relationship. Claire sold the Holbrook Street homestead in 1968, but it was bought back by the L.L.Bean Company in 1987. I would be willing to bet that Claire's French Canadian heritage added zest to her life in Freeport and gusto to those around her.

It's interesting that Mr. Bean, in *My Story*, said that Claire had never fished before they were married. However, from birth in Nova Scotia and residence in Boston, Freeport, and the east coast of Florida, she never drifted far from Atlantic fishing grounds. I'm forever grateful for Stan Rogers' songs of Canada, and learned that he summered among relatives in Guysborough County, Nova Scotia where Claire was raised. I wonder if she enjoyed the music of Atlantic Canada.

Claire died on January 7, 1974, almost 80 years old, at a Pompano hospital. She lived on Southeast 8th Street in Deerfield Beach, Florida, the Bean's winter home. Her surviving three sisters and two brothers were: Theresa Lucy of Deerfield, Florida (probably living with Claire), Louise Bleakney of Needham, Mass., Maria (possibly Evangeline) Foucher of Long Island, New York, and Alfred S. and William J. (Reginald) of Allston, Massachusetts. Alfred later lived with the Bleakney family.

The *Portland Press Herald* obituary did not include Rita, Alphonse, or Daniel who, I presume, had died as unmarried. Subsequently, William J. departed in 1977, Alfred in 1978, Louise in 1980, and Theresa in 1999 at Fort Pierce, St. Lucie, Florida, at age 95.

Like Mr. Bean, who chose to be buried in Freeport next to his first wife, Bertha, and his brothers, Warren and Carl, Claire was interred in a grave near her parents at St. Joseph Cemetery, West Roxbury. Three of her Boudreau siblings, William J. (Reginald), Alfred S., and Louise M. Bleakney repose in Claire's grave group. From day one to death, Leon L. Bean worshiped his family, and Claire Boudreau Bean, remained devoted to hers.

Charlie Bleakney, grandson of Louise M. (Boudreau) and Charles Y. Bleakney of Needham, MA, told me that among his family, Mrs. L. L. Bean was "Aunt Claire." She would always give him a dollar when they met. Charlie's grandmother, Claire's sister Louise, got a 1960 and a 1972 Cadillac when Claire got a new one. Another inheritance was an Old Town canoe with a five-horse outboard motor. When his father, Philip T., went up to Freeport as a boy, Mr. Bean took him fishing, and kindly acted as a guide rather than fish himself. Meanwhile, the Bean boys were cavorting around in other boats. Charlie, at 15, attended Claire's funeral and was impressed with the bronze casket, fancy funeral, and all of the limousines, some occupied by members of the Bean family who came down to Massachusetts to pay their respects.

Laurie and I, by our own design, have hiked many trails that the Beans had blazed. We walk Main Street in Freeport, occasionally drive through the Haynesville Woods, and instinctively return to New Brunswick's hospitality. I'm delighted to share these stories about Leon and Claire with the extended Bean family and with Claire's Boudreau descendants.

Like Claire and Leon Bean, my cousin Joyce Briggs Jones, her husband Percy, and son Jason, spend the winter in Pompano Beach generously inviting family and friends to share in that southern bliss. It's warmer than Temperance Vale, New Brunswick in winter (no kidding!), and they pursue cross-border harness racing honors with their trotters, go to hockey games, and play golf. Percy won't fly and has no problem making the round trip with his truck and multi-horse trailer.

To conclude, Leon L. Bean, a perpetual steward to his State of Maine, rests in glory and at peace, in hometown Freeport. When walking through central Discovery Park from one Bean building to another, I stop to say hello to L. L.'s bronze bust. I have yet to find his grave in Freeport and pay my respect. It's on my 2014 must-do list.

TURF BLANKETS

When I'm cross-border at Otis Cemetery in Nackawic, it's like walking through a town forest with familiar family trees. Climbing them furnishes a better view of landscape legacies. A Nackawic ridge outline seldom changes, unlike life below it. This continual sense of place or "Terroir" preserves the old among the new.

While I'm walking among the tombstones, it's either a "Wish I knew ye" to great grandparents of English and Scottish birth, "Nice to say hello again" to Valley acquaintances, or "I miss you" to those that I walked with. Our Mary Ann McGowan Mulkern had her fifth generation photo taken beside John Munro's 1914 marble stone in 1991. Loved ones or neighbor's names and dates are either clearly etched in granite or dim in marble. Turf blankets cover all beneath. It's a place that helps me to retrieve memories. Searching the "Find A Grave" website, I entered Otis in "Cemetery," Canada in "Country," "Search," and in Otis Cemetery, York County, New Brunswick, "861 Interments." The surnames listed in alphabetical order are a virtual encyclopedia often leading to remarkable clues.

One paid off, and hit me like a hammer! It was discovered while perusing New Brunswick's York County Cemeteries on RootsWeb-Ancestry.com under Southampton Parish. Among 15 cemeteries, including our Munro/Baylis section in Otis at Nackawic, I came across "Lower Southampton-Calder Cemetery <near Nackawic>" and retrieved the burial list. Number twenty is "20. Rockwell – George Rockwell d. 26 Apr 1886 ae 29yrs & 10 mos." George Rockwell, unknown to me and my living kin, was probably my Uncle George Rockwell Baylis' namesake! I was immediately intrigued that there might be a connection, since both are buried in the same graveyard only a few hundred yards apart.

Both of my Baylis uncles died in the fall of 1965. I was 34 years

Mary McGowan Mulkern, 1991, 5th Generation Descendant of John Munro

George Rockwell's Buried Stone Found by Rose Staples

George Rockwell's Stone Uncovered, Aug.3, 2010

old, and, upon reading their obituaries, their middle names left no meaningful impression. Delving deeper into their past, full names at passing became more important; Ronald Kitchener Baylis, age 50, and George Rockwell Baylis, age 56 are ancestral markers.

In 2009, I engaged Rose Staples of Broad Meadow Genealogy, Maple Ridge, New Brunswick, to help me explore my family history in Southampton Parish. With one return visit a year, fact-finding 500 miles from Rossville, wouldn't be practical. Rose, fortunately, was reared with and married into many of the families that I know. This obscure thread of a graveyard clue was immediately passed on to her. On June 25, 2010, she and her father, Eugene Bradley, searched and by chance spied the corner of a sunken gravestone. It was George Rockwell's! She subsequently did a lot of legwork, had a keen eye for detail, and persisted in unearthing new facts about George Rockwell and his life.

Rose and husband, Geoff, came back to the cemetery on August 3rd, and a worker helped to unearth the gravestone, broken in eight deteriorating pieces. She further found its caringly composed epitaph:

Fair well wife and baby dear
I am not dead but sleeping here
I am not yours but Christs alone
He loved me best and took me home

I was consumed with the inscriptions. Why did he die so young on April 26, 1886? My great grandparents and his half brother, William my grandfather, and half sister, Aunt Lucy Ann (Baylis) Fox, were an intimate part of his life. Through them, did my mother or her siblings not know about his passing? I had an intense desire to find the answers.

Even negative circumstance has its way of opening doors. I've talked about the St. John River Mactaquac HydroElectric Dam project and how it imposed upriver home and hallowed land loss. Thanks to provincial foresight, a historical commission was created to collect and record data and gather artifacts before the head pond rose in 1967. Rose found a photocopy of the original stone, taken prior to its relocation to Otis, at the Provincial Archives in the 1966 Macquatac Dam Historical Project, Calder Cemetery file. The photo and records show a serpentine-topped, decorative monument as a fine example of late 1800s art of final farewell. Except for "GEORGE ROCKWELL" in Roman lettering, all inscriptions were italic and difficult to decipher. Funeral director Wendell Flewelling offered to remove the remnants and store them until we decided what to do about a replacement.

I often communicate with Wendell, whose family has compassionately put souls to rest for five generations, four known in my time. Coincidentally, Hayward Johnson, an uncle of Wendell's wife, Judy, was one of my patients. We compared as much of New Brunswick history as we could during his appointments. Wendell recalls working with his grandfather Fred in 1961 to clear the Calder Cemetery of brush and overgrowth to make it look presentable only to have it moved uphill six or seven years afterward before the flooding. Wendell identified the original Rockwell stone slab as marble, probably from the local Oldham Brothers stone works in Southampton. After 81 years above ground, and then buried for some part of 42 years, the white or gray became brown. Wendell frequently sees Otis Cemetery visitors walking among the gravestones with notebook in hand searching history.

*Original Stone,
from Mactaquac Files,
Provincial Archives, N.B.*

I continue to follow Flewelling Funeral Services, Ltd. website for current obituaries. Each tells of a person passed, those before them, and their living relatives. When I recognize one of those names, a personal history often expands upon what I remember about the deceased and their family.

When standing at the Rockwell grave, I think not only of George's hopes and schemes of earth, but wonder if we will someday meet as kindred spirits? Ron Trammer offers an answer in "The Broken Chain."

Our family chain is broken
And nothing seems the same
But as God calls us one by one,
The chain will link again.

Alive and kicking at 81 in this summer of 2013, I had an eccentric burial wish granted. In senior jest after having a tooth extracted by Dr. Jeff Stone (whose group carries on my old surgical practice in Lowell and Nashua), I asked for the tooth and received it in a plastic box. Since Jim, Jean, and Kelley Burbine and Chip and Joanna McGowan were going up to Harpswell, I thought that it would be a rare opportunity to have a part of me buried in Maine. The tooth went with them!

I'm told that the ritual overlooking Middle Bay, was "Picture perfect." At sundown with Burbines, McGowans, and golden retriever Bailey at graveside, Jo said prayers while Jean shed tears hoping it wasn't an "Almond." Jim reassured her that it was not an omen. She provides the family with other "Jean-isms" such as "Like a bum on a log." Affectionately called "L.L. Jean, our Harpswell Queen," she has a heart as big as a boulder and warm as a wood stove, which suits her well for nursing. They ceremoniously poured Dewars whisky on my plot for earthly esprit de corps.

BOOK II

FOREST

And the forest echoes clearly...
John Greenleaf Whittier

New Brunswick Landscape by Wm. G.R. Hinds, c.1884

Woodchoppers
Painting by Oliver
Kemp, 1917

Book I defined my upbringing, cross-border bonding in Massachusetts and New Brunswick, climbing to Katahdin's cloud nine, and how Laurie and I hitched up for four exciting decades of heir-raising and homesteading. High spirits were never at a loss in camps, on coastal capers, and at Freeport frolics. With sentimental deep breaths, I covered the cemetery scene. Now I'm onto the lore of logging.

Behind it all, "Trees are my comfort!" I'm happy when around trunks, boughs or branches. From skyline crowns to good-earth roots, I've a soft spot for their natural history. "Going to town" is grand, but give me evergreen or familiar foliage anytime. I'll tell you why.

I'm fascinated with turn of the century logging and river drives when logs were long and drives defying. There are sounds and sights of the seven month harvest process that mark the hardy lives of loggers: the sharp ring of the chopper's axe and a resounding crash to the forest floor; commands of teamsters yarding and horse teams heaving; bobsled loads slewing and pounding; crashing and splashing break-aways at the landings; rebounding concussion of the tumbling log mass in its watery descent; and hearty bean-hole bean "logging berries," biscuits, salt pork, potatoes, molasses, and tea served at driving camps. Upon delivery, different sounds and sights arose: the repetitive buzz of steam sawmill blades; rattling wagon and rail carriage of lumber to factories and wharves; the creaking of planks, frames, and decks of wooden riverboats, coastal, and deep-sea schooners loaded for near or distant market.

Certain logging scenes are clear to me. I think of Uncle George using his axe, saw, chains, and twitching horse. Remember, he never owned a tractor! I watched him peel spruce bark off pulpwood. I recall swollen Penobscot and Nackawic Streams with massive ice-slabs crunching up on the shore at the start of the spring freshet, primeval tree stumps around Katahdin, and Corey's sawmill in Pokiok. Not as a logger, but as a hiker and hunter, I've had lunch next to campfires in all kinds of weather. I've only read about the last Penobscot log drive in 1928, but I have seen the St. John full of four-foot pulp runs through 1957. That's a lot of paper floating in the raw!

St. John River Pulp Jam at Pokiok, 1954

CHAPTER ONE

CHERISHIN' CEDAR AND SUCH

New Brunswick Cedar Rail Snake Fence

I have a thought and a story, whenever woods, wood, or woody enter a conversation. In his epic "This Land Is Your Land," Woody Guthrie put everyone who loves our Country and countryside on patriotic soil.

Cross-border, the song reminds me of walking along and climbing over an old zig-zag, field and pasture, cedar fence in Rossville. Those interwoven stacked poles have charisma, being strong, veined, and weathered-gray. Most poles were straight as an arrow and ancient, and many were twisted and knarled with knots. Crisscross stacking at the end of each rail, created a series of alternate, wide-angle (about 120-degree), triangular spaces on either side for cleared fieldstones, brush, and berry bushes. Any hollow rail was a haven for a bee's nest; we were wary berry pickers!

When hand-harvested close to wetlands over 150 years ago, the abundant eastern white cedar was affordable, sizable, and fit my family's need for simple and strong fencing. It was and easy to gate, move, or remove. Grandfather's eye or surveyor's chains laid out its course. It needed no pole digging, adapted to the terrain, and didn't decay. My uncles gradually replaced their old cedar fencing with dug-post and wire fencing in the mid-1940s after WW II. Come to think of it, I can't ever recall seeing a stonewall property divider around Rossville. Since the 1950s, it's hard to find a weathered cedar, snake-fence on farmland. Like the salmon, maple leaf, ancient galley, violet, fiddlehead, deer, and wampum found in the Coat of Arms, the cedar fence represents New Brunswick history.

Maine lumberman Bruce Ward started the ball rolling by selling a commercial Northern White Cedar cabin in 1923. The Ward Cabin Company gradually grew and relocated to the town-owned Houlton International Airport, about as close to the border as you can get. There were masses of cedar growth on both sides of the border. Ward established a first-of-its-kind pre-fab plant in 1955, and now Wards sell everything from basic camps to custom log homes. In our neck of the woods, Walpole Woodworkers is a major distributor of cedar garden sheds, fencing, and furniture.

In line with Maine's steadfast northern white cedar, Don Ellis, of the Southwest Harbor fine-boat-building family, told me that he had a grandson named "Cedar." The cedar shingles that I first saw on the Baylis outbuildings have never gone out of fashion. Here on Cape Cod we use them as tried-and-true Yankee siding in historic restoration and new construction. In New England, we see cedar used for snow and residential fencing, patio furniture, house lumber, and ribs and plank-ing for hand-crafted canoes. When we had red-cedar lined clothing closets built into our Chelmsford homes, opening the door automati-cally made me inhale and recall the smell of mother's cedar chest that kept moths away from her woolens. When I have salmon served on a cedar-plank, it arouses my appetite more than if baked in a dish.

How could I help not being among trees when my childhood home was on *Woodside Road*, and I walked to the Wyman Elemen-tary School along *Wildwood Street*? Attending the 1930s and '40s New England Sportsmen's Show in Boston was an experience symbolic of the Great North Woods. Our neighborhood chestnut tree hut and Horn Pond rope-swing were courageous conquests of youth. My Boy Scout camping experience kept me in touch with woods lore. Our

Chelmsford nine acres had both hard and softwood species. The kids learned how to tap maple trees and boil down the sap in March. They climbed on every branch of the old copper beech. After a horrific storm, I used my Ford tractor, axe, and chainsaw to clear felled trees and limbs in our neighborhood.

I thought that a mackerel net over our pool would catch fallen leaves before they sank to the bottom. It was a disaster because some debris still got through, and the net with leaves froze before I could remove it! There's a side story about that mackerel net. Laurie made a trip to F. J. O'Hara & Sons marine supplies on the Northern Avenue, Boston waterfront. Brad O'Hara not only supplied her with the net, but invited her to lunch and sent her to a fish dealer as a "cousin" wanting to buy some cod. Lunch was in the middle of the warehouse cement floor where they set up an electric burner, fried fresh fish, and dished out salad. I'll bet dollars to doughnuts that Laurie had a smoke and, to the guys' delight, fed them some of her stories!

Anyway, to continue with some serious tree stuff, skiing and snowmobiling among New Hampshire's tree-lined trails was fresh-air splendor. Shogomoc Sporting Camp's access to 5000 acres of New Brunswick woodland became treasured hunting and tramping grounds. Furthermore, my peavey has been retired and gifted to John Adams, the proprietor of our local Cataumet Sawmill, and my "Logging" is occasionally using a chain saw. I am endowed with a respect for woods-work, and survival among trees is not necessarily a rocking chair experience.

I have an ongoing garden-in-the-woods project between our back boundary granite fieldstone wall and the landscaped slope down to the back lawn. It has involved three years of clearing, burning, and finally planting bushes, perennials, wild flowers, and ivy. Year-round indoor gardening consists of watering plants and placing fresh flowers in vases. Laurie and I are just fine living with four seasons where changing tree color and form are "Pleasin' to the eye," our simple standard.

Our family tree began with seeds planted from across the Atlantic and sprouted branches across borders. My Canadian ancestors left a legacy of stamina when manpower, horsepower, and waterpower delivered the goods. From woodland tales of yesteryear, let's shift to forests of our time.

In New Brunswick and Maine, 85 to 90 percent of the land surface is timberland. We make sure that our Christmas balsam fir, the
official tree of New Brunswick, is Maritime grown. Maine's Paine
Company balsam incense and pillow stuffing are my back-to-camp
aromas. Heavy snow on balsam branches dropped down the neck of
my Filson Seattle mackinaw (No offence Beans or Orvis!) when I was
in the winter woods hunting deer. The wetness annoyance when it
melted was offset by the splendor of green boughs draped with white.

During the fall rut when bucks chase does, hunters look for "Deer
sign." Some are pebbled droppings, fresh or old. Others are hoof
scrapes under overhanging branches, or rubs on bark or branches,
bruised or broken by thrashing antlers. A buck's snort or "Blow" ain't
a sign, but it's a heads-up that he's nearby!

After a few hardy frosts that set the needles (sap ceases to flow),
folks go on a safe No-Hunting-On-Sunday "Tipping" (bough gathering) harvest to make holiday wreaths. Pam Douglas, third generation
at wreath making in Harpswell, does our wreaths to perfection with
help from children Sterling and Krystal, and husband, Gregg (and any
willing friend that walks in the door). We've watched the whole process in Pam's shop and sent her wreaths to our families in Texas, Virginia, and here up north as Christmas gifts.

It's said that a remote Maine island resident with multigen-
erational credentials describes family trees as wreaths! If one of our
bachelor grandsons hitched up with a Harpswell girl, we could graft
that branch to our family tree. No need to press the point any further.
I do have sap in my veins.

Now friends, let's get right into what loggin' is all about.

CHAPTER TWO
Downeast Logging

Downeast, I've seen forest fire devastate standing timber, and I've felt flame warm a farmhouse, cabin, or campsite. Rafts of logs were my boyhood fishing and swimming platforms. I love the lore of lumberjacks who harvest logs and river drivers who transport them. Whittier said it well in the "Lumbermen" of those who sought distant woods work, and the reason for its worth:

> Up, my comrades! Up and doing! Manhood's rugged play,
> Still renewing, bravely hewing through the world our way!

> But their hearth is brighter burning for our toil today;
> And the welcome of returning shall our loss repay,

> When, like seamen from the waters, from the woods we come,
> Greeting sisters, wives, and daughters, Angels of our home!

Romantic as those crews of yesteryear who cut and moved logs along to be sawed might be described, every family could recount a personal or village toll of tragedy as with my grandfather, Willie Baylis. To them, work meant good wages, and its hazards were worth the risk. To break boredom, loggers in the remote camps jumped to have fun as quickly as moving from a falling tree's path or leaping "Cattyfooted" with a pike pole across a rolling jumble of floating logs. Let's delve deeper into what Downeast logging was all about.

New Brunswick's St. John River, Maine's Penobscot River, and their tributaries were the main channels to float logs from distant cuts to settlement sawmills. Both rivers discharge billions of gallons daily into the Bay of Fundy or the Gulf of Maine. Both originate from Maine and Quebec headwaters above Northeast Carry on Moosehead Lake. The "Carry" is a two-mile portage between North Bay and West

Branch of the Penobscot. The West Branch tributary flows from near the Quebec border for 117 miles and drops 1,174 feet, to meet the East Branch that drains the area east of Baxter State Park at Medway. Except in winter, men, goods, and logs were constant commuters on downstream or upriver runs.

Men going to the north woods or returning home passed through Bangor on the railroad. It was an exciting place for many loggers. The 1937 *Maine, A Guide 'Down East'* explained the Washington, Hancock, and Exchange Street vicinity as "This riotous quarter, where salt-water shellbacks and tall-timber men swapped tales, drinks, and blows." There were 17 lumber establishments on Exchange Street, along with diverse listings of barbers, ice dealers, saloons, and timber-land dealers. Bangor was the commercial distribution center for rough and sawn timber going to Kenduskeag and Penobscot River schooner and steamship wharves. An 1886 *Bangor Daily Whig and Currier* article reports: "The barkentine Eyvor arrived here last night with 940 tons of coal for the Maine Central [Railroad] from Newport News."

As logging fed Downeast ports with wood for the world, Whittier romanticized the trade and the Caribbean riches brought home. Though he didn't mention molasses, Medford Rum might have been in his tumbler when he composed this verse:

Strike, then, comrades! Trade is waiting on our rugged toil;
Far ships waiting for the freighting of our woodland spoil.
Ships, whose traffic links these highlands, bleak and cold, of ours,
With the citron-planted islands of a clime of flowers.

In 1881, 111,814,920 feet of surveyed lumber passed through Bangor. When I say "Feet" in terms of lumber, understand that a "Board Foot" is 12 inches long, 12 inches wide, and one inch thick. A more practical explanation for non-loggers is that 20 full-grown spruce tree logs make for a thousand board feet of lumber. In any case when quoting millions, that's a heck of a lot of wood out of the Penobscot cuttings. *Barnes's N.B. Almanac and Register, 1851* had "Port City of Saint John Fees for Surveying Lumber." Terms lost in today's world, listed export categories: "Saw Logs and Deals [usually exported fir, spruce, or pine 2 and 3 inches thick, 7, 9, 11 inches wide, often 12 feet long], Plank, Scantling [small dimensional lumber for building or shipbuilding], or Boards; Masts under 17 inches diameter and over 17 inches; Spars under 9 inches and over 9 inches; Lathwood per cord; Pine and Cedar Shingles per thousand; Hogshead and Barrel Staves." It is no wonder that New Brunswick was called Great Britain's Woodyard.

Ice on the St. John River restricted lumbering activities and navigation. Records show average closing in late November with opening in late April, but the Port of Saint John did not freeze. The Penobscot River average 1880s freeze-over and breakup was mid-December to mid-April. While frozen, the head of navigation was Bucksport, Maine. Both the town of Bucksport and city of Saint John flourished as the closest Downeast ice-free harbors to Europe and Atlantic ports of call.

The sight of a river full of logs or pulpwood could be compared to thousands of match sticks tumbling in a rain-filled gutter. Whether long logs or pulp sticks, timber still had to be cut and laboriously hauled to landings by loggers. In order to describe how a logger makes a living, I might as well start at the beginning.

When combined, the harvest and waterway-drive to the mills was seasonal from November into May or later. By day, it was according to the amount of available light. Loggers recruited from Maine and the Maritime's were often hired out by the same outfit year after year. After an operator (contractor) with sufficient money, equipment, and logging expertise obtained an area permit from the state, province, or timberland owner, men called "Timber cruisers" were sent in. They scouted desirable cuts, estimated the standing timbers' linear footage, and determined suitable logging road-hauling distance to drive sites. The latter was as important as a choice timber stand in order to have better access to drivable streams or a lake to get the logs out. As those prime cuts became less convenient, the hauls deeper into the forest, or over rough terrain, became more difficult for men and teams to make a "Turn." A turn was a round trip haul of logs between the chop and yard, or the yard and a landing.

The summer work of swamping roads into an area and clearing streams for log passage was cursed by millions of mosquitos, midges, and black and moose flies. A complex of living quarters, barns, and outbuildings in isolated and cleared timberland, was called a "Farm" by logging operators. Hay, grain, and vegetables were grown, and cows pastured. In summer, "Put up" hay and kept-over horses were ready for the crews to arrive in late autumn. One of those farms was the 200-acre Grant Farm in Piscataquis County, Maine, three miles from Ragged Lake. Horse teams brought supplies to these depots for winter and spring operations, and men in transit were afforded room and board.

In the 1880s, the tool for tree falling was the axe. Whittier's script of camp and chopper in "The Lumbermen" bespeaks the setting. I'm riveted to every logging line!

Through each branch-enwoven skylight, speaks He in the breeze,
As of old beneath the twilight of lost Eden's trees!
For His ear the inward feeling needs no outward tongue;
He can see the spirit kneeling while the axe is swung.

Make we here our camp of winter; and, through sleet and snow,
Pitchy knot and beechen splinter on our hearth shall glow.
Here, with mirth to lighten duty, we shall lack alone
Woman's smile and girlhood's beauty, childhood's lisping tone.

Cheerly on the axe of labor, let the sunbeams dance,
Better than the flash of sabre or the gleam of lance!
Strike! With every blow is given freer sun and sky,
And the long-hid earth to heaven looks, with wondering eye!

A man's ability to chop could be closely scrutinized by brethren and boss during the three to five month stay in camp. I found a compact, all-inclusive reference for loggers in the pocket-sized *Scribner's Lumber & Log Book, 1882*. One of my copies has front and back pages covered with penciled ciphers of estimates; a brief note of interest was "Sow bred January 5." In it is detailed perspective of "Woodsmen and Axes." It's a long paragraph of quotes, but well worth grasping, as the variety of burly axemen perform their swing.

"The styles of axes differ with nationalities. A Canadian chopper prefers a broad square blade, with the weight more in the blade than elsewhere, the handles being short and thick. A down-East logger, one from Maine, selects a long, narrow head, the blade in crescent

SCRIBNER'S
LUMBER & LOG BOOK;

FOR SHIP AND BOAT BUILDERS, LUMBER
MERCHANTS, SAW-MILL MEN, FAR-
MERS AND MECHANICS.

BEING A CORRECT MEASUREMENT OF

SCANTLING, BOARDS, PLANK, CUBICAL CONTENTS OF
SQUARE AND ROUND TIMBER,

SAW-LOGS, BY DOYLE'S RULE;

STAVE AND HEADING BOLT TABLES, CORD WOOD, PRICES
OF LUMBER PER FOOT, SPEED OF CIRCULAR SAWS,
WEIGHTS OF WOOD, STRENGTH OF ROPES, FELL-
ING OF TREES, GROWTH OF TREES, TABLES
OF WAGES BY THE MONTH, RENT AND
BOARD BY THE WEEK AND DAY,
COST OF FENCES, PRICE OF
STANDARD LOGS, INTER-
EST TABLES, &C., &C.

BY J. M. SCRIBNER, A. M.

AUTHOR OF "ENGINEERS' AND MECHANICS' COMPANION,"
"ENGINEERS' TABLE BOOK, &C."

ASSISTED BY

DANIEL MARSH,

CIVIL ENGINEER.

TO WHICH IS ADDED SIXTY PAGES OF NEW TABLES AND
OTHER MATTER TO THE PRESENT.

REVISED, ILLUSTRATED EDITION OF
1882.

BEING THE MOST COMPLETE BOOK OF ITS KIND
EVER PUBLISHED.

Nearly a Million Copies have been Sold.

ROCHESTER, N. Y.:
PUBLISHED BY GEO. W. FISHER.
1883.

LUMBER AND LOG BOOK. 145

Lumberman's Shanty.

MANY a backwoodsman will recognize this
picture of a lumberman's camp in the wilderness. No matter how poor the lumberman
may be, and whatever his trials, and they are
many,—whether he is known or unknown,
rich or poor, in the lumber camp a stranger is
made to feel at home, if worthy; if not, woe
betide the wary traveller or wild woods tramp
who seeks shelter beneath the hospitable roof
of a chopper's dwelling.

CONTENTS.

4 CONTENTS.

Scribner's Lumber & Log Book, 1882

shape, the heaviest part in the top of the head above the eye. New York cutters select a broad, crescent-shaped blade, the whole head rather short, and the weight balanced evenly above and below the eye, that is, where the handle goes through. A West backwoodsman selects a blade, the corners only rounded off, and the eye holding the weight of the axe. The American chopper, as a rule, selects a long, straight handle. The difference in handling is, that a down-Easter takes hold with both hands at the extreme end, and throws his blows easily and gracefully, with a long sweep, over his shoulder. A Canuck chops from directly over his head, with the right hand well down on the handle to serve in jerking the blade out of the stick. A Westerner catches hold at the end of his handle, the hands about three inches apart, and delivers his blows rather directly from over the left shoulder. In fact, an expert in the woods can tell the nationality or State a man has been reared in by seeing him hit one blow with an axe. It is, however, an interesting fact to know that a Yankee chopper, with his favorite axe and swinging cut, can, bodily strength being equal, do a fifth more work in the same time than any other cutter, and be far less fatigued. This, in a very large degree, will account for the great percentage of Maine men who will be found each year in the woods." Around the turn of the century, the axe was replaced by the two-man cross-cut felling saw. Then, in the early 1900s, a versatile one-man buck saw was introduced to fell and cut logs.

Here's some more basic history of logging. Before the chopping began in late fall and early winter, log camps were built for a bunkroom and a cook space, and hovels (huts or lean-tos) were put up for horses or oxen. Literary logger of the era, John S. Springer, says of the teamsters with oxen (the same attention applies to horses): "Every shoe and nail, every hoof and claw, and neck, yokes, chains, and sled claim constant attention." Horses gradually replaced the stronger oxen, because they were faster at hauling.

While opening the camps, paths were cut, trimmed, and cleared for the usual four to five months of hauling long logs on bobsleds over iced roads to waterside landings, also called rollaways or brows. Winter means of hauling logs from chop to yard or landing required maintenance men, so-called "Road monkeys," to either water the tote road to get a smooth iced surface or to spread hay on downgrades to help slow the sleds and keep them under control.

*Oliver Kemp Painting
of Logger and Team
Unloading, 1917*

 If timber cuts were near to a drive-lake, yarded logs were piled on the ice to await the spring melt and start of the river drives. Small operations on branch streams, like on Temperance Vale's Nackawic Creek, had short drives directly to the sawmill head pond at Pinder (Mother's recorded birthplace). Men working in local lumber woods came home to spend Christmas and New Year's.

 Other than axe or saw, another hand-held contrivance of lumbering stands out. The cant hook or cant dog was a tool that early loggers used to move logs. A log is a cant when slabs are sawn off four sides leaving edge strips of bark before being cut into dimensional lumber. The cant dog's shoulder-height shaft was rock maple. About a foot above a toothed metal tip on a steel socket, a C-shaped steel tong, or "Dog," swung up and down and rotated around the shaft on a ring or collar. When the tip was struck, and the pivoting hook gripped the timber, the logger could leverage the shaft to roll or shift the log. The improved "Peavey" was invented in 1858 by Joseph Peavey of

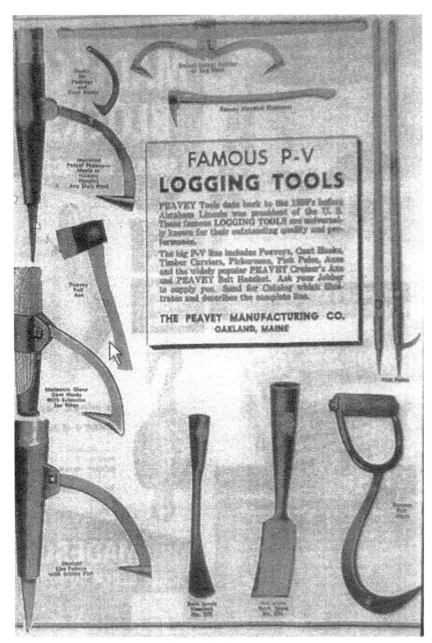

Peavey Co. Ad, 1946

Stillwater, Maine, who made a stationary collar with two lips that had holes for a bolt. The bolt passed through the lips and the shaft-end of the C-shaped dog so that it could still pivot up and down but not move sideways. He changed the blunt tip to a sharp spike. Loggers found the peavey their more stable and versatile "Wrench." To lift and pry, the shaft tip pierced the bark and the thumb hook, on the open tong, grabbed another point for leverage. That grasp could be released rapidly if necessary. It's a rare picture of loggers moving timber on land or water that doesn't have men working "Peavey-sticks." Can you believe that in the early days, a peavey cost as much as two dollars each! As time went on, woods talk and writings twisted the name to now and again be "Pevy" or "Pivie." Even with my light logging experience, I know that the peavey has tremendous leverage. Snow and Nealley of Bangor leveraged the name "Peavey," because they held the title.

Peaveys were used from the time a tree was felled, limbed, sawed into lengths, and "Twitched" by a horse (dragged and maneuvered) on bush-cleared tote roads or skidding trails to a yard or skidyard (a temporary log-storage clearing). Most yards were not at a waterside crest or landing. When loading and transporting logs to landings on single or double bobsleds, teamsters employed peaveys. The peavey moved logs, broke jams, and performed tasks such as tightening chains or working at the sawmill carriage whenever a purchase point and leverage was needed. They accomplished what the pike poles could not.

The traditional pike pole, or "Pick pole," river driving tool had a 12 to16 foot long spruce or fir shaft with a metal pike (point) to prod logs from a safe distance. There were some with a spiral tip to penetrate and hold a log more securely and, with a quick opposite twist, would let go just as easily. Others had a forged side-hook gaff above the point for snatching or pulling. Drivers with pike poles guided the log flow from river bank, bateau, or while riding on the floating mass. When balancing on a moving log, the driver looked like a circus tight rope walker using a pole for balance. Along with peaveys, pike poles helped to break a jam, steer logs through a dam or saw-mill sluice, and move logs out of the sorting booms. A boom was a string of floating logs, chained end-to-end, that either served to hold-back a mass of river-drive logs for sorting, or gather them, like a raft, to be towed across a lake.

Reports from the logging camps contributed articles of fact and fun. *The Daily Gleaner* carried the following bit of news from Hallett's Camp in Davidson, Maine (Herseytown Township):

"Having seen news of other camps we wish to let the public know something of our camp. We are quarter of a mile from the B. & A. R.R. and about forty miles from Houlton. Our foreman, Mr. Hallett, is a jolly good fellow and is well liked by all the boys. Our cook is a beaut; the cookees are A. McMillan and E.S. Grant, two Canadians. We have twenty teams hauling off the yards, all doing good work. One team is yarding yet; it is driven by Joe Blaney. The choppers are Chas. Scott and John Merrithew, two men who have no equal for brushing lumber and making roads. The men who make the roads are Dick Hull and Suscarsk. The yard tender is H. Wallace. The road monkeys are under J. W. Godsoe."

From the smaller New Brunswick camp of Harvey B. Biggars, a February *Gleaner* relates: "Is it not time you heard about our big concern. Well, our crew consists of six jolly good men. We have three teams hauling off the yards. First is Red Rube the trapper. He says he can haul as many spruce logs as any other man, and next is Elbridge Redstone, who says he will beat him or leave his hide in the woods, and last but not least comes Seldon Brooks, who says he has no wings but he can get there just the same. Pearl Harrington and Harvey Biggar are the yard tenders and they are struck [set] on themselves, and last comes our road monkey, who says he can make the snow fly almost as well as any other man. Our largest day's work is 215 [loads of logs]. We expect to finish up soon. We have quite a little town here now, as there are 7 teams of Mr. McBreen's and Harvey U. Biggar's team hauling here betimes. Snow is very scarce just now. Mr. and Mrs. Edward Brooks and Mrs. Leo Brooker visited our camp this week."

In a February excerpt: "We share with us here a good sample of the shanty man. Among them is a musician we call Orpheus of Johnston Brook. Then we have a man who has a special license to tell the biggest yarn. He is our boss. Besides good singers and dancers we have several jokers, so the entertainment provided is rather in the nature of continuous entertainment." Another large camp reports: "We also have a fine machine known as a graphophone ['phonograph' to my parent's generation or 'record-player' to mine]."

Any opportunity to break camp doldrums was laid out on the

Fiddler in the Logging Camp by Oliver Kemp, 1917

table, except for mandatory silence during meals. The last name of New Brunswick lumber baron, Jabez Bunting Snowball, was subject to camp humor. I suppose that Maine loggers in Hodgdon, Aroostook County, mocked the family name of a settler from Nova Scotia named Joseph Outhouse.

After all the cutting and hauling was over, the practice of breaking up, springing out, or closing up a camp operation is expressed in "Songs of the Maine Lumberjacks."

"Now we leave the old camp All covered with straw

Where the squirrels do chitter, And the hedgehogs do gnaw."

I've found no better way to describe a logger's lifestyle than what Fannie Pearson Hardy Eckstorm, 1865–1946, wrote in 1904. A Brewer Maine native, she attended Abbott Academy and graduated from Smith College in 1888. By canoe, Fannie and her father, Manly Hardy, travelled up into Penobscot's West Branch region, east of Moosehead

Lake. He traded with Indians in the territory and spoke their language. Fannie observed and absorbed what she saw and heard. She recorded (by pen and box-camera) lumberjack and river driver tales, detailing place, character, dialect, and dialog. By her own words, she was "Bred up to the Maine woods and its speech." She gave credit to men who carried heavy bateaux and cargo over rough and uneven portages. Shoulders were chaffed by gunwales and shins were hammered from jibes of sharp obstacles as they strenuously stumbled, in order to by-pass falls, rapids, and shallow water or to cross between rivers and lakes.

In the mix of Yankee and Irish Mainers, French Canadians, and Province Men at the logging camps, there was a lot of opportunity to poke fun at the other guy. To the same mix in the river driving crowd, add the Indian, not at all times reserved and serene as often portrayed. John Ross, the most acclaimed West Branch master driver, captained that diverse bunch of "Bear-cats" or "Bangor Tigers" into a sought after group on the drives.

Fannie phonetically had Indian English and that of the lumbermen, down pat. To know the lore of lumberjacks of old, read Fannie's book, *The Penobscot Man.*

I'll also refer you to a Northeast Folklore book called *Fleetwood Pride, 1864–1960.* It has 60 pages of tales, notes, and extensive bibliography about Fleetwood, a cross-border woodsman. You'll learn firsthand about Downeast logging and loggers from his penciled manuscript and interviews with two of the most informed University of Maine, Orono, faculty members, Edward D. Ives and David C. Smith.

CHAPTER THREE
THE WILD RIVER DRIVES

When nature made its April move, "Ice out" happened, and the log drives of old were on. They hoped for high water, and boldly faced the hell that comes with or without it. In the 1850s, Whittier announced the explosive arrival of the spring freshet. It ruled river drives for another 80 years.

> When with sounds of smothered thunder, on some night of rain,
> Lake and river break asunder winter's weakened chain,
>
> Down the wild March flood shall bear them to the saw-mill's wheel,
> Or where Steam, the slave, shall tear them with his teeth of Steel.

In that last passage, do you suppose that Whittier subscribed to Thoreau's fear of woodland devastation?

The rapid melting of snow and ice provided a high-water force for driving crews. If water was low in upper-branch streams, driving was intense to avoid leaving part of the log crop behind. To compensate for low water, dams were built to create reservoirs and holding ponds. The flood-gates were opened when stream water got low, providing a fresh rush to carry the drive. As logs accumulated in holding ponds, men with pike poles guided logs through sluiceways (artificial wooden channels or troughs controlled by flood-gates) to shoot onward through fast water. Slanting "aprons" of small logs or planks as part of a sluiceway or on top of jagged ledges in a stream allowed the flow of logs to move along easier.

Granted, the dash of water carrying logs through rough and tumble channels is what text, paintings, and photographs might imply, but he drive is not all on feeder brooks, creeks, and rivers. They're only part of the route by which logs floated to market. The West Branch of the Penobscot is the best example. Interspersed are level

River Drivers in Bateau Moving Camp Downstream, Oliver Kemp

lakes of considerable size, occasionally stormy, that required towing of corralled or boomed logs to another surging waterway. At first, a set anchor and capstan-winch system slowly advanced the log mass. Then, steam towboats hastened the process.

From the lake, logs entered a river surge, and men in bateaux with long set-poles guided the drive through twisting rocky currents. Their famous shallow draft bateau was a rugged double-end river workboat designed to ride up on logs or land on shore. The Bangor made Maynard rode many a drive. John Ross said that Maynards and peaveys in the hands of six men did the job better than any other driving crew. Set-poled or rowed, they had flared sides with bow and stern bottoms curved upward and were 18 to 30 feet or more in length. The simple lapstrake-and-plank construction allowed easy repair after wear and tear from gouging river rocks and driver's "corked" (spiked) boots. Aside from being platforms for guiding the floating logs, they moved drivers, cooks, and supplies downstream. Maine's famous boat builder and designer, John Gardner, reiterated the rugged capability and responsiveness of the bateau in fast, rocky shallow currents, and its portability, though hard-on-the-shoulders, over uneven land between waterways.

Once piles of up to 300 logs were let go into the drive stream, they pitched, bumped, and rolled with a thousand others. If one got "Jill-poked," others hung up on it, and a jam formed that had to be broken. To do that required "pulling the middle," so that the king-log could be identified and worked loose for the others to follow. Otherwise, dangerous "powder" (dynamite) would have to do the deed. Some jams occurred on rocky outcrops or curves in a stream, others were midstream in narrow gorges, or some filled an entire stream from shore to shore. All halted the drive and tested the drivers' ingenuity to break them. They sometimes claimed lives as in a verse from the unidentified song, "When the Drive Comes Down."

> But break the roll-ways out, my lads, and let the big sticks slide,
> For one man killed within the woods, ten's drownded on the drive.

Adventurous river drivers stood out from woods loggers as matchless in agile mind and body. Their dangerous daily duty was keeping logs moving. Propelled by pride, they lived (or died) in step with their reputation. Trademarks of river drivers were red flannel shirts and greased leather boots with one-inch "Calks" on the soles. Those spikes were sharp as needles to grip the bark of a stationary or moving log. Every bunk house and boom house floor bore their battering. When a "Redshirt" died in the line of duty, his boots were nailed to a nearby tree.

Though river runs were cold, wet, and eat-on-your-feet, young men accepted the challenge, prestige, and thrived on the thrill. A carefree verse from Roland Palmer Gray's *Songs and Ballads of the Maine Lumberjacks*, reflects on beans as justification for a tough job.

> For eating we had plenty
> Of those grand and glorious beans,
> Lots of ham behind the dam,
> On old Penobscot stream."

Holman F. Day plugged that daily diet in the *Kin O' Ktaadn*, "Cook Song."

Perhaps there are cooks who in slapping up grub
Have got eddication clear up to the nub.
There are cooks for the rich men and cooks for the queens,
But here's to our cooks of the pork and the beans.

Aside from singing, there must have been a lot of orchestrations throughout timber cutting, log driving, and bunkhouse snoring, thanks to the cook's musical fruit!

Each part of logging involved high risk, but driving, from the time a log plunged from a landing to the time it floated into slow moving boom waters, was daringly dangerous. A top choice of river bosses, were the "Bangor Tigers," many Irish, who came from that city. Bloodied knuckles and noses before and after the drive, in the bars around Exchange Street, earned them a reputation of being untamed. Verse in "The Black Stream Drivers' Song" proved the point.

Who makes the big trees fall kerthrash
And hit the ground a hell of a smash?
'Tis Johhny Ross and Cyrus Hewes.

Who gives us pay for one big drunk
When we hit Bangor, slam kerplunk!
'Tis Johnny Ross and Cyrus Hewes."

Fredericton's *Daily Gleaner* readers in April, 1906 could follow what was going on in the drives faster than by word of mouth or mail. I'll start with the St. John River Log Driving Company:

April 1: The estimates sent in by different operators would be just about 150,000,000 feet. The driving will be done upon contract with Mr. George Moore of Woodstock at 20 cents per thousand. The lumber operators and millmen were very much pleased with the manner he did his work last year. They look to him to get the logs within the boom limits at the earliest possible moment this season. On the Tobique, the estimated 25,000,000 driving feet will be done by Archie Fraser on contract. There is now about four feet of snow and the prospects of stream driving could not be better.

April 5: A great deal of lumber always goes down river with the ice and the owners put forth every effort to catch the lumber, have it placed in booms and towed to a place where it may be sorted and sent to the different mill owners. Within the next few days hundreds of men will be taking the trains from here en route to the scene of the stream driving operations. Some of these men will go into Maine and a great many will not leave the province at all. Operators are offering from $1.50 to $2.25 per day.

April 17: River is rising. In all between 200 and 300 men will be wanted on this drive and a crew is gathering here today at the Waverley and Lorne Hotels to start in the morning. Woodstock, Water raised about eight inches last night. Ice gradually weakening.

April 25: A sad catastrophe occurred on the Pokiok river this morning when Gilford Morecraft of Hartfield, Southampton lost his life by drowning. The unfortunate man was cutting some logs when he suddenly slipped and fell into the stream and disappeared from view. He sank beneath the logs and water and his fellow workmen were utterly unable to render him any aid. His tragic death has cast a deep gloom over the surrounding community.

April 26: Mr. M. Welch, who came in from the Miramichi today, said that the Bartholemew river drives of the Gibson Company were out.

May 22, Southampton: Mr. Charlie Allen is doing a rushing business this spring rafting. [I remember mother's Aunt Hughena and Uncle Charlie. He was moustached, short, wiry, and spoke crisply. He dressed smartly in a shirt, tie, suspenders, and trim felt hat and gave the impression of a person in charge.] He rafted a large body of lumber for Mr. Ezra Cronkhite and he has between twenty and thirty men. It is a good thing for the place as it makes a market for our produce. Ingraham mill is running full blast, cutting from thirty to fifty thousand lath [thin spruce-strip backing for plaster] per day.

Saw mills were plentiful, and lumbering had become mechanized, but the mills still got their logs from the drives. I never knew any men who worked a drive.

New Brunswick-born Hiram Alfred Cody, a noted clergyman and writer, wrote a narrative poem called "Glasier's Men." "Main John" Glasier was a famous New Brunswick lumberman who once employed 600 men. One verse told the tale of "The Mighty Drives" in two tributaries of the St. John that I know well. They drove on the Tobique to Plaster Rock for 75 years until 1960.

Shogomoc is running wild
Tobique's white with foam.
Once again the mighty drives
Are sluicing grandly home."

When the last logs left the brooks, streams, lakes, and rivers, there was still work, called "Sacking" to be done. Men and horses scoured the banks to refloat logs that remained.

When the drives reached wide stretches of slow water in the watershed above Bangor, retaining chains of logs (booms) were strung from shore to shore or between rock-and-log crib piers and islands to round up logs for sorting. As a youngster, I recall seeing pier remnants on the Penobscot near Old Town. The four-section Penobscot Boom was the largest employing as many as 300 men in a season. It had two booms upriver, Nebraska and Argyle, and two others above Old Town, Pea Cove and Mexico. Companies evolved as drives became larger. Foremost were the Penobscot Log Driving Corporation, for driving, and the PLA (Penobscot Lumbering Association), for booming. They put bids out for managers to coordinate driving, booming, and rafting. An operator's unique registered log mark was axed on each end of a log by a yardman at the landing prior to the drive to show ownership at sorting. At each boom, sorting gap channels funneled the logs through a checkerboard of connected floating logs upon which the boom tenders would run with their pick poles catching and sorting out the logs of registered permit holders.

PLA pay record files showed earnings from $16.30-$30.00 a month with the majority of loggers being paid from $20.00-$22.00

per month. Among Holman F. Day's *Pine Tree Ballads*, "Ballads of Drive and Camp" versed the voice of the drivers:

> Twenty a month for daring Death; for fighting
> from dawn to dark—
> Twenty and grub and a place to sleep in God's
> great public park;
> We roofless go with the cook's bateau to
> follow our hungry crew—
> A billion of spruce and hell turned loose when
> The Allegash drive goes through.

In hitching grounds after sorting, an owner's "Rattlings" of 30 or so parallel log units were made into "Joints" held together with rope rigging, half-hitched to wood or metal wedges, and hammered into the end logs. Sometimes, a diagonal pole or spar was lashed down for added stability. Next, in the "Bracketing ground," an average raft contained a dozen joints slashed together. Passing Southampton on the St. John in my grandparent's time, 100-log rafts bound for Fredericton and Saint John had bunk and cook shacks aboard and were steered by long oar "Sweeps." With larger drives and more sawmills, rafts were made up of both logs and sawn lumber; bateaux boatmen and raft pilots guided them downstream to sawmills.

Forest industry communities with steam powered saw, lath, planing, shingle, and clapboard mills thrived. On the Penobscot, Old Town and Stillwater, in Orono, became "Boomtowns".

Logs that escaped the booms of the Penobscot, St. John, and Kennebec floated into harbors and were hazards to navigation. Sawdust, bark, and waste from upstream sawmills, accumulated in downstream millponds making it hard to get logs out of the water and led to ensuing pollution.

From sawmills, lumber went to a planing (smooth sawn for lumber) mill or directly to the wharves for sailing ships and steamers which may have just arrived with tons of coal from the South. Cut and stored ice was also an important Bangor export up until 1890. Its warehouse harvest was shipped to cities down along the East coast for refrigeration in city homes and eateries. In Southampton at the turn of the twentieth century, natural ice was in demand, because The

Daily Gleaner reported "The Nackawic Ice Company is doing a rushing business in building ice houses."

A boon to booming and sawmill employment above Bangor was the Penobscot Chemical Fibre Company, the first pulp and paper mill in Maine, which opened at Great Works, Old Town, in 1882. As well as logging in the winter and river driving in the spring, there were opportunities for Maritime loggers to work cross-border as long as the mills were operating. A Province Man may have worked at any or all of those cutting, driving, milling, or shipping trades, which governed the time of year and length of stay when "Over the Lines."

CHAPTER FOUR
LOST AND FOUND

Not all logs made it through the drives to sorting booms and saw-mills. Some hung up and rotted on shore, a few, that could not float on their own, were part of rafts that broke up in sluices, gorges, rapids, and storms. Others laid in river pools or lake water too long and sank.

Logging, believe it or not, does have a lost and found. Maine and New Brunswick log recovery companies sustain a unique version of the lumber industry. During a 1920s winter, a logger named Louis Woodbury "Woody" Eaton did it out of immediate necessity on a drive through a log-holding bay in the St. Croix River.

Born in Calais, Maine, in 1892, he grew up working in the lumber woods. He advanced to top level management in family owned Eaton Land Company that had holdings in Maine and New Brunswick. In 1954, he wrote *Pork, Molasses and Timber, Stories of Bygone Days in the Logging Camps of Maine*. Woody probably had a license to hunt and fish, but his trademark was a literary license to play with place names by spelling them backwards. "Notae River", probably the St. Croix, was derived from Eaton. "Hamot" was Tomah Mountain and Stream in Washington County, Maine (Tomah was once the head Chief of all the Saint John River Indians). To say the least, he made it hard for me to trace actual geography…I gave up on his arse-end-to talk! I wonder if he was carried backwards from his birthplace and permanent residence, Calais, when buried cross-border with his parents in the St. Stephen, New Brunswick Rural Cemetery? Far from the Maine border in Montana, the Cheyenne had tribal members known as "Contraries," because they did everything backwards. Do you suppose one of them drifted over to Passamaquoddy Indian Township, and became a counselor to Woody?

Now, I'll get back to Woody's pioneering in the lost-and-found log business. Hardwood, unless hauled, sank when floated. Even on spruce and fir supportive rafts, rough driving conditions caused breakups and logs were lost. Those held back from the drive by low water sometimes sank. Woody's challenge was delivering enough logs to the mills when they ran out. Though underwater then for only a few seasons, he raised and recovered those lost logs and sent them to the mills keeping men busy and food on their tables.

That era had a total 5-15% loss of river driven logs. The lumbering economy took "Sinkage" for granted. Through modern search and retrieval methods, preserved logs that were under water for over 80 years, have been raised for lumber. The tight grain and aged finish, when sawn and milled, produces prized furniture and musical instrument stock. Cross-border companies have reclaimed Bird's-Eye Maple, Yellow Birch, Red Oak, White Pine, Spruce, Eastern Hemlock, and a few less known species such as Butternut and Basswood.

Shaw & Tenney paddle and oar makers of Orono, crafted a limited edition of L.L.Bean centennial paddles in 2012. We often went there with Chris in her UMaine days. If you ever get the chance, visit 20 Water Street and take in 1890s history combined with 2013 variety and quality. The Bean-paddle wood was retrieved from the depths of Quakish Lake on the Penobscot (there's a dam at the outlet) by West Branch Heritage Timber of Millinocket. A lightweight centennial paddle at Beans drew my attention, because it had a unique grain. That beavertail blade haunted my mind; on the next trip I bought one! How did I choose this genuine specimen from the drive from other offered grains? Some were clear and handsome from the grip to the tip, and others had conspicuous dark lines. I picked the in-between in favor of its strong bright shaft-likeness to a bateau or canoe set pole and blade semblance to flowing streams or rock ridden rapids.

Reminiscing one evening, I gazed at the paddle and grain and wrote (giving Whittier a run for his money):

"The mother softwood once stood tall,
Till flashing chop and crashing fall.
From stump to stream to final float,
'Twas doomed to lie 'neath man and boat.

But see! Once more again to rise
For man to craft as ancient prize.

By grip on grain each stroke will guide
Canoe and cache in dreamlike glide.

As a matter of fact, sunken pulpwood was raised from the bottom of the Madawaska River by New Brunswick's Fraser Company from 1955 to the early '70s because it was becoming a pollution hazard. In winter, they would cut holes in the ice, use pike poles to find and "fish" the four-footers out, and slide them out onto the ice with a pulp hook. When there was no safe ice, they worked from rafts. Much of that salvaged was reusable went to the paper mill in Edmunston, New Brunswick.

A surprising 2010 discovery of submerged lumber happened in Boston Harbor, only 70 miles from my Cape Cod home. A water-front construction project exposed a hand-hewn numbered cache in briny mud. The underwater "Timber Basin" stored specific wooden shipbuilding lumber, called Live Oak for the Boston Naval Shipyard in Charlestown. The 1797 built U.S.S. Constitution of War-of-1812-fame, still commissioned at Boston, is a living example of Live Oak durability.

Fifteen truckloads of those retrieved timbers arrived at The Museum of America and the Sea at Connecticut's Mystic Seaport in time for restoration of the 1841 built Charles W. Morgan. As a museum member, I've watched that progress. It's the last wooden full-rigged whaling ship in the world and oldest commercial American vessel in existence.

The Charles W. Morgan has a Massachusetts and New Brunswick connection. New Bedford builders and brothers, Zachariah and Jethro Hillman, were cousins of Capt. Tristram Hillman, and all were born on the island of Martha's Vineyard.

Tristram, left America (evidently a Loyalist) and became a lieutenant and ship's master in the British Royal Navy. As a discharged Crown officer, he sailed from England to British North America's New Brunswick with his wife and children. He sought a Land Grant, and in1787, became the first grantee in the parish of Woodstock at Shogomoc Stream (by Charlie Lake, New Brunswick).

Five of my deceased friends rest with Tristram in the Hillman Cemetery at Ritchie: Harold Davidson; his brother-in-law Neil Grant (wife Myrtle will join him); and Willard, Muriel, and Mark Way.

Between the TransCanada Highway and the St. John River, it's located on high ground at the river bank. As the river winds downstream and curves up into the Nackawic Bend, so does this story to another cemetery on the east facing bank in Lower Southampton.

CHAPTER FIVE

THE LEGEND OF GEORGE ROCKWELL

In the same way that precious lost logs from old time drives are reclaimed, I literally and figuratively raised a tombstone, retrieving the name of a great uncle, George Rockwell. Until four years ago, my cousins and I didn't know that he existed in our Baylis and Munro lineage. His first and middle names matched those of my uncle, George Rockwell Baylis.

As said earlier, I was researching burial lists of the Munro, MacFarlane, and Calder cemeteries relocated to Otis Cemetery, and discovered that George Rockwell's grave was among those in the Calder records. I passed it on to Rose Staples, who unearthed the shattered monument and found a cemetery site photo of the original in the Provincial Archive Mactaquac file.

That beginning introduced me to George Rockwell. Knowing nothing about him, this tale developed strictly through documents and Rossville relationships or happenings. When writing about long ago events in settings where I've walked, *The Tales of Tappan Adney* (friend of Dr. George Frederick Clarke) straightaway bring me back to what went on around the turn of the nineteenth century. It provides a feeling for George Rockwell's world and helped me to walk in his shoes. Adney's New York City 1883-1887 art studies taught him to sketch details of maps, campsites, birch bark canoe excursions, river tow-boats, snowshoe making, a Woodstock sawmill, and best of all, "Myself [Adney, snowshoeing] at Nackawick."

I will, however, try to tell the tale as humanly as possible. To make it realistic, let's pretend that we are gathered in the Baylis kitchen of my youth. A narrative about the kitchen of 91 year old Baylis cousin, "Grandma" Nettie Fox Bull of Maine, also sets the same scene. It's described in her 1982 *Presque Isle Star Herald* interview by Hazel Cameron. "The wood snapped and crackled in the cook stove as the rays of sunlight filtered through the kitchen window. The warmth and aroma from the wood made a pleasant setting. One felt the warmth and love that surrounded each visitor to the homey kitchen. In the quiet setting, with steam rising from the teakettle on the stove, there was a feeling of peace and serenity seldom experienced in these harried days of anxiousness."

As I start my story, there's quiet anticipation. Only the clock ticks with its time-telling. Oh how I wish that Guy Davidson, 40 years older than I, was here to tell what he knew. Guy spoke with kindhearted wisdom. After all, he identified the photograph of my Baylis family and horse in front of their farmhouse that burned c.1905. When I asked his daughter Myrtle if Guy had ever discussed his paternal Aunt Ellen or her first husband, George Rockwell, she had no recall. Ellen's second husband, Whitfield Grant, was interred at Upper Southampton in 1931. I do know that Guy, a nephew through marriage, was a pallbearer.

Every seat is taken at the table, around the room, and on extra dining room chairs. A dozen children are shyly watching and quietly listening on the couch and on the steps leading up to Mabel's bedroom. Through the front and back kitchen screen doors, a few folks can be seen on each porch. With this as the setting, I'll commence.

I've not yet found a picture of George Rockwell to preside (I silently pay particular attention to my relatives, wondering if they carry a Rockwell likeness). I was given one of Ellen and son John taken in Saskatchewan. Maybe a Davidson present has their features. Elmo Stairs, from across the river at Hawkshaw, is here with his fiddle. As he bows "The Piper's Refrain," I'll sing a verse to honor George, son of my Highland Scot great grandmother, Annie Munro Rockwell, substituting a few of my own words.

> I'll tell it to you as they told it to me,
> By the glow of the [stove]fire burning-
> By the banks of the [St. John], where [he]
> Sported and played,
> [George] once faced the [forest so bravely.]

When George and Ellen Rockwell were married in 1883, "Nackawick" was a small settlement in Queensbury Parish on the bend in St. John River at the Southampton Parish line. In 1885, George bought a

350 acre farm on the Southampton side of the parish line. After the Mactaquac Dam head pond got higher in 1967, a new Nackawic was created on the opposite bank of Nackawic Bend. Let's talk about this Nackawic Town that was incorporated in 1976, its Culliton Cove, and how they relate to the legend of George Rockwell.

With its long lumbering history, Nackawic was chosen "Forestry Capital of Canada" in 1991 (Fredericton's motto translates: "Noble daughter of the forest"). The community planned and preserved water-side property to perpetuate the honor. A cove-side acre of paths, patterned on the course of the St. John River was planted with worldwide tree and shrub species, comprising an International Garden, once a Munro potato field. A prestigious landmark in the park is "The World's Largest Axe." It is a testimonial to the past, present, and future forest industry in Nackawic and New Brunswick. "Driven" at an angle into a 33-foot diameter concrete "Stump," it has a 23-foot wide, stainless steel, double-bitted head, a 49 foot high handle, and weighs 55 tons.

I perceive George Rockwell as the mighty Nackawic lumberjack whose semblance swings the giant axe. He typified the seasoned and proud woodsmen and farmers who were recruited as Province Men for the timber harvest in Northern Maine. This story is about how George came to be the first of our family to cross the border from New Brunswick, and why he has a new memorial stone in Otis Cemetery.

Looking across Culliton Cove from the International Park, the Rockwell farm site lies between the pulp and fiber mill to the left, and the woods at the Queensbury Parish line, eastward to the right. It's amazing that the bulk of that farm remains forest, and even more miraculous that the bit (cutting edge) of the axe is permanently pointed directly at that historic spot. Below Route 105, a portion of that acreage is under Culliton Cove waters.

George Rockwell's beginning starts with the document of his parents' marriage, their wedding witnesses, and land grant petitions of Rockwell and Baylis. "William Rockwell, b. abt. 1825 and Anne Munro b. abt. 1836 both of Southampton, York Co., N.B." are recorded as married on June 16, 1855, by Rev. John M. Brooke and co-signed by George Baylis and Rebecca Hamilton at St. Paul's Presbyterian Church in Fredericton. My great grandmother, Ann Munro, was of Scottish birth, but William Rockwell's origin is unknown. Upriver couples often made that trip by steamboat, for a dollar each way.

On July 1, 1855, William petitioned for a land grant of 90 acres in the "Nackiewikak" area with the names of J. Davidson, Deputy Surveyor, and John Munro on the document. At the same time, his wedding witness George Baylis petitioned for land "Adjoining Rockwell." I've found no record of those petitions being granted.

A son, George Rockwell, was born to Annie and William at Lower Southampton on June 25, 1856. I don't know why or what happened, but William either died or departed. Annie united with his friend George Baylis, my great grandfather. A formal record of that union has not been found. Rose Staples explained to me: "Early Southampton families that were Presbyterian had a hard time getting married by their own minister. Travel was hard and ministers were few and record keeping was often poor."

There are no accounts about George Rockwell, from birth in 1856, until he became a member of the Baylis family. After 1861, census records and land investment papers verify his whereabouts and prove that he was my great uncle.

The Southampton, York Co. 1861 provincial census lists the "Baylas" household as "George age 32, Ann age 25, and George Rockwell son by 1st husband age 5." An 1871 census "Bayliss" household was "George age 45, Ann age 35, George Rockwell age 14, Lucy Ann age 5, and William James age 10/12." Fact is, George Rockwell grew up on Rossville Road. Variations in the Baylis name were recorded

World's largest Axe Monument, Nackawic, N.B.

according to how the census taker viewed the spelling.

At 19, George Rockwell is among 12 names in a John McFarlane Land Petition for York County. As I see it, he had a mature interest in settlement land.

The census year 1881 listed "George Bayles age 54, Ann age 45, Lucy age 14, and William James age 10, George Rockwell age 24 Farm Lab'r, and Thomas Gorman age 28 born in U.S., R Cath, Irish, Labourer."

As this census was taken April 20, 1881, I speculate that Thomas Gorman may have worked with George across the border in Maine and returned to help at the Baylis farm for the summer. Curious, I came across a Thomas Gorman born at Portland, Maine in 1859 in the 1880 U.S. census. The New Brunswick 1881 "Age 28" may not be accurate. With logging in mind, I found a Thomas Gorman in the Bangor City Directory as boarding on Washington Street in 1884 and on York Street in 1892. If it's the same Gorman, George Rockwell may have started working in Maine as early as 1881.

With farm neighbor Ross F. Woodman, Sr., 44 years of age, George Rockwell, at age 25, acquired a Registered Land Grant on May 26, 1882 for 100 acres from farmer George Brymer for $400. Note that it was the second time that George was included in a land deal. That registered grant in British legal language must have made George, a young and single farmer, feel quite proud!

"Victoria, by the Grace of GOD, of the United Kingdom of Great Britain and Ireland, Queen, Defender of Faith, &c. To all to whom these Presents shall come, *Greeting:* KNOW YE, That We, of Our special grace, certain knowledge, and mere motion, have given and granted, and We do, by these Presents, for Us, Our Heirs and Successors, give and grant unto *Ross F Woodman and George Rockwell as tenants in common and not as joint tenants, their Heirs and Assigns* a Tract of Land situate in the Parish of *Southampton* in the County of *York* in Our Province of New Brunswick‑‑‑‑‑‑‑WITNESS Our trusty and well beloved *His Honor the Honorable Robert Duncan Wilmot* Our Lieutenant Governor of Our said Province, at Fredericton."

As to the history of George's courting and marriage, I'll start with Corbett and Marie McGuire's farmhouse across the road. It was built by John and Isabella Trail Davidson after they migrated from Scotland in the 1860s. After the birth of John W. (Guy Davidson's father), daughter Ellen was born on March 12, 1863, followed by sister, Louise, and son, George. Ellen was six years younger than George Rockwell. They grew up together when he lived at my great grandparent's Baylis farm as a step-brother to my great aunt Lucy and my grandfather William.

Ellen and George were married on October 23, 1883 at the manse (parsonage) in Prince William by Rev. William Ross. Prior to wedlock, George farmed and worked in the woods. To support Ellen, he made frequent border crossings to and from the better paying lumbering jobs in northern Maine, where skilled lumberjacks were in demand. Maine's hiring bosses looked upon men from an Atlantic Province as hard-working, low-priced labor. Developing railway routes enabled Canadian workers to travel cross-border to "Ameriky" when the logging camps opened in the autumn and return home to their farms in the springtime.

In the late fall of 1883, George took up woods work with John Morison, age 65, and Col. Elbridge H. Hunting, age 46, both from East Corinth, Maine. There was a stage line passing through Corinth, and they could commute to their office at 50 Exchange Street in Bangor and residence rooms at the Penobscot Exchange hotel. As early as 1850, Orono, Maine, census records gave the names of logging workers from New Brunswick who lived in the Morison household and probably worked at his Island Mills property. Through that tradition, or newspaper and boarding house advertising, George and other Province Men came to Bangor and were hired. After that first year, he signed up with Morison and Hunting for two more years.

Neither the hardships of being distant from family life and comfortable quarters, nor long work hours and harsh weather conditions, deterred George from returning to the woods when farming was slack and jobs were scarce at home.

The Hon. John Morison (spelled Morrison in Hempstead's 1975 *Penobscot Boom*) "Was known over the entire length and breadth of Maine. He was a kindly man of simple ways who well deserved the fortune that by his industry, ability and sturdy integrity he won from the forest of Penobscot." John was one of the Lumber Kings of Old Maine on the Passadumkeag, and later on the West Branch of the Penobscot with Elbridge, where they cut as high as nine million feet in a season hiring crews of 100 to 150 men. Elbridge Hunting had the confidence of the Penobscot Log Driving Company, because he "Had the drives" (was in charge) from 1881 to 1887.

George saw his share of hard times. Work around Rossville, before and after marriage, was sometimes scarce. The Eastern hemlock tree was readily available in ample quantities in and around York County. The hemlock bark became more valued than its soft wood that was mostly used in rail-tie and coffin construction. Boiling the bark in vats extracted tannin that was used to process hides into leather. Local to where George made a living, the areas of Tweedie Lake, Allandale and Shogomoc are remembered as "Bark woods." From full moon in May to full moon in August, tan-bark sometimes three inches thick, was peeled while the hemlock sap was seeping, piled to dry, and measured to sell by the cord for about five dollars. Upon the first snowfall, loads were hauled to the local extract operation and very large tannery in Pokiok beside the St. John.

F. Shaw & Sons of Boston, the largest leather-tanning firm in the country, had almost exclusive control over stumpage holdings in New York, Maine, Quebec, and New Brunswick. In the mid–1880s, disease distressed the hemlock resource. The industry gradually failed financially and relocated closer to the shoe-shops farther south. Pokiok, Millville, and Woodstock harvesters, haulers, and extract-worker's jobs were lost, and the slow-growing hemlock reserve was depleted. Lumbering in general was also falling off. The wage earning potential of the hemlock bark resource ceased to exist. It was one less opportunity for George Rockwell to find work locally.

As Father Time forced ups and downs on the economy, Mother Nature challenged lumbering with drought or mighty freshets, deep snow or lack thereof on tote roads, frigid winters or premature mild melts, and strong winds or lightning strikes. Within the 1883–1886 years that George worked for Morison and Hunting, an autumn "Cyclone" in 1883 devastated the second-growth pine creating a decline for a number of years. Some crews sought and salvaged tangles of blow-down spruce and fir stands in spite of snarled undergrowth; the result was fewer logs brought out. Though progressive pulp wood demand was creeping up on the saw-log industry, it too felt the impact of spruce budworm plagues of 1884 and 1885. In those years, very heavy annual snowfalls and subzero weather occurred with excesses of over 100 inches and 40 degrees below zero.

Weather was no obstacle to a logger's motivation. George had a pregnant wife at home in Rossville to support and the get-up-and-go to face adversity. The average wage for a raftsman, woodchopper, or an unskilled laborer in 1883 was $1.24 a day; it increased to $2.00 in 1886 when good drivers commanded $2.25 to $2.50 a day.

When the drives were over, crews were disbanded. Some drivers went to work in the mills to saw the logs they just ran. Maine held work assurance in spring at the villages of Old Town, Orono, and Stillwater, which were the principal mill sites. The July 9, 1883 *Bangor Daily Whig and Courier* notes: "Messrs. Morison & Hunting take possession, to-day, of the steam saw mill at Upper Stillwater recently purchased by them of Gilman, Webster & Co." No doubt, it was an investment expanding their and their workers' wage earning after winter logging and spring driving. It's recorded that Stillwater's Basin Mills consisted of 12 saw mills, two lath, two clapboard, one shingle, and two rotary saw mills. Quite likely, expectant mother Ellen Davidson Rockwell moved cross-border to be with George, when he was working in one of the mills.

The company owners given names, John (Morison), and Elbridge (Hunting), became those of the Rockwell newborn. Southampton census records verify John Elbridge Rockwell was born cross-border in the U.S. on June 17, 1884.

Ellen and John came back to Rossville to be with her mother and father, Isabella and John Davidson. Isabella was a Trail, as were my mother's aunts, uncles, and Trail cousins. That's another example of how many Lower Southampton folks have ancestry within other large families in the community. To carry it one step further, Ellen Davidson Rockwell was my great aunt by marriage.

George, as far as I know, never gave in to hard times. He had high hopes and enough savings in 1885 to purchase a 350 acre farm on land adjacent to where the Nackawic Stream joined the St. John River. The Land Purchase Deed of 128 years ago had boundaries described in 100-link units called a "Chain." Some surveyors' chains were not always the standard 66 feet. I used Land Grant, atlas, and cadastral (surveyed property lines) maps to compare that original purchase with current linear feet landmarks. Loyalist land grants, whether to a soldier or to an influential evacuated citizen, defined the early York County property ownership.

By an 1881 map, the property was that of Captain George Shore of the New Brunswick Fencibles regiment, acquired in 1828 from his wife Ariana's father, Chief Justice John S. J. Saunders who had been a Loyalist Queen's Ranger captain from Virginia and received 6000 acres of Crown grants of land. Mr. Shore passed the 350 eastern acres along the Queensbury line on to his son William. When William died, it passed back to Eliza Saunders Stewart, another daughter of Justice Saunders, and her husband Captain William Little Stewart who were living in England. They sold the property to George Rockwell.

In the Deed of September 30, 1885, British legal terms prevail; date is by day, month, and year, and currency is in shillings. The document margin stamp reads "T. Lewis Not. Pub. [until] 16/12/95 one shilling." Payment by George is stipulated in Canadian dollars.

Bear with me as I present this long and meticulous conveyance, because it brings us closer to George. It was his document of dreams. Don't feel obligated to dwell on the details, but to me and those of George Rockwell's ancestry, it is vital.

William Little Stewart &
Eliza Saunders Stewart
No. 35560 This indenture made
George Rockwell

This thirtieth day of September in the year of our Lord one thousand Eight hundred and Eighty five Between Willian Little Stewart of Dover in the County of Kent in England A Colonel in the British Army and Eliza Saunders Stewart his wife of the first part, and George Rockwell of the Parish of Southampton in the County of York and Province of New Brunswick Farmer of the second part.

Witnesseth that said William Little Stewart and Eliza Saunders Stewart his wife for and in consideration of the sum of Ten Hundred and fifty dollars of lawful money of Canada to them in hand with and truly paid at or before the ensealing and delivery of these Present by the said George Rockwell the receipt whereof is hereby acknowledged have granted, bargained, sold, aliened, released, conveyed and confirmed by these present do grant, bargain, sell, alien, release convey and confirm unto the said George Rockwell his heirs and assigns, All that certain Lot, Piece, or Parcel of land and premises situate lying, and being in the Parish of Southampton in the County of York and the Province of New Brunswick (being part of a Block of land formerly owned by Colonel William H. Shore) and bounded as follows viz: - Beginning on the Easterly Bank of the Saint John River at the point of intersection of said Bank with the Parish line dividing the Parishes of Southampton and Queensbury, thence following the said Parish line in a North Easterly direction Two hundred and fifty (250) chains; thence at right angles in a North Westerly direction fourteen (14) chains; thence at right angles and parallel to said Parish line in a South Westerly direction to the Nackawiciac Stream, thence down the said stream to its mouth, and thence down the Easterly bank of the Saint John River to the place of beginning containing Three hundred and fifty acres more or less. Together with all Houses, Out Houses, Barns, Buildings Edifices Fences, Improvements, Profits, Privileges and appurtenances to the same belonging or in any manner appertaining and the Reversion and Reversions, Remainder and Remainders, Rents Issues and Profits thereof and also the Estate, Rights, Title, Interest, Use, Possession, Property, Claim and demand either at Law or in Equity of them the said William Little Stewart and Eliza Saunders Stewart his wife of, in, to, or out of the same and every part and parcel thereof with the appurtenances To Have and To Hold the said Lot, Piece or parcel of land and premises hereby granted, bargained, and sold or meant mentioned or intended so to be and every part and parcel thereof with the appurtenances unto the said George Rockwell his heirs and assigns to the only, proper use, benefit, and behoof of the said George Rockwell his heirs and assigns forever.

In witness Cohere of the said parties hereto of the first part have here unto set their hands and seals the day and year first herein before written.

Signed Sealed and delivered W.L. Stewart (F.S.)
E.S. Stewart (F.S.)

In the presence of Fred J. Sargeant
Arthur Brooke Elwin
Clerks to Mr. Thomas Lewis, Solicitor in Dover, England.

Be it remembered on the Sixteenth day of December in the year of our Lord One Thousand Eight Hundred and eighty five personally appeared before me Thomas Lewis a Notary Public for England and elsewhere by lawful authority admitted And sworn residing and practicing in Dover in the County of Kent in England, the written named William Little Stewart and Eliza Saunders Stewart his wife the Grantors in the foregoing Deed freely and voluntarily for the uses and purposes therein mentioned and the said Eliza Saunders Stewart being by me examined separate and apart from her said husband acknowledged that she executed the same freely and voluntarily without any fear threat or compulsion of from or by her said husband.

In testimony whereof I the said Notary Public have hereunto set my hand and affixed my Notarial Seal the day and year last above written.

Thomas Lewis, Notary Public (F.S.)
New Brunswick, York County
Registered this Nineteenth day of January,
One Thousand Eight hundred and Eighty Six.
A.D. Terxa, Reg

That transaction across the Atlantic in 1885 would take three-and-a-half months to carry out. When George finally read the registered deed, I'm sure he devoured it again and again. Dedicated to the prosperity of his household, he could hardly wait for homecoming.

Locating George's whereabouts in the winter of 1885, I'll assign "High water" to his river driving escapades. It was said that George left for Maine, "About Christmas last" 1885, to work through the spring drive. A November 12, 1865 *Bangor Daily Whig and Courier* news article read: "Morison & Hunting will send another crew of men up to the West Branch on this morning's train. This firm are getting ready to do a heavy business in the woods this winter."

Just before the drive, the last logs cut were hauled to landings, and the watercourse obstacles of ice and debris were cleared from the smaller branch streams. Toward the end of April 1886, George was on a Morison and Hunting crew of 14 men booming logs on Ragged Lake in Piscataquis County. Ragged Lake sits 15 miles east of Moosehead's North Bay in line with the lower border of Baxter State Park to the east.

The Penobscot River West Branch linked chains of lakes through which driving channels coursed. From Ragged, the next chain to require booming and tows are Caribou and Chesuncook Lakes. The Penobscot flowed on for 25 more miles to the Pemadumcook Lake chain: Ambajejus (famous Boom House at its head), Pemadumcook, South Twin, North Twin, and Elbow; the North Twin Dam was at Elbow's outlet. Then, the West Branch proceeded through Quakish and Ferguson Lakes, and past Millinocket, to join the East Branch. The drive would be long one for Morison and Hunting, taking the average of a month, or maybe six weeks, to reach the sorting booms around Old Town and Orono.

It's not hard to imagine his thoughts of home-coming, best described as yearning, a nostalgic craving. Poetic, but with gist, a copy of verses from "The Logger's Boast" might be tacked on a log next to George's bunk.

> When winter's snows are melted, and the ice-bound streams
>   are free,
> We'll run our logs to market, then haste our friends to see;
> How kindly true hearts welcome us, our wives and children
>   too,
> We will spend with those the summer, and once more a
>   lumbering go.

> And when upon the long-hid soil the white Pines disappear,
> We will cut the other forest trees, and sow whereon we clear;
> Our grain shall wave o'er valleys rich, our herds bedot the hills,
> When our feet no more are hurried on to tend the driving mills.

What were George and Ellen's thoughts on that Easter Sunday, April 25, 1886? George would be thinking of his wife and son and plans for his newly acquired farm. Ellen might have watched young John playing on the floor, picturing George walking through the door. "Home soon, surely home soon."

In camp, the boss might have referred to the *Maine Farmer's Almanac* to find that sunrise on the next morning, April 26, was at five o'clock. That's when, after an early breakfast, George and the crew went off to work at booming on Ragged Lake. Overhead, the last quarter moon was still in the sky. Most of the lake was open, but the edges and coves were still covered with ice.

Suddenly, the unthinkable was reported in the April 29, 1886 Bangor *Daily Whig and Courier* "Local Matters" column:

SAD DROWNING ACCIDENT

George Rockwell, one of Morison and Hunting's Crew, Drowned in Ragged Lake. William Snow, of this city, who has been in the woods this winter with Morison & Hunting, arrived here on the train yesterday noon bringing the news of a sad drowning accident which occurred at Ragged Lake Monday. A crew of fourteen men had been engaged in booming some logs in the lake which were owned by Morison & Hunting. They finished this work at two o'clock and were headed for the camp. The distance was much shorter across the ice, but eleven of the crew, knowing that it was unsafe to cross, started along the shore. The other three, all Province Men, were repeatedly warned of their danger, but decided to try the experiment and so struck boldly out upon the ice.

They had proceeded but a short distance when they dropped through into the water. Two of them easily broke their way to the boom, a distance of over one hundred feet, but the third man George Rockwell, evidently lost his presence of mind and could only call to his companions on the shore to save him. This they were unable to do, although making the utmost exertions and he sank after remaining above the water for ten or twelve minutes. He never rose afterwards.

The men immediately commenced trying to recover his body, but it is not thought that they will be successful. Rockwell was about 25 years of age and had been in the employ of Morison & Hunting for three years. He was a steady and industrious man and a general favorite with his employers and fellow workmen. He purchased a farm this spring at his home in Lower Southampton, N.B., with his savings and was soon to settle upon it with his wife and child. The latter are in the place above mentioned and were notified yesterday of their loss."

With telephone service not yet established, news of loss probably went by Western Union Telegraph Company through railway station agents.

After the notification of next of kin, widespread news of Rossville's sorrow soon appeared in the *Bangor Daily Commercial, Lewiston Evening Journal, Fredericton Capital, Woodstock Press, Saint John Daily Sun*, and *Saint Andrews Bay Pilot*.

Lines of "The West Branch Song" were foreboding.

And as he started for the shore,
He fell, alas ! to rise no more.

And within three minutes all was done,
When the work of eternity begun.

Three times he rose, all in our view, As if to bid us all adieu."

What caused George, a veteran to logging, to falter? Did thoughts of home distract him, or was he not cautious about walking on thin ice in that much warmer April? As agile as George may have been on a floating boom log, ice cold water disabled mind and muscle overcoming efforts to survive. Two Canadian companions amazingly did stay alive.

Other *Whig and Courier* "Local Matters" columns provide a better insight of conditions: "The ice in the lakes up river [Penobscot] is ready to break up. It is very soft and in none of the lakes is it safe for a man to cross. The Moosehead people think that boats will be able to run from Greenville to Kineo Saturday or Sunday. If so, this will be the earliest that the ice has been known to leave the lakes for a number of years. A correspondent writing us from North Twin Dam

[Elbow Lake outlet in the Pemadumcook West Branch chain of lakes] under date of April 27th says: The ice in the lakes is weak and will all be gone in a few days if the warm weather continues. There is still quite a body of snow in the woods about here. Nearly all the farmers in this vicinity have been sowing their grain this week. Many of them have been planting potatoes, and in fact, everything that will not be injured by the late frosts. Planting operations have not been carried on so early here for many years."

When Mrs. F. Beavan wrote *Sketches and Tales Illustrative of Life in the Backwoods of New Brunswick*, she advised "Travelling on the ice is not altogether free from danger; and even when it is thought safe, there are places where it is dangerous to go."

The April 30 *Bangor Daily Whig and Courier* "Local Matters" column reads: "Contrary to expectations the body of George Rockwell, drowned in Ragged Lake, Monday, was recovered Tuesday. The water was very deep, but Rockwell went straight to the bottom when he sank. The remains were hauled forty miles through the woods [only a winter road] brought down from Greenville on yesterday morning's train and sent to his home in New Brunswick last night by order of Mr. E. H. Hunting of the firm of Morison & Hunting."

Jabez Osgood Bradbury, age 27, also a young farmer from the Rossville area, worked with George for Morison and Hunting (I alerted you to "Remember the name!"). Like Ellen and son John, Jabez' wife, Barbara (Morrison) and year-old son Harry were at home. Rose Staples diligently searched the York County newspapers of the day and found Jabez' account of the drowning in the May 5, 1886, issue of the Fredericton *Maritime Farmer*.

DROWNED IN MAINE

George Rockwell was a well to do young man, living at Lower Southampton, York County, up to December last. He had purchased part of the Stewart farm in that locality, married a wife, a daughter of Mr. John Davidson of the same place, and was getting along nicely in the world. There being a small debt on his farm, he went to Maine about Christmas last to work in the lumber woods, and to earn enough money to clear his place. His friends heard from him that he was doing well, and would be home as soon as driving was over, but instead of his returning in life, his remains arrived last Friday [April 30th], in charge of Jabez Bradbury, a young man belonging to Temperance Vale, Southampton but who had been working with Rockwell. It appears that the deceased was drowned while building a boom. Bradbury was fifteen miles away when he heard of his companion's death, and, with much discomfort, hastened to the spot to pay what respect he could to the remains of his friend. He secured the body, with much difficulty, and brought it home, having had to make his way for thirty miles [to Greenville] through the woods, [by train to Bangor and thence to New Brunswick,]and having to bring it down the river from Lower Woodstock in a catamaran [small raft of lashed logs] alone. The relatives of Rockwell feel much indebted to young Bradbury, for his efforts in bringing the body home, and there is a general feeling of sympathy in Southampton for the friends of the deceased, especially for his young wife who is left with one child. The remains of the unfortunate young man were interred last Saturday, the funeral services, which were conducted by Rev. Mr. Ross, being very largely attended.

The long and grueling journey from Ragged Lake would require a day or more to travel over 40 miles by horse drawn sled or buckboard on a winding winter tote road to Greenville and its railroad connection. In 1887, the March snow depth reached seven feet and prohibited travel. That route today would be called the Greenville or Baxter State Park Road.

From Ragged Lake, Jabez took George's body past Morison and Hunting's Grant Farm property (1878–1901), and over half-mile Sias Hill (a height of land that no longer exists) to First Roach Pond. The Roach River Farm and hotel, presently Kokadjo, was owned by Morison and Hunting since 1844. They had a stage line, quoted as "Seven miles in length," to Lily Bay on Moosehead Lake. The rough ride took about two hours and a half. From Lily Bay to Greenville, the distance was about 18 miles. Jabez, with George's remains, then rode 60 miles on the Bangor and Piscataquis Railroad morning train from Greenville and arrived in Bangor at the Exchange St. Railway Station on Thursday, April 29th. George and Jabez probably passed through that same station on their way to the woods.

That night Elbridge Hunting sent Jabez with George's corpse 120 miles on the eastern division Maine Central R.R. to connect in McAdam Junction with New Brunswick Railway Company. From McAdam, it was 25 miles to Canterbury Station where the rail-bed was ten miles distant from the St. John River over rustic roads. Past Canterbury and somewhere closer to the river near Woodstock, Jabez Bradbury rafted George's remains down to Lower Southampton on Friday, April 30th. Overall, the long sad journey back to New Brunswick took four days and covered about 230 miles.

By an act of God, the goodness of his employers, and Jabez Bradbury's brotherly will power, George's remains were not destined for a boots-nailed-to-a-tree grave site at distant Ragged Lake. He was home.

On the next day, Saturday, May 1, the grief stricken community gathered for the interment in Calder cemetery. Rev. William Ross, who officiated at George and Ellen's marriage just three years prior in 1883, now presided at his burial. At graveside, the 5th verse from "Burial of a River-Driver" reflects Ellen's suffering:

A fair young maid with pensive face,
Looks forth upon the silent night,
Her heart sweet memories doth trace,
Till future years glow in their light.

Alas! For life's all changeful scene,
How soon must perish that fond dream
For him on whom her thoughts doth pore;
His hopes and schemes of earth are o'er!

Among the community clustered at the burial, immediate family would have been my great grandparents, George and Annie Munro Rockwell Baylis, great aunt Lucy Ann, age 19 (soon to wed Wilmot Fox in October), and my grandfather William, age 16. Ellen's family, included parents, John and Isabella Davidson, sister Louisa, age 20, and brothers George, 11, and John W., 24 (Guy Davidson's father).

Grieving Ellen, left intestate, had to deal with supporting infant son John. The issues of property were promptly brought to the

Supreme Court in Equity by Alfred Bartlett, James K. Pinder, and John Davidson (her father), each a Justice of the Peace. I've transcribed six handwritten documents of the process. The J. E. Rockwell Guardianship, Petition 1, specifies the same location and boundaries of George Rockwell's deeded Lower Southampton 350 acres. "The River Saint John and Narquewickac Creek" were on the southeast Rockwell boundary.

The asking price document as mandated by the court, has language like that of the Land Purchase Deed: "By an order of his Honor John James Fraser one of the Judges of the Supreme Court in Equity dated the 16th day of October A.D. 1886 his Honor did order of the said Ellen Rockwell Mother and next friend of the said Infant John Elbridge Rockwell should have leave to absolutely sell and dispose of all the right title and interest of the said Infant of in and to the lands and premises in said order particularly mentioned and described to such person or persons and for such price as she the said Ellen Rockwell should in her judgment think fair and right no less however than the sum of Seven Hundred and sixty Dollars."

Infant John's interest was purchased by his grandfather John Davidson. In 1886, that figured out to be a fair two dollars and fourteen cents per acre for John Rockwell's upkeep.

Seventeen months after George's death, The *Woodstock Carleton Sentinel* of September 24, 1887, and *Saint John Daily Telegraph* of September 27, 1887, announced that Ellen married George Whitfield Grant of Southampton. George "Whit" Whitfield Grant first married Emma Armstrong of Lower Woodstock in 1880. A son, George Armstrong Grant, was born March 14, 1882, and Emma, age 27, died two months later. Whit's home was near the Middle Southampton School House, the Free Baptist Church, and the Blacksmith Shop and Store along the St. John. John Elbridge Rockwell then became a step-child to Whitfield Grant, as did George Rockwell to my great grandfather George Baylis.

Now I'll tell you what I know about Ellen Grant and her son, John Elbridge Rockwell, after they became members of the Whitfield Grant family. The 1889 Southampton School District registration lists "Johnnie Rockwell 5 and George A. Grant 7." The 1891 census reads: "Grant Whitfield-38-farmer; Helen [Ellen]-Wife-28; Grant George-9; Rockwell John-7-born U.S." Once again, I note that John E. Rockwell was born in the States, probably Maine. Another half-brother, Harry

Gordon Grant, was born in 1892. A Culliton School class photo c.1897 (not 1889; Guy Davidson was at least six) identifies each pupil. George Grant is on the left in the back row, and John Rockwell is next to the teacher. Harry is on the left in the front row. At the time, the Grants may have been living in the Bellamy house on "The Lane," which ran above the Nackawic Stream, opposite and parallel to Rossville Road. John might have heard, from his mother and her Rossville relatives, that his father's skills in farming and logging would become second-nature to him.

A 1901 Southampton census reads: "Grant, Whitfield-Head-47-Farmer; Grant, Ellen-Wife-38; Grant, George-Son-19- School Teacher; Grant Harry-Son-9; John [Rockwell]-stepson-16; White

This old photo may not provide much information with regard to the educational standards of one room schoolhouses in the year 1889, when it was taken, but it is one indication of how time changes all things. Because the site of this schoolhouse -- at neighboring Culleton in York County -- is under 30 feet of the waters of the Mactaquac headpond now and there is no possibility of the eloquent words of the dapper teacher, Mr. H. Fraser, on the right, echoing down through the hallways of time. But they raised a hardy breed of youngsters in that 81 year ago period. It's a remarkable fact that of the 24 students in this picture, five are still living. The class members were, left to right, back row: George Grant, Ida Munro, Mary Woodman, Maud Bradbury, John Rockwell. Middle row: Ralph Stairs, Willie McLeod, Ezra Woodman, Ada Munro, Ella Hagerman, Ethel Bradbury, Fred Ackerman, Percy Hagerman, Minnie Davidson, Laura Munro, Mary Munro. Front row: Harry Grant, Hazel Munro, Bessie Stairs, Stanley A. Stairs, Guy Davidson, Gracie Stairs, Gertie Munro and Muriel Munro.
We are indebted to Mr. Guy Davidson for allowing The Sentinel to use this picture.

Culliton School Class, c.1897

Ada-Domestic-35." I note that Ellen and Whit were well enough off to have a domestic in residence. At age 18 in 1902, John contracted scarlet fever, which exposed him to future kidney and cardiac setbacks.

Nackawic Bend quotes James Culliton: "Johnny Rockwell worked on the boats [river steamboats between Woodstock and Fredericton]." Violet Stairs Davidson said of the Cullitons: "I can just remember the smoke from the steamboat at Grant's Landing the day they took James [maybe John W., Irish origin and Roman Catholic, age 18 in 1881 census] Culliton to be buried at the Catholic cemetery at Kingsclear." Steamboat schedules were seasonal, determined by ice in the winter, log drives in spring, or low water in warmer weather.

On the final 1906 trip of the river steamboat "Aberdeen," Johnny Woodman said "The deck hands were John Rockwell [age 22] of Southampton, Bill Embleton of Dumfries and myself."

Patricia Gunter's *The Trail Line* speaks of John Rockwell: "He had worked in the lumber camps and had spent time riding the logs down the St. John River to the sawmills."

According to the 1911 Southampton census, John Rockwell was still a bachelor living at home. Whitfield Grant purchased the Alice and Mary Grosvenor store across from the steamboat landing at Lower Southampton. The Grants also kept Post Office and Mrs. [Ellen] Grant tended the first switchboard in the area.

George Armstrong Grant, Whit's son by first wife Emma, was 29 and had moved elsewhere. Listed as a school teacher in 1901, he boarded at the James K. Pinder place in Temperance Vale to be near where he taught. I discovered that the same George A. Grant migrated to New Westminster, British Columbia, on the Lower Fraser River Valley beside Vancouver. The 1913 Vancouver City Directory listed "Grant Geo A clk P O [Post Office] r [residence] 1266 Richards." In 1915, the same reference book listed "Grant Geo A clk P O r 365 Royal Hotel." He married Ethel Wynter Maxwell, originally from Charlotte Co., New Brunswick in 1925, and they moved to Point Grey, Vancouver. That union introduced a new British Columbia family branch to the Rockwell-Grant family tree and indirectly to our Munro and Baylis line through Ellen.

Since George Armstrong Grant was the first of the Southampton Grants to venture West, I'll come back to his British Columbia lineage after I complete the rest of his family history in Saskatchewan.

In 1912 Whitfield and Ellen heeded the popular cry to "Go west" and sold their store in Southampton. In that major relocation, John Elbridge Rockwell and Harry Gordon Grant went with them to Saskatchewan, a prairie province between Manitoba and Alberta. The Canadian Pacific Railroad expanded westward in the 1880s, and Saskatchewan opened to migration about 1905. When Whitfield, Ellen, Harry, and John arrived to farm, the provincial population was about 500,000. Like Scottish, English, Irish, and Loyalist migrations

Ellen Davidson Rockwell Grant &
George Whitfield Grant

John Elbridge Rockwell

to Canada, they joined a Maritime migration to the prairies, settling between Regina and Saskatoon in Craik, founded in 1907.

I found the following in *The Craik Book of History*: "They settled on the farm [four miles west and north of Craik] on Section 25 across the road from the Alfred Holland farm. "Later, the Holland children spoke of John Rockwell's kindness to them. "These people [the Grants] never lost their love for New Brunswick. Whitfield was lame but he managed to do the farm chores and raise a big garden. He died at the age of 75. Ellen was a real 'down homer.' She spurned the use of a washing machine and all her life washed her clothes in a tub with the help of a rubbing board. She never used [bought] yeast to make bread, but had a crock in the basement where she had hops, sugar, water, and flour. The starter for this she brought from New Brunswick when she came out, and on each trip back she brought a fresh container of 'my yeast.'"

Fitting to their farming, the 1916 Census of Manitoba, Saskatchewan, and Alberta recorded: "Saskatchewan, Last Mountain District, Craik: Grant George W.-Head-65-Farmer; Ellen-Wife-53; Harry-Son-23-Farmer; Rockwell John-Lodger- 32-Labourer." That changed in 1917, when Harry bought the farm [from a Frank Orchard] south of Craik.

The Craik history book further quoted: "Each year some of the family went east for the winter." This was a long trip by train. After one such trip, Harry returned in the spring with his bride, Etta Maude Fraser, of Prince William, New Brunswick. They were married January 2, 1918. He and Etta moved to the farm and set about the task of adapting to life on a western farm. She learned to bake her own bread, churn butter, raise poultry, and feed the hungry men "Who drove teams of horses long hours in the field."

In 1930, as a consequence of his scarlet fever in 1892, John was ailing for one year with rheumatic carditis. G. Whitfield Grant died at Craik on March 10, 1931, according to his tombstone inscription. Accompanied by Ellen and John, his remains were brought to Lenentine Cemetery in Middle Southampton, New Brunswick. *The Trail Line* and *Daily Gleaner* show a March 17, 1931 date of burial. Once again, and 45 years later, Ellen had a husband brought home to New Brunswick!

In Saskatchewan, John farmed and supported his mother Ellen. That same rheumatic fever of yore however, resulted in terminal Bright's Disease, a chronic kidney condition. Ellen and Etta nursed him at home. He predeceased his mother on April 23, 1940, at age 55 years and 9 months, just about 54 years after the sad drowning death of his father, George Rockwell. Ellen passed away, at age 78, on December 9, 1940 after a lengthy battle with cancer. She and son, John, share a headstone in Craik, where they toiled for 28 years.

It's gratifying that this George Rockwell story relates to the Grants

George Rockwell's Original and New Gravestones

of Southampton and the Canadian West Grant history in fact and fellowship. Fact includes the discovery that there is a Munro, Rockwell, and Grant linkage. The fellowship connection is "The Grants of Southampton New Brunswick" clan, and their mission fits mine by paying tribute to ancestors, the beautiful province where they settled, and from which some migrated.

Neil Grant from Temple, New Brunswick, married my friend Myrtle Davidson in 1949, and was the first of the Grants that I came to know. He was the youngest brother of historian Ruth Winona Grant. I recently came to know Ruth's son, Nelson P. Grant of Waterloo, Ontario and Southampton, through inquiry about his mother's books (available through Nelson's listing in the Southampton Grant website). Nelson told me that his mother, in spite of severe arthritis, avidly pursued Grant and Hillman history.

The Southampton Grant Clan has members in New Brunswick, Ontario, Quebec, British Columbia, California, Utah, New Hampshire, and Massachusetts. They gather at summer reunions at the Middle Southampton Hall. The graves of Whitfield Grant, first wife Emma, and Ruth Winona Grant and husband, Ernest, are close by at New Lenentine Cemetery in Upper Southampton.

The Grants can conveniently visit the Davidson plot in Otis Cemetery and pay respect to Ellen's first husband, George Rockwell. With Wendell Flewelling's support, the new memorial was erected in October 2010, and the original stone remnants were gently matched and buried in front of it. "George Rockwell" and his epitaph are inscribed on the front. Engraved on the back, are the names of his kin and "Erected by Dr. and Mrs. Charles E. McGowan in memory of the Baylis and Munro families."

I'll conclude this Rossville cross-border tale as I admire and show this stone that I picked up on Route 105, the lower road across George Rockwell's farm, where he walked in 1885. It's history in my hand!

BOOK III

FIREWOOD

*Age appears to be best in four things; old
wood best to burn, old wine to drink, old
friends to trust, and old authors to read.*
Sir Francis Bacon

Baylis Woodpile and Ronald, c.1923

Cousin Gwen Briggs Bradbury recently asked "Did you keep a diary?" My quick reply was "No." My conscience cut in saying "You've kept everything else." The farm custom of saving old hay wire, nails, and string has evolved into my trait and obsession to save the whole shebang! I told Gwen that I had a "Woodpile" of the goings-on in and around the Baylis farm, and that I had accumulated a lot of "Firewood" from cross-border travel.

Among samplings of gathered firewood, I inherited family pictures from my mother, and fortunately saved prints of my childhood and youth. Photos from New Brunswick were given to me by cousins Ella and Alton. I look at them and compare the facial and physical features of a long-gone family member to more recent photographs. My mother had a close resemblance to that of her aunt Lucy Baylis Fox in Maine. A few of my children have some of the freckle-face features of Uncle Ronald and my mother. Red-hair genes have resurfaced in my cousin Brenda Baylis Nicholson, and my grandson Ted Donahue.

In my childhood and teenage years, adults rarely disclosed their personal past or showed emotions in front of children. However, I do know two things about my great grandmother Annie Munro Rockwell Baylis. The spinning wheel that I have was said to be hers, and I was told that she sometimes smoked a pipe!

Charles & Cousins Ella Stairs and Alton McElwain

What will I be remembered by? Close friend, Joanne Moynihan, called me, "A Chatty Mick." Another acquaintance told Laurie that I'd "Talk to a telephone pole." No question, I'll talk with anyone who'll listen, and try to listen to anyone who talks (as best I can...I'm deaf as a doornail). Laurie says that she should write a book on the way that I interpret things that she tells me. Yarns, accurate or not, are best told around a cozy camp stove filled with firewood. Here is my first armful.

CHAPTER ONE
MY KIND OF KINDLING

Dr. George F. Clarke was the first author to kindle my fondness for the New Brunswick out-of-doors, and he continues to be an inspiration in writing and lifestyle. He was a humanitarian at heart in health care, conservation, and respect for his fellow man. In 1964, I wrote him a letter of appreciation and included a donation to help the struggle against the Mactaquac project. At age 81, he courteously took the time to pen, in long hand, a three page reply on December 2, 1964. Up and awake at four a.m. from disabling arthritic knee pain, he was openly upset about the impact of the dam, so much so, that he put aside writing another book about rivers. He said that "Cullerton, Nackawick, and Pokiok would be under water should the dam be built." He went on to say that he told a visiting fisherman that "the books are not all about catching fish." The man replied "That's what charmed me: you brought the rivers right into my room," and said that he'd read *The Song of the Reel* eight times. I often think of the last sentence in the letter: "In the meantime and for all time may the good God bless and keep you all [my family] in good health."

Upon meeting genealogist, Rose Bradley Staples, for the first time about four years ago, I didn't realize that we had so many mutual family and community links. Taken from her grandmother Edna Jane Bradley, and Aunt Ann, and Aunt Jen's old scrapbooks, she often sends newspaper clipping copies of bygone local news that I can use in my tales. It's incredibly easy for Rose and me to communicate electronically with my inquiries and her replies. Her kindling keeps my fire burning.

I seriously required the aid of a professional writer who could relate to the sense of place, event, and personality that I portray in *Cross-Border Tales*. In the 36 years that I practiced oral surgery, accurate documentation of patient data has been my forte. The summary of chief complaint, history of present illness, past medical history, social history, list of medications, and review of systems told a story…

Holman Day Book,
My Student Award
from Elizabeth Peavey

but certainly not a tale. My found friend is Elizabeth Peavey of Portland, Maine-of-course! Her attributes are a logger's "Peavey" in name and know-how. Born and bred in Bath, she's transitioned in travel and returned to stay put (no, not always) in Maine with fervent commitments to writing, teaching, performing, fun, friends, and marriage.

In *Maine and Me*, the cover shows her under a vintage "Welcome to Maine" sign, sitting on a travel trunk under fir trees, while wearing a red and black mackinaw. With one hand on her chin, and looking mischievous, guess what the other hand holds? A peavey, obviously! I found *Glorious Slow Going* at the Portland Museum of Art store. In it, Elizabeth combines travel and friendship tales with the western Maine paintings of Marguerite Robichaux. After reading Elizabeth's articles in *Down East* magazine, I knew that her expertise and interests matched my quest. After chasing her by phone, I proposed by mail. When I sent additional manuscript, she accepted my pitch. We trade my drafts and her critiques by snail and e-mail and occasionally discuss progress on comfortable Marriott bar-lounge settees in Portland. When daughter Mary drove us up one day, she was Elizabeth's first sample of our young-uns. Vivacious Elizabeth and shining Mary hit it off right away.

After a year of tutoring, Elizabeth flattered me with a copy of *King Spruce* by Holman F. Day, 1908, the cover flanked by two peaveys.

The Honor Student
Just a little something to add to your logging library.
From your North Woods pal, ep.

Three hundred miles north of that congratulatory send-off in Portland, I was suddenly stymied at Harriet Irving Library on the University of New Brunswick grounds, but walked away fulfilled. Wasn't it just yesterday when I was a student or strolled across a college campus with my kids? In the cafeteria, a sudden sense of age disparity hit me hard! It didn't seem to faze any of the students around me who were taking breaks between classes. Maybe they assumed that I was some sort of an entitled emeritus who continues to poke around the maze of research stacks. I adjusted to, and actually enjoyed, the status of a student collecting my kind of kindling.

CHAPTER TWO
CHUNKS THAT FEED MY FANCY

Countrified poetry, music, and art are my choice chunks of firewood. Douglas Malloch's 1917 published poem, "When the Drive Goes Down," sparks my imagination. It's about river men full of pride in the bravado and busker of their trade. Let's grab a pike pole, jump in a bateau, and listen to them boast!

> There's folks that like the good dry land, and folks that like the
>> sea,
> But rock 'an river, shoal 'an sand, are good enough for me.
> There's folks that like the ocean crest, 'an folks that like the
>> town—
> But when I really feel the best is when the drive goes down.
>
> So pole away you river rats from landin' down to lake—
> There's miles of pine to keep in line, a hundred jams to break!

For the past 70 years, the music of the Maritimes has been a pleasure that I inherited from my folks. At home in Massachusetts, station WWVA in Wheeling, West Virginia had the best of country music. On Saturday nights in Canada, the Baylis farm radio was always tuned in to station CFCY in Charlottetown, Prince Edward Island, to listen to Don Messer and his Islanders. Presently, I listen to John Valentine Devine's 1912 "The Badger Drive" on CD. It's a foot tapping Newfoundland ballad. Here's a sample of the lyrics.

> There is one class of men in this country that never is mentioned
>> in song.
> And now since their trade is advancing, they'll come out on
>> top before long.

They say that our sailors have danger, and likewise our
    warriors bold,
There's none know the life of a driver, what he suffers in
    hardship and cold.

With their pike poles and peavies and bateaus and all
And they're sure to drive out in the spring, that's the time;
With their caulks on their boots as they get on the logs,
And it's hard to get over their time.

I've talked about Charlie Chamberlain of Don Messer's Islanders, cowboy singers Wilf Carter and Hank Snow, and Aroostook's
Dick Curless. Lately, my favorite songs are Roger Miller's "King of the
Road" and Arlo Guthrie's "City of New Orleans," when played by Joe
Sutton and Friends band from Woods Hole. Joe plays acoustic guitar
and does baritone vocals. Rusty Strange self-crafted his eight-string
steel guitar. Tom Renshaw fingers his big bass strings. Ted Fill picks
the four-string banjo and sings. John Ferreira perfectly plucks his
yellow electric guitar, and Mark Fuller bows the fiddle with fervor.
Each adds style to group harmony. They smile when I suggest that a
National Geographic photographer should film the venue, and laugh
when I request "I'll Never Smoke Weed with Willie Again." Laurie and
I agree that a caricature of each band member would be delightful.

In another venue, we've seen Bill Staines on stage at the Woods
Hole Community Hall. Since I've heard him sing "Walker Behind the
Wheel," I've called our daughter, Laurie Ann, in Fredricksburg, Texas.
I always sense a smile on her face when I warble:

Do the bluebonnets carpet the fields in the spring?
Does the Brazos still run to the sea?
Does the sun still shine down on those Texas girls?
Once one, gave her love to me."

With YouTube on full screen, I can't get enough of Merle Hag-
gard singing "When My Blue Moon Turns to Gold Again" with
Janie Frickie, or Willy Nelson doing "Blue Eyes Crying in the Rain"
with Shania Twain. When Emmylou Harris and the Cheiftans do
"Nobody's Darling But Mine," Laurie and I think that the song is

dedicated to us. Laurie usually asks the pianist at the Silver Lounge restaurant in North Falmouth to play her favorite, "September Song."

Thanks to our Saab's CD player, music travels with us. Laurie favors Kate Wolf doing "Give Yourself to Love" and Judy Collins Colorado classic, "The Blizzard." My current Atlantic Canada favorites are Stan Roger's renditions of the "Badger Drive," "Northwest Passage," and "Cliffs of Baccalieu." We carry enough Maritime Canada and Downeast discs to fill a shoebox.

In tune with our "Pleasin' to the eye" standard, painting, illustration, art-form, and sculpture are chunks of firewood that warm us up. I proudly remind you that Laurie's Trout Brook watercolor, hanging in my den and on the cover, is my favorite painting. Her watercolor teacher, Arthur Corsini, Professor of Painting at Mass. College of Art, commended the pièce de résistance. That same year, she did another watercolor of deserted St. Dominic Church in Allandale. We lost the art but found the dedication page photo. Go back to that page for a moment. Note Laurie's liquid refreshment, Moosehead Pale Ale, I think!

I've found two artists whose illustrations match the honest-to-goodness rudiments of Maine and Maritime logging. Oliver Kemp, 1887–1934, a *Saturday Evening Post* illustrator, did six illustrations in color for Malloch's *Tote-Road and Trail*. In the truest of logging tradition, each title speaks for itself: "It's chuck in the day and a bunk in the night," "While us poor skates in regions cool go out an' make his money," "An' ev'ry time you turn a bend the next bend looks the best," "For there are the woods to people, and there is the trail to make," "I'd like to just come walkin' in an' find you all a-settin' here," and "Worked a peavey, pulled a saw, rode the river in a thaw." Four of them are in Book II.

The next painter and illustrator is Rev. Randolph Hubert Nicholson, 1909-1989, a son of the Upper River Valley between Woodstock and Meductic. His paintings bring to mind the writings of Ruth Winona Grant. Randolph and Ruth were of like age, lived locally, and each accurately recorded history. Jean Elizabeth S. Irving's 1982 *R. H. Nicholson, Painter and Man of God* has pages of paintings and drawings inspired by his life's farm, woods, and ministry experience.

I treasure paintings by Rev. Nicholson's nephew, Arnold Cowper of Woodstock who told me that he watched his uncle paint. Laurie bought three of Arnold's landscapes for me over the past 23 years. I titled two "Shogomoc Stream in Fall Foliage" and "Trout Fisherman with a Rise on a Beaver-pond." He titled the last purchase "Deep in the Woods," a scene on the cross-border Maliseet Trail, called the "Old Trail," from the St. John to the Penobscot.

Cast bronze sculptures exist, side by side, that epitomize two sports celebrities zeal for hunting and fishing in New Brunswick. At the entrance to the National Baseball Hall of Fame in Cooperstown, New York, Babe Ruth and Ted Williams are at bat!

At the Bangor Public Library, near the Penobscot River "Turnpike" for log drives, I've seen a sculpture entitled "The Last Drive." It's a granite-base Charles Eugene Tefft bronze casting of three drivers using an axe, a cant dog, and a peavey breaking a log-jam. Cross-border in Saint-Leonard, New Brunswick, J.D. Irving Ltd.'s Forestry Division erected a granite monument to river driving. It's an etching of four rivermen guiding logs with pike poles in a traditional bateau. Remember, Nackawic has the world's largest axe sculpture!

CHAPTER THREE

FROLICS IN THE FIREBOX

I find entertainment in the show-of-lights wood-stove firebox. Once a scratched match head ignites dry cedar, the snappy crackle of kindling at peak performance nourishes its hardwood audience.

Ever since Uncle George took me to the Harvey Fair in New Brunswick a long time ago, country fairs have been one of my favorite treats. When our kids were young, we always went to the Sandwich Fair in New Hampshire. It was a one-day event that always fell on the 12th of October. Laurie and I favored gentle oxen or spirited horse pulling competitions. We saw that teamsters too, can be gentle or spirited. Most gave quiet commands to the teams, and a few hollered, jumped around, and feverishly snapped a whip. My Maine delight is the Fryeburg Fair Woodsmen Field Day. Ready-for-action loggers, root for their sturdy womenfolk who compete in skillet and axe throwing. Chopping contests on terra firma and on narrow springboard slats wedged into an upright pole, have chips flying and contestants sweating.

Sit-down entertainment, at a fair or a feed is having a "Charge" where bean-hole-beans are baked. That tin plate "Friend-of-the-cook" staple of camps and river-drives still survives where country folks celebrate the ritual. Expressed in downright Downeast, Robert E. Pike in his *Tall Trees, Tough Men* said: "There is nothing better in God's sweet world, when it [bean-hole-beans] is cooked right." From my point of view, eateries and oven cookin' can do a good job, but beans baked in the ground and 'et at long supper tables are special actuals. "Fixin's" that usually accompany the beans, are coleslaw, ham, red hot dogs, relish or ketchup, fresh rolls, real boiled tea or coffee, and…pie!

An anecdote as garden-grown as the beans is John McDonald's famous gag of three hungry coastal fishermen sitting at Moody's Diner counter in Waldoboro, and the genteel old couple seated behind them. It was an explosive scene. When the proper old man confronted a fisherman about breaking wind "Before my wife," the reply was "If I knowed it was her turn, I'd let her go first."

In Boston, "You don't know BEANS till you've 'bean` to BOSTON" is a cartoon claim. Up north, your credibility is at stake if you are accused of "Being full of beans." Anyone in Portland who has been around since 1920, know the baked bean aroma wafting from the Burnham and Morrill plant stacks. I wonder why we got away from buying B& M brown bread that was served with beans and hot dogs. Laurie steamed it, and we lathered the slices with butter. Yum!

A glowing chunk of firewood is the accent, dialect, or whatever you want to call the way a word or phrase is spoken in a particular place. I'll limit my interpretations to those that I've been accustomed to hear along the northeast coastal region from Newfoundland to Cape Cod. A Newfie song, "Salt Water Cowboys" that I heard, hits the nail on the head:

By da Lord dyin', By da tunder and Gee,
How are ya doin' ya son-of-a-B?
Ya can't fool your old man by dressin' like dat,
Yer still just a Newfie in a Calgary Hat.

Some native New Brunswickers have what Dad called a "Twang." It is unhurried and clearly articulated. The "Rs" are particularly distinct, as in calling me "ChaRles." However, I can't recall hearing the Canadian "Eh," said around York or Carleton counties.

Coastal Maine dialect is a unique birthright. You'll hear "Bahth," with a wide-open mouth, in Bath, Maine. In Brahmin Boston, a tub-soak (said closed-mouthed) is a "Bahth." "Grahssin'" in Maine differs from idling on the "Grahss" at Boston Common. Of course, one place has boats and Iron Works on the Kennebec and the other has chandeliers and paneled libraries on Beacon Hill.

Downeast diction is often best heard around the docks. Not taught by William Strunk and E. B. White's 1959 writer instruction book, *The Elements of Style*, the guideline of "Omit needless words" rings true here! It's a no-time-wasted choice of words spoken forthrightly, ample though brief, and paced according to need, like "You got it," the fast answer to a request.

Now and then, from Maine to Cape Cod, a Toyota is a "Toyoter", and Boston's beloved Mayor Menino is "MAY-ah." My Falmouth friend, Darryl, whose son took tuba lessons, quotes a lady as saying "That's sup-ah that Andy is playing the tuber."

Disappearing, but occasionally heard from Maine male elders is "DEE-ah." It can begin or end an eye-to-eye affirmative sentence: "Let me tell you, DEE-ah." or "Enough, DEE-ah!" It is also the 240-pound ten-pointer shot up in Sebec. As big as that "Dee-ah's" antlers were, no sane Mainer would say "Horny"…except…if the deceased was said to be runnin' around in rut! For "Dee-ah" in Newfoundland (an endearment, where there are no deer), they fondly throw in "Me old trout," "Me love," or "Me ducky." Don't try them Downeast, because you're apt to get slapped, snookered, or find yourself swimmin'!

Our "Dee-ah" old friend, Captain Elliot Allen Billings, at almost 99, never lost the native tongue. Born in 1912 near Baxter Boulevard in Portland, he took off, literally and figuratively. As a commercial and military pilot, he flew Sikorsky, Martin, and Boeing PANAM "Clipper" flying boats during the '30s and early '40s through Cuba to South America and across both oceans. As a Marine pilot in WWII with transatlantic experience, he ferried propeller-driven planes overseas for the Air Force Air Transport Command. On stopovers in Iceland, he said that the government would not allow servicemen to mingle with Icelandic girls in hopes of safeguarding their blonde beauties. Returning to commercial aviation, his last command was flying Boeing 747 jets. Elliot lived all over, except Maine, between 1936 and 1972 while he was with PANAM and the military.

He told me of piloting an amphibian with Ernest Hemingway and "Hammered" friends aboard. They would reach forward and mischievously fool with the trim wheel between the pilots, slightly disrupting a level flight path. Encyclopedic in story-telling, he remained Maine coast Yankee as did his accent. He was always USMC "Shaap" with spit-polished shoes, a quick step, bright eyes, and a crew haircut. There was no dilly-dallying with Elliot in perception, query, advice, or memory! He'd say: "My brother was the smartest of all to never leave Maine" or, when I told him that I spotted a guy stealing lobsters from my Buzzards Bay traps on a foggy day, Elliot counseled, "Shoot him!"

Christmas arrived early last year with a present from Elliot and Priscilla's son, George, with a note reading: "In my continuing excavations of Pop's and Mom's prodigious accumulations, I unearthed this guide from 1937. I can think of no one better to appreciate and enjoy it more than you! George, 12/18/12." *Maine, A Guide 'Down East', by Workers of the Federal Writer's project of the Works Progress Administration for the State of Maine* has 476 pages describing where-to-go, how-to-go, and what-to-see-and-do. Among Maine gems, an off-coast tour of Monhegan Island goes like this: "alt. 40, Plantation pop. 109, has three summer hotels"...etc., "All summer long, fishing smacks unload cargoes of green lobsters along the waterfront. 'Cheap-livin' fish, lobsters are [explained an old fisherman]. Kin eat barnacles, seaweed, mud, anything. Even live in the well of a smack five or six months an' come out all right, less they chaw each other up, an' they're mostly doin' that. Don't seem to hurt much, though. I've found lots o' claws broke off in fights, an' they grow back just as good agin.'"

George also dropped off *The Maine Atlas and Gazetteer* by Delorme on which Elliot wrote "15 Aug. 89, Billings." To bear out my memory for Maine yarn and place accuracy, I pick a location and jump to the Billings gift book index or map page, and hope that my recollections of three quarters of a century ago are true!

CHAPTER FOUR
TINDER TALK

63 Woodside Road, Winchester, MA, 2013

This is a "Local News" kind of commentary, and I'm the columnist. My tinder (and tender) typo deals with what's going on "Around town" and in my mind. I'll start with items from the archives, update tales, report new stuff, and fling out a philosophy or two. Thanks for being a subscriber to this sequence of events.

Laurie and I tenderly speak of our parents, Larry and Ella Louis, and Charlie and Lucy McGowan and all that they gave us. Pictures are fond reminders. If we're near Holyhood Cemetery in Brookline or Woburn's Calvary Cemetery, we pay a quick visit. Either we, or one of our children, place Memorial Day flowers on their graves. Otis Cemetery holds the same sentiment when we're in New Brunswick.

I can't go any further without telling you that Laurie often says that she fortunately has had three mothers. Her birth mother was Phyllis Reilly, a nurse supervisor at Falkner Hospital, and the name of her father is speculative. Phyllis was a patient of Dr. Louis who delivered Laurie at Phyllis' home on Thaxter Street in Hingham, Massachusetts. She offered the child to him and Mrs. Louis who had no offspring. They accepted, took Laurie home in a basket, and adopted her as born in Newton, Mass., where they lived at 1515 Center Street. Ella became her second and forever real mother. Six months after that, Loretta Putnam came to work in the household. She too lovingly mothered Laurie, and was looked upon as another grandmother to our children. From my perspective, that's why Laurie is so precious.

I seldom walk into a post office without proudly recalling Dad's letter-carrier service.

There are other reminders of Dad in Winchester. There wasn't rentable power masonry equipment in 1931 like we have today for those who choose to "Do-it-yourself," but his cement and stone wall still stands solid. His blue spruce, planted in the 1930s, is now a 60 foot giant, and the front yard maple that had a three-inch trunk, now measures to more than a foot in diameter. Go back to "The Beginning"

24 Lake Avenue, Woburn, MA, 2007

chapter for comparison. While Dad's landscape trees are lofty, my hair and my height are short. We occasionally drive past that home, as well as the last nine (Can't believe it!) that Laurie and I have owned…so far.

The Lake Avenue, Woburn, home, where Dad, Mother, and I lived with my grandparents, had what we called a cupola, a Victorian roof-top structure with windows on four sides. As kids, we were thrilled to climb up there with a ladder from the attic. We would often open a win-dow and sneak out onto the roof. Here's how a house can change after 80 years in contrast to the 1920s photo on page 26. In the late '40s and early '50s there was only one bathroom with a tub on the second floor.

Cousin Frank Murphy, Jr., who I was close to growing up, went on to work for the *Boston Post* and then, after U.S. Army service, had a career with the *Baltimore Sun*. I was the best man at his wedding. Flying, as a private pilot and instructor, was his passion. His daughter, Lynne, became an officer in the Military Police, married Doug Lam, has a son Ryan, and is retired. She still is a military criminal investiga-tor in Washington State.

I have a 1956 U.S.N.R. Commissioned Officer's Mess card from the Boston Naval Shipyard with expiration marked "Indefinite." The Navy is long gone from Boston Harbor (except for USS *Constitution* and WWII destroyer USS *Cassin Young*), but though discharged in 1958, I have the *official card* to drink and to dine there indefinitely! It's archived with my photo as a commissioned USNR Ensign at Tufts Dental in 1954, and my Selective Service (draft) registration and clas-sification cards. Those, the birth certificate from Woburn City Hall, and my Social Security (now good for a monthly deposit!) card once resided in a strong box or in wallet slots now occupied by credit, health, license, and travel IDs.

Boston City Hospital (BCH), where I spent three years of spe-cialty training up to 1961, was the first municipal hospital in the U.S. As an intern, my room was in the old South Department build-ing where patients with tuberculosis were housed, and where there had been an alarm that sounded when a child with influenza had an airway obstruction and needed a tracheotomy. BCH, combined with Boston University Schools of Medicine and Dental Medicine, comprise the present Boston Medical Center.

The Kennedy name kept emerging in our lives during courtship, marriage, until Dr. Louis died, and finally, forever after, as it has with our generation. Before JFK, and in succession, came his family. The Kennedy name echoes globally. I've told you about Dr. Louis filling us in with accounts of Boston medical history, and his tales carried over into the times of JFK's parents, Joseph P. Sr. and Rose Fitzgerald Kennedy. Anecdotal stories of Kennedy fortunes, misfortunes, foreign friendships, and faith came forth from what Dr. Louis absorbed from the '20s, '30s, '40s, and '50s. Robert Luddington of Jordan Marsh Company, Rose's interior decorator, helped Laurie and me choose furnishings for Bob's and my Lowell office. The Kennedy reality came

Me at Tufts Dental in 1954 as Ensign, USNR, My Service Cards

closer when our Chelmsford neighbor, friend, and dentist L. Rodger Currie and his wife Pat, were Kennedy Compound neighbors in Hyannis Port. Our Mary Ann's baptism coincided with JFK's burial. In the '60s, Rodger invited local dentists, and sometimes wives, to Hyannis Port to relax, play cards, and/or play golf. I was introduced to Ann Gargan, a Kennedy cousin from Lowell, who was intimately involved with Joe and Rose' care as they aged. Laurie, I, and friends were hosted on the iconic motor yacht "Marlin" that was known from homeport Hyannis Port, to West Palm Beach. It was captained by friendly, sea-seasoned Frank Wirtanen who, I observed, casually accepted guests as they came and did his job. I told you about our Hyannis Port vacation rental, seeing Ted Kennedy, Jr. standing, or Pierre Salinger walking, alone with their thoughts, Laurie's acquisition of Jackie O's Sunfish, and Chris Currie's horrific plane crash. When John Kennedy Jr.'s body was being brought into Woods Hole from another aircraft tragedy on July 21, 1999, I happened to be alone on my "Lan Mara" in Woods Hole Passage. With a multitude of photographers lining the roadways, a solemn, dignified respect prevailed on the water and at Station Woods Hole. An escorting Coast Guard boat asked me to temporarily secure one of the channels from traffic. I turned on my strobe light and sat steady in mid-current. As Laurie and I visit her parent's grave in Holyhood Cemetery in Brookline, we say a silent prayer knowing that our ashes will be mixed and lie there in repose. Neighbors (under Elliot Billings' "Turf Blankets") will be the Senior Kennedys, offspring, and grandchildren. If things go right, and our kids carry out our wishes, other vials will hit the wind and water along the New England coastline and sacred soil up into Downeast New Brunswick.

Rossville-raised Harold Davidson and wife, Loverine, reared their family at Temple, on the St. John River. They worked together in the auto repair and trade business. He did the repair, and she was a sharp trader. Harold's sister Myrtle married Neil V. Grant. Laurie and I vividly recall Myrtle's impeccable housekeeping on a visit to their home in Temple. Neil served in the army and fought in Normandy at the same time as Myrtle's step-brother, William. They relocated to Moncton in 1962. Neil worked on the railroad and has since passed away. Myrtle worked as a cardiology technician at Moncton Hospital. In the autumn of 1998, Laurie and I went with Harold and Loverine to see Daisy, his mother, in a rest home. Though in her late nineties, Daisy recognized us. It was like old times again at their farm. She passed away on Christmas Day, 2000.

In June of 2002, we attended the Genesis Fund fishing tournament at Martha's Vineyard with John Reichheld, and I was a Mate on his boat. At a benefit auction for their Child Development program, I bid on and won the ABC Private Studio Tour for two to be hosted by the network medical director, Dr. Tim Johnson. A week before leaving for November hunting in New Brunswick, we flew to New York City. That evening, Dr. Johnson brought us to meet Peter Jennings on the set of *World News Tonight*. Peter introduced us to Michelle, the production coordinator, who made us feel welcome and relaxed. We were the only audience in the studio. Familiar with Peter's Canadian nationality, we talked about his upbringing in Ottawa, his farm retreat in Quebec, and our connections to New Brunswick. He teased Dr. Tim about his neckties, took his own off, and handed it to Tim. Dr. Johnson had a full plate of programming to prepare for the next morning on *Good Morning America*, and he asked me if I might make a few comments thinking, for some reason, that I was an obstetrician. I forthrightly said that I only delivered impacted third molars or stones from salivary glands! He left us off at a marvelous Italian restaurant near North Central Park.

Up early the next morning for a waiting ABC limo, we drove to the Times Square studio. In the make-up room prior to the feature entitled "Baby, Oh, Baby," we sat and chatted with host Charlie Gibson and Dr. Tim. Once again, we were the only spectators on site and sat up front on folding chairs among a maze of cables, suspended lighting, and mobile camera units. An exceptionally attentive production staff directed the show. It featured impending births in San Francisco, Cleveland, and Falls Church, Virginia with Dr. Nancy Snyderman, Elizabeth Vargas, and Claire Shipman as roving reporters. In addition to Charlie Gibson and Diane Sawyer on a section of the set, an incredible group of TV celebrities, as I remember it, acted in sync: Joel Siegal, Robin Roberts, Cynthia McFadden, and Tony Perkins.

We spoke with co-host Diane Sawyer about her home on Martha's Vineyard at Tashmoo, where we often fished and cruised. She referred to it as "Across the Pond" from Woods Hole. Diane, her hairdresser Vincent, and set staffer Ed Harding (now host on Boston Channel Five) were friendly and made things easy for us. Vincent said "I know Diane better than her mother does." Ed was concerned about his sick dog that was going to the vet in the Boston area. We rode the elevator with George Stephanopoulos and with Lara Spencer, who was attentive to the beautiful infant in her arms.

Mind-boggling were those precise November six and seven, 2002 *second-by-second* program sheets which we had in hand (and still have). The whole experience made for wild tales to be told when we came north to New Brunswick that fall.

In 2003 while in Fredericton, I visited Arthur Ingraham in the York Manor nursing home. Seeing one another and talking about old times, gave me the feeling that we were boys again. His wife, Donna, died three years prior. With George Ingraham's sudden passing in 1962, my times with Arthur and Harold Davidson (who died in January, 2002) lasted longer. In 2004, my silent togetherness with Arthur was at his bedside in Dr. Everett Chalmers Hospital. He was unaware of my presence. Laurie and I had to leave for home, and I paid Arthur a final farewell at Flewelling Funeral Home in Otis. The Ingraham family said that my letter of consolation was read at his service. George, Arthur, and Harold's friendship stays inside me.

When my Katahdin climbing friend, Francis T. "Frank" Lawton died, his obituary read, "A true gentleman, Frank had a huge heart and helped many people during his lifetime. He will leave behind a legacy of hard work, dedication, friendship, and love." His youth was that way. My junior high school friends and Old Scouts, Jim "Red" McLaughlin and Art "Junior" McGonagle still sound the same on the telephone. When we get together with a cocktail, I can still croon my Boy Scout "Fellsland, Camp Fellsland, On the Pow-wow River Shore!" None of us kept our 1949 graduation picture pompadour hairstyles. We look forward to seeing Nancy O'Rourke Martin whose aunt, Annette Mulhern, was a student nurse classmate and longtime friend of Laurie's mother. At my 50th reunion, classmates Peter Kirwan and "Joe" Stover Donnell told me first-hand stories about my parents. Pete said that he remembered my mother as maybe from Scotland with

*Robert Vernon
"Bobby" Lowe, c.1939*

red hair, and always fun to talk to. When Dad was delivering mail to the Donnell home, Stover's pet squirrel ran up Dad's pant leg! Like Dad in uniform, Stover wore one as the admiral in command of the U.S. Navy Atlantic Fleet. Paul "Pete" Dillingham, who usually attends, was an admiral in naval intelligence. He now enjoys driving his John Deere tractor in Maryland. I attended my 60th high school reunion in 2009, appreciate the lasting lifeline of Winchester, Massachusetts friends, and look forward to a 65th reunion in 2014.

Reunions and obituaries resound with forgotten and new facts that capture lifetimes. After the most recent Winchester gathering, Dick Richmond and I had a long phone conversation that just wasn't possible among those of us in aged ecstasy and cocktail euphoria. We had been acquaintances, but not buddy-buddy. I never knew that Mr. Bob Keeney, a favorite teacher was Dick's uncle, that Richmond and Ann were his cousins who grew up in my neighborhood, and that Mrs. Keeney taught math at Newton High School. He reminded me that Mr. Keeney called all of us boys "George." Dick commented that I was always "Well met, with a smile." That took me back! It never occurred to me that my happiness flew like a flag.

The Winter Ponds in Winchester were playgrounds for a familiar few that followed my generation. Alison Hersey Risch name is in the U.S. Field Hockey and Lacrosse Halls of Fame. We knew Captain Richard Phillips' parents, Jim and Virginia, when they lived on Woodside Road long before he was captured by Somali pirates and freed by Navy Seals in 2009. Dr. Stephen B. Murphy, who performed Laurie's 2011 hip replacement, is forever from Winchester, but occasionally stays on an island in Maine. Dr. Murphy developed a unique computerized surgical navigation system to enable minimally invasive hip surgery, and provide pre and intra-operative measurements, thus affording Laurie, a more rapid, uneventful, and less painful recovery.

I've minimal hip or knee dysfunction, but there's not much trail hiking in my future, so I thrive on a recollection of those that I've taken. Route 1 was my auto trail (and parts still are) prior to the turnpike era. Admittedly, I never got to uppermost Fort Kent (Paula's going there snowmobiling), but I went with Chip, Charlie, and Matt McGowan to Key West in 2009, to celebrate Chip's 50th birthday. While standing under a sign that marked southernmost Route 1, I looked north and, for the moment, was lost in magnetic melancholy.

During a visit to Larry and Layton Ford's Brown Lake Allandale, New Brunswick camp in 2010, we chatted about Bobby Lowe, the legendary woodsman. I've told about Uncle George taking me to meet him when I was 14 at his camp on the other side of the lake. Layton gave me a photo of a bear on Bobby's back with the write-up that said the bear was alive. Bobby, cheek to cheek with the bear, appears unfazed with a long-stem pipe clenched in his mouth. All of that and high-laced leather boots suggest that he was a time-honored story-teller-guide. In any case, the bear was said to be real. It's one of my favorite photos. Layton kindly sent me a copy of the hand written obituary of Bobby Lowe's 1968 death at age 89.

I'm reminded of climbing Katahdin, as often happens, 12 years after the celebrated survival of Donn Fendler in 1939. I've acquired, and reminisced over copies of Donn's 1978, *Lost on a Mountain in Maine*, and his 2011 sequel, *Lost Trail*. There may be a movie version of the latter. Stephen King reviewed *Lost Trail* as a "Terrifying and uplifting story of survival in a format that will introduce it to a whole new generation of readers. Here's a graphic novel about a real American superhero." It's different and done in comic book style throughout, just like the comic strip escapades that I enjoyed as a boy.

Among good and bad "Local News," I'll relate the bad news first. Though the Mactaquac Dam turbines produce one-fifth of New Brunswick electric power, and the head pond is hosting more and more bass fishing, boating, and sailing, the concrete integrity is deteriorating. The predicted life-span expectancy has been reduced by 40 years. Dr. George Frederick Clarke's spirit of resistance to the dam, in the sense of aboriginal sites, homesteads, and hamlets lost, haunts its presence.

I followed the triumphs and troubles of woodland economy during the St. Anne-Nackawic Pulp and Paper Mill Company existence. It began operations in 1970 with impressive benefit to the area and collapsed in 2004. With little or no notice, my friends, who were employees, lost their jobs and hard-earned pension. A 1,000 plus millworker protest was held in September, 2004 at the World's Largest Axe in Nackawic. Reopened in 2006 as AV Nackawic, the Aditya Birla Group textile company from India successfully put into operation a process for producing rayon fabric using cellulose fibre from native hardwood. One of my friends, Larry Ford, recovered part of his pension and returned to the mill as a supervisor.

Among five items of good news, the first is that Dr. Mary Ann Bramstrup is carrying on her father, Dr. Peter's, medical practice in Nackawic. More good news comes from Cousin Joyce Jones who says that there is talk of a second edition of *Nackawic Bend*, one of my best historical resources. I've two copies, and both are well worn. Published twenty-eight years ago in 1985, it has 17 pages of Munro descendants. Most descendants still live in New Brunswick. Near the water's edge in 2007, the Nackawic Waterfront Development Committee placed the engineering steel plaque from the demolished and original Hawkshaw

Bridge as a historic monument. Before the Mactaquac flooding, it served generations for 60 years. My next cheery update is from Gwen Bradbury. She sent a Christmas photo of McAdam Station where the village people do a great job decorating the first floor, and others are working to open the hotel rooms on the second and third floors. When driving through, I see 285 feet of restored Chateau-style railway station and former hotel, unhurried, sitting proud, but solitary. Tourism and function facilities hopefully can keep it active and open. Rail traffic may someday return. It's good to see the hustle and bustle return from the days when Claire Bean, my mother, and so many Atlantic Canada folks passed through there on their way to New England and came home again for visits! My last good news item is that Bill Miller will retrieve one of the early canoes that he made about 30 years ago in Nictau, New Brunswick, from the estate of Mary Buckley here in Woods Hole by Mary's wishes. Only in the water about four times, it will glorify Bill's shop back home beside the Tobique River.

From settlement surnames carried to the present, I recognized some at the 39th "Festival on the Bend" last August. Valley beauty and flair are not confined to farm and forest. The 2011 and 2012 winners

Shogomoc Stream by Arnold Cowper

of Miss New Brunswick Pageant at Woodstock Old Home Week were Chelsea Grant and Kaitlynn Bragdon, both from Nackawic!

I frequently bring Rossville up on satellite earth search sites or GeoNB and reflect on the cedar-fence parcels of the past. I trace Trout Brook and then look up at Laurie's watercolor of my trout pool. Trout Brook was not always tranquil. Other than being subject to the fury of spring freshets, a 1970 Woodstock *Sentinel Press* article showed an early 1900s photo of Eddie Woodman's sizeable and active lumber mill complex. When built in 1897, only Trout Brook water supplied the power to saw long-logs. Possibly Ross Woodman used that lumber when he built the Baylis home after the first farmhouse burned. When steam power came in 1910, they sawed lumber, lath, and shingles. The Woodman brothers also ran a water power carding mill for sheep wool on the opposite side of the brook. Travelers on Rossville Road would have full view of the operation until it closed in 1925.

Among many keepsakes in my den, is a panoramic photo of Mt. Katahdin, where gazing eastward, I viewed cross-border New Brunswick. An autumn foliage oil painting by Arnold Cowper, has a vivid reproduction of the furrows of Shogomoc whitewater rushing in rocky descent. In the distance, a metallic silver barn roof (a landmark

McGowan Family, 2009

for my hunter's eye) is prominent among blue sky, ridges, and autumn colors.

Almost daily website photos by Paul Cyr, from Aroostook County, are another way that I stay in touch with woods and wildlife, farm-fields and festivals, and barns and backbone. He did a classic photo of a full moon over Katahdin. Whether shot with a zoom lens from a tripod or from his powered parachute, the scope and variety keep me connected. Outside, I started flying the Maple Leaf flag with the ever present Stars and Stripes on July 1st, Canada Day. Now, they fly together year round.

My son-in-law, Jim Burbine, who has a collection of vintage 8N Ford tractors, brought the Way green game-carrier tractor down to Massachusetts. Remember, it transported my bear out of the Charlie Lake woods. The tractor is another family trophy brought cross-bor-der along with my bear rug, the Chestnut canoe, and Lottie Steeves' quilts. As said before, we've donated Lottie's "City of Saint John, 1985 Bicentennial Quilt" to the Carleton County Historical Society Con-nell House Museum in Woodstock, New Brunswick. Rightly so, it was superbly hand-sewn at her home in Hartland. I saved this prac-tical Canadian comment on quilts: "Bedrooms were not expected to be warm" and shared it with Myrtle Davidson Grant. She told a story of her quilt-making that Laurie would have pursued if known while "Trophy Hunting." Before she and Neil moved to Moncton in 1962, she was "Putting on quilts" (assembling the quilting frames and attaching the backing fabric). To date, she has an accurate record of 143 completed hand-quilted heirlooms. One, with panels of each Canadian provincial emblem, flag, and flower, was bought by the Boy Scouts in 1968 for a Jamboree in Australia. It hangs, proudly on dis-play in that continent.

I'll now reintroduce Bill Miller in the Tobique River settlement of Nictau above Riley Brook in northern New Brunswick. Bill is a first-rate canoe crafter, whom I've mentioned meeting while on a hunting trip. We "Paddle together" (by phone and mail) on the Tobique with stories of Leon L. Bean at Gulquac Lodge and local goings on. Bill established the annual "Fiddles on the Tobique" festival in 1994, with one fiddler and two canoes participating. June 2012, expected 1500 canoes, about 75 musicians, and over 6,500 people for the weekend. It rained a torrent, and hindered scheduled river activities. However, I heard that Bill Miller's place resounded with music. I'll bet that the Don Messer "Mouth of the Tobique" fiddle tune is played on site as it should be. Cousin Gwen Bradbury attests that the annual event is a sight and sound to behold, since she has paddled in that fiddling flotilla many times.

To celebrate our December 31, 1952 first and blind date with Jim and Peg McLaughlin, we've got together each New Years Eve with them and friends for 55 consecutive years. In their homes, ours, and restaurants up until the last few years, midnight was the magic hour of toasts and kisses!

This June 9, 2013 was Laurie and my 57th privileged wedding anniversary. Take a deep breath, because a long list of our family's "Who" and "Where" will hit you right between the eyes! Oldest daughter, Laurie Ann, was 56 in July. She, husband Dave Dionne, and children Lindsey, Cassie, Andrew, and Patrick plan to relocate from the Houston area and build a new home on the Cool Water Ranch in the Texas Hill Country at Fredericksburg. Next in line, Chip, his wife, Joanna, and sons, Charlie and Matt, live in Scituate, Massachusetts, when not in Harpswell, Maine. Jean, Jim, Jackie, and Kelley Burbine, also part-time in Harpswell, live in Westford, Massachusetts. So do Mary Ann Mulkern, husband Matt, and daughters, Shannon and Meaghan. Peg, John, Sarah, Jack, Kelan, and Maggie Mahan have a new home in Andover, Massachusetts. Larry, retired from 29 years in the Navy, lives in Chesapeake, Virginia, with wife, Nancy, her mother Selma, and daughter Lauren and her children, Courtney and William. Their youngest daughter, Nikki, is spending time in Germany with her Army brother, Larry Jr., and his Army wife, Nicole, and our third and fourth great grandchildren, Katelynn and Kristian. Beth and Len Jolles have homes in Framingham, Massachusetts and Newfound Lake, New Hampshire. Her children, Katie and Paul Throckmorton, live in Denver, Colorado. Christine, Paul, Ted, Ella, and Kiera Donahue live in Winchester, Massachusetts, my hometown. Paula and two daughters, Lily and Ruby Kondos, thrive in York, Maine, one of our stopovers on travels to or from Canada. Kate, Hilary, Meredith, Colby, and Charlotte Davis live near us in Falmouth. They're always around when we need them, they and watch over Barney, our beautiful, friend-to-all, Brittany. Every so often, Barney stays with Laurie and me for a sleep-over.

As our grandchildren grow, we hear good things about their participation in charitable events. Meaghan Mulkern travels to Gulfport, Mississippi, or Port Au Prince, Haiti with a church group that helps to restore storm-damaged lives. In summer, great grandchildren and other pre-teens enjoy swimming and the beach or just plain playing at home. A few teenagers get away for a week or two at camp (where, thank goodness, electronics are not allowed). Others have summer jobs at restaurants or golf clubs. I'm grateful to those who have helped me with my woods-garden project. Those in college subsidize their expenses and earn spending money by working more than one job. Young adult grandchildren are out in the workforce in their own apartments. We are very proud of Lindsey Dionne, our oldest grandchild, who graduated from the University of Houston, went on to earn her law degree at Thurgood Marshall School of Law, and passed the Texas Bar. She did it on her own while working for Starbucks Coffee Company.

Laurie and I hope that our children and their children can benefit from principles that worked well for us.

Do your best each day and enjoy life.
Be proud as "*Me,*" and coexist as "*We.*"
Say "*Please*" often, and "*Thank you*" always.
Giving, more than taking, enriches being.
Practice and teach spirituality.
Share as much as you can.
Take care of one another.
Stay healthy, delight in nature, and live long.

We wish them the wisdom to set aside time for free play and family. An excess of undertakings can mess up what's right for the individual or for the clan.

Our sons frequently travel across this continent and worldwide as easily as we take occasional trips across borders. Larry continues to use his naval expertise in the private sector of Naval Communication and Missile Defense in assignments from Hawaii to Europe. Chip is North American president of a global German zinc fabrication group. When he walked the game trails with me in Riley Brook, New Brunswick, little did we know that part of his corporate territory would be the whole of Canada! He regularly does business in Montreal, Toronto, Winnipeg, Vancouver, and occasionally travels to Mexico and Germany from Boston. He is my ambassador to Canada (I claim to be a Downeast diplomat). Chip encountered time consuming U.S. border security checks. He obtained Nexus and Global Traveler clearance cards by driving 350 miles up to Calais, Maine, since it took a long time to schedule an appointment in the Boston office. He stuck to my "I told you so" philosophy of "Go north young man!"

The idea of writing an account of my life has advanced to the point of completing the manuscript for publication. There is a force at work that helps me recall happenings from Cape Cod in Massachusetts to Rossville in New Brunswick, Canada, including Maine of course. As an example, I've been back on Katahdin paths reading *The Call of Katahdin, Life in Werler's Woods* by retired ranger Ed Werler, 2003 and *Chimney Pond Tales, Yarns Told by Leroy Dudley*, first printing in 1991. Remember, Ed Werler was the park ranger who signed Frank Lawton and me in at Roaring Brook campground in 1951. From our next camp at Chimney Pond, we climbed the trail named after Leroy Dudley, who told tall tales about episodes with Pamola, the phantom, playful, but sometimes ferocious mountain storm spirit. Roy was not shy about embellishing encounters with Pamola. Roy possibly read what a Penobscot tribe elder simply wrote in 1916: "Every mountain he got Injun in it...Katahdin...he man...Katahdin...he different... mountain once was man."

Ed Werler and Ralph Dolley (twice met on my hikes) were close friends in the woods-work days before they became rangers. Ralph was local, introducing the Connecticut Werlers to northern Maine plants and trees and to many couples in the area. From photos in Ed's book and the timeline described, Ralph and Ed couldn't have been too much older than me.

In his epilogue, Ed talks about being a Park Ranger Supervisor at Two Lights State Park in Cape Elizabeth, Maine. He received a phone call from a rescue crew at Katahdin, because a woman climber and Park Ranger Ralph Heath, who set out to find her, were lost in an October 29, 1963 horrendous snowstorm on the mountain. Ed coincidentally left to join the rescue team at about the same time that Chip and I were driving up past Katahdin to New Brunswick, because my mother had become ill. Mother returned with us, but the Park Service did not find the two bodies until spring.

After crossing the border in Houlton and travelling downriver toward Rossville, there's a great German food restaurant and motel not far below Woodstock named after John Gyles. The ten-year-old coast of Maine (Pemaquid) lad was kidnaped by marauding Maliseet Indians in 1689 and brought to their stockade in "Medoctec" (Meductic), New Brunswick where he lived among them for over six years. He was sold and indentured to Louis Damours at Jemseg until his release in 1698. He gave an account of his captivity, *Memoirs of Odd Adventures, Strange Deliverances, etc.* in 1736. It had a tale of a beautiful Indian maiden taken wife by a Spirit, "Gulloua," of the "White Hills," a hallowed peak that the Indians called "Teddon." He heard an Indian, who lived on the Penobscot River, talk about seeing Teddon through the smoke hole at the top of his tepee, making a climb, and because of spirits, would not go up it again. Teddon is the earliest published English reference to what we know as Mt. Katahdin.

I always enjoy learning more about Percival Baxter and Baxter Park. In 1931, when Dr. Kelleher was delivering me in Woburn, Mr. Baxter was delivering his gifted deed of 5,960 acres of Great Northern Paper Company land to the Department of Inland Fisheries and Game for its 90,000 acre game preserve that was established in 1921. Twenty-three thousand acres was his largest purchase, and 11 acres was the least. It took him 25 years to reach his goal of over 200,000 deeded acres. On November 30, 1941, the Portland Sunday *Telegram* quoted the words of Governor Percival Baxter:

> Man is born to die, his works are short lived. Buildings crumble,
> Monuments decay. Wealth vanishes but Katahdin in all its glory,
> Forever shall remain The Mountain of the People of Maine.
> Throught the ages it will stand as an inspiration to the men
>   and women of this State.

In discussions held between 1994 and 2002, there were private venture proposals to add a 1900 mile cross-border section to the Appalachian Trail (AT), extending to the tip of Newfoundland, and call it the International Appalachian Trail (IAT). The linking plan needed trail authorization from Baxter Peak, the terminus of AT, to the northern edge of the privately managed Baxter State Park. Governor Baxter's stipulation prevailed: the area "Forever shall be held its natural wild state." Not changing Baxter Park management or trail policy, the park's white trail marker signs did not become a white-rectangle, blue-border IAT marker, till outside the park limits. The continuity has worked out fine. Hikers hoping to cross the border had better not forget a passport at the Fort Fairfield, Maine, and the Perth/Andover, New Brunswick, border stations! The IAT logo in New Brunswick is combined with Sentier Internationale des Appalaches (SIA), and part of the trail passes along the Tobique River area up through Mt. Carleton Provincial Park before heading west toward Mt. Jacques Cartier in Quebec.

Transitioning from when Frank Lawton or Elmer Clark and I were the only climbers on Baxter Peak summit 62 years ago, Elizabeth Peavey describes a crowd scene in recent years, as a "Political rally."

O.K., though I've told you just about anything that I've done or know concerning Katahdin, I just got re-educated. Anyone who wants to touch "Ktaadn" in any way, shape, or form should read *Wildnotes, A Visitor's Guide to Baxter State Park* available in Maine State Visitor Information Centers. The Park Director, Jensen Bissell, lays it out in his welcome by reminding us that the 209,644 acre parcel is independent in agency, funding, and management.

But that ain't all. Baxter State Park, at 310 square miles, has a cross-border counterpart, the 72 square mile Mount Carleton Provincial Park in north central New Brunswick. When Cousin Gwen Bradbury stays at the Jones' in Riley Brook, she and friends climb Mt. Carleton. I've never made it past Nictau, but my times on the Tobique, the Bean family's association with the Gulquac Lodge, and the Miller canoe heritage spurred a need-to-know-more. I inquired through the Tobique Valley Genealogy and Local History Group website, and Patty Corey steered me to *Mount Carleton Wilderness, New Brunswick's Unknown North* by Marilyn Shaw, 1987. It's a book about the Tobique Highlands that's like *Nackawic Bend* in geography, First Nation inhabitants, settlement, and growth. Marilyn's folks ran a lodge, and she lived, absorbed, researched, and wrote this first class piece of history. Until I read it, I thought that I had mentioned about every celebrity who hunted and fished the Tobique Valley and Mt. Carleton backwoods. Marilyn's got an international list, I mean England, Chile, and Cuba, as long as your arm, and a New York to Hollywood list as long as your other arm. Don't get me wrong, the aboriginals, settlers, and subsequent residents with the outfitters and guides among them, are the best bit of this book. If anyone's lucky enough to find a copy, grab it. Also grab Dr. Clarke's *Six Salmon Rivers and Another*, as his tales of the Tobique and St. John humble mine.

Call it a coincidence, a connection, or both. When I learned that Bill Miller once lived in Presque Isle, I asked him if he knew any of my great Aunt Lucy Baylis Fox' folks named Fox, Blackstone, or Bull. He sure did! Dr. Donald Blackstone came to his mother's funeral a few years ago, and Bill's sister, Julie, worked for Donald. He also knew Arden Bull (who would often come to Rossville and the Baylis farm). It's also been gratifying to connect with Dr. Don and trade eight decades of family tales. I speak and write to his cousin, Carolyn Dahlgren, of Yarmouth, Maine, and we too share history and old pictures. As a Fox descendant, she sent me a silver foil potato chip bag labeled "Fox Family Potato Chips Inc." owned by Rhett Fox and family of Mapleton. The eye catching five red-fox faces, "Get real. Get Maine!" and "O grams Trans Fat" memos are on the front. On the back, with "Plain, Salt & Pepper, and BBQ" flavors are the nutrition facts, AND a family history. I can only smell the chips, but know that many stores, including Hannaford Supermarkets, carry them. I can't wait to buy 'em and try 'em!

Before I leave cross-border and Maine matters, I've another recent Freeport tale worth telling. Eating alone (I bring Laurie a breakfast tray) in the Freeport Inn's cozy Café, I noticed a young mother with a blonde curly-head little girl who sat across from me in a booth beside the kitchen. As they left, she came over and said, "Your breakfast is on me. Have a good day." Taken back, I said thanks, and was prepared to tell her all about my clan and politely decline, but she left quietly and quickly. In some vital way, she must have felt fulfilled. I asked the waitress if she knew them, but she didn't. I was overwhelmed!

Back again on home turf, Laurie and I have a superb Wednesday routine. Since Laurie has had mobility problems, our St. Anthony Parish secretary friend, Connie Kiss, brings us Holy Communion and good cheer after breakfast. She opens scripture with "Bless this house and all who live in it." She is native to Falmouth, and of Portuguese heritage. Her grandparents were farmers who raised vegetables, chickens, and strawberries; my kin harvested timber, hay, and grain. Both of our forebears worked with horses. We trade stories of our countrified past on Cape Cod or Downeast.

After I drive to the West Falmouth post office before lunch, Laurie opens and separates the mail. I probably use scissors as much as any barber. Most publications have snippets of interest that I send to family and friends. It is my clip-and-mail addiction and pleasure! We read the daily delivered *Cape Cod Times*.

Oops! I forgot to mention a delicious Downeast dip in my menu of memories. *Uncle Henry's Weekly Swap or Sell It Guide* "Serving ME * NH * VT * MA * NB, Canada" is yours for two bucks, and worth every cent. *Uncle Henry's* sponsors Dickerin' Days at Lewiston in August and "Down East Dickering" on TV.

When the weather cools down, I pick Barney up at Kate and Hilary's home, and we go to the Falmouth Skeet Club. Skeet shooting is a year round sport that fits my age and ability. I can stand on shooting stations and not feel wobbly, whereas imbalance and arthritis now deter most boating and hunting excursions. Rich Cole, a Beretta gunsmith and stock-maker from Harpswell, Maine, fitted me to one of his custom 20 gauge over-and-under models (two barrels, one over the other). The Falmouth club is handy to our home, the members are good company, and I'm getting better at the sport!

My skeet shooting mentor, Brad Varney, of Richmond, Maine and owner of Varney Clay Shooting Sports and I have a great time shooting the breeze as well as clay pigeons. Brad talks about his boyhood clam-digging days in Scarborough, Maine. He is authoring a sporting clay instruction book. Other loves are wife, Allys (originally from Caribou), and his bird hunting dog "Moonie." He teaches (attempts to tutor) me on the basics of the eight-station sport: "Be confident, mount the shotgun properly against shoulder and cheek, focus on the front of the flying target [not on the gun barrel], swing according to target speed, and pull the trigger when just ahead of the orange clay target." That's a long explanation for the short, rapid series of movements necessary to break a fast flying clay disc.

In a pressured state of disillusionment, I (not Laurie) was proposing a move back to Westford or Chelmsford, because the location is more central to family, and downsizing made sense. Since retiring to Falmouth 21 years ago, our homes, friends, recreation, health care, and places of worship have been fantastic. That part of separation would be difficult. We're not at the assisted-living level yet. Our home is handy to most of our needs. It is in good shape and nicely landscaped. We have bright and spacious one-floor living space with an open rear deck that overlooks a large lawn, oak, pine, Leland Cypress and holly trees, rhododendron and azelea bushes, and lily and hosta beds. Song birds and doves, hawks and crows, squirrels and chipmunks, rabbits, and the occasional fox and coyote enjoy the setting. Barney does too.

I started sorting, saving, gifting, and reorganizing. Garage tables hold boxes filled with volumes from multiple bookshelves. My paper and photo collections are the most time consuming challenge. Daughter Christine gave me a shredder, and it has been handy! I've only peeked at the 35mm slides and 8 and 16mm film collection in the cellar that could be a 50-year manuscript resource. Laurie rightly wants her dining room and kitchen counter space free of my treasured clutter. Each item brings out memories, and the process is slow...slow...slow.

I frequently wonder if my children will value and pursue their ancestry. I've been blessed with that appreciation, but my focus 40 years ago on making history, not researching it, is the same as their goal today. Some undoubtedly will live mostly for today and tomorrow, occasionally reviving yesteryear, and others will have an interest in from whence they came. Grandchildren are already doing a semester in Europe with never-to-be-forgotten memories of being where an ancestor once walked. Father Time will determine who will join our family tale-telling relay team, pick up the baton, establish a record run at the finish line, and look forward to participating in the next clan sprint.

I've come to the conclusion that *preparation* to move, *not relocation*, is my comfortable priority. Laurie and I are committed to remain in Falmouth as long as we can.

CHAPTER FOUR
Fire-Pit Finale

This long week-end, we're heading to Harpswell, Maine, to celebrate my birthday with family.

On the way, we stop in Yarmouth at the Royal River Grillhouse to meet Elizabeth Peavey and husband John for the first time. Initially, Elizabeth and I mull over my manuscript, and Laurie and John chitchat. Then, we all join in a ping-pong conversation. We learn that John's 93-year-young father, Jim McLoughlin, lives in Harpswell. He regularly shops at the Vegetable Corner, where our kids go for fresh garden goodies, berries in season, meats, groceries, and news. John markets wine in Maine, and Elizabeth professionally writes, gives lectures, and teaches writing and public speaking. They travel extensively, and in two days, they're driving up north to trek around Katahdin.

We overnight at the Freeport Inn and stay in one of our usual first floor rooms that overlook the pool and fountain or the iced pond, according to season. Next morning, after a home cooked Café breakfast, we do our regular L.L.Bean cruise and head for Harpswell. Though I refer to it as our halfway point, there is nothin' halfway about Harpswell in scene or spirit!

Now it's Thursday night. Jean, Laurie, and I are having dinner (supper) at Morse's Cribstone Grill next to the granite-woven bridge between Orrs and Bailey Islands. We're enjoying food, drinks, waitress Haven from Cundy Harbor, guitarist Keith Lowell, and the rocky ocean views.

Come Friday morning, Chip and I tour the coves off the Dolphin Marina on Basin Point in his center console boat. Bad balance prohibits me from keeping a boat, and old fishing buddies are gone or at anchor. Boats and fishing may be things of my past, but I'll never lose interest in them.

I think of the 40 or more years that Laurie and I took as many people, as often as possible, out on our boats. I dearly miss being out on the water with family and friends. On Hilary, Kate, and their kids Mere-C's from Quissett Harbor, we cross Buzzards Bay entrance to Woods Hole passage, and moor in coves on Naushon Island for picnicking, swimming, and fishing.

Chip is my host today in Harpswell. I work the helm and throttle while Chip is at some task, and relive piloting Lan Mara along the Elizabeth Islands, all around Martha's Vineyard, and on trips to Warren and Newport, Rhode Island. We see no seals nor catch any mackerel, but we and lobstermen wave as they come back to their moorings. Afterward at the Dolphin bar, I order dark rum on the rocks and Chip chooses a beer. Our hot cream-and-buttery fish chowder is loaded with haddock, perfectly cooked potatoes, and onions. That and their famous wild blueberry muffin finish off our cruise. I tell him about Mom and me sitting there recently, comparing notes with local fishermen, and talking to the bartender. We told owner Mimi Saxton that we liked the bar because we could watch the action. She retorted "You are the action!" I wondered if Linda Greenlaw, whose Downeast books I like, might be there as she was with her family two years ago. Wedding congratulations will be appropriate when we meet again.

As we leave the Dolphin, Erica's Seafood (named after daughter Erica Hunter) is on the right in a summer season take-out trailer. That's where we order fabulous Maine crabmeat rolls and sides of chowder and salad. We first met Erica's mother, Andrea, when she was a waitress at the Dolphin. She and husband, Tom, have a year round retail and wholesale lobster business on their wharf. After December, they have fresh scallops for sale. Tom and Andrea have recently offered the best of both crab and lobster meat in their *out-of-this-world* Crabster Roll.

I'm unequivocally happy driving back to Sunset Cove. Soon we'll pass through tall fir and pine tight to the road like the back roads up north. In daylight, dusk, or dark, a deer can jump out of nowhere into our path. We see grassy lawns and farm fields, some sloping down to the bays. Woodpiles or stacks of lobster traps are common sights near dwellings. One house has quilts for sale hanging on clothes-lines close to the pavement. On Sundays, the small, white steeple, Baptist church has worshippers cars parked across the street in a lot and others that line the side of the road. Village homes are well kept, and usually painted white. Chip and I pass Harpswell Neck Fire and Rescue station where Laurie and I had a fun time last August, buying crafts, consuming clam chowder, and making acquaintance with folks at our table. The next landmark is Mitchell Field, formerly used as a military fuel supply depot for Brunswick Naval Air Station, where town-folk now have a large recreation area down to the bay. As Chip rounds a certain sharp turn, I've come to know that the first road on the left leads to Burbines. As soon as we arrive, Jean insists on taking a picture of Laurie and me on their deck with "Old Glory" in the background.

In the evening, Jean, Jim, and Kelley Burbine host a lobster boil starting with drinks, dips, and steamers. Then Jim brings in trays of lobster and corn on the cob that he boiled in a big stockpot where the propane inferno roars like a jet afterburner. With us, packed around the huge kitchen island, are neighbors Chuck, Missy, Phil, and Mary, Jim's mother Barbara, and Chip and Joanna McGowan. After we are full of good and plenty, guests depart. I step out onto the deck for a moment and look down at my Maine burial site. My silent vow is "Here's to my tooth, the root of my tooth, and nothing but my tooth, so help me God." I raise my glass to good fortune, good company, and a good night.

I awake to a sunny, calm, and clear Saturday morning. Suddenly in spirit, I'm with my manuscript mentor Elizabeth Peavey and her husband John, as they hike Katahdin Land. Being on Baxter Peak again and reliving my treks of 62 years past, requires no stretch of the imagination. In fantasy, I'm not winded but very excited to be walking behind them glancing eastward at New Brunswick across the border.

Departing from my daydream of Elizabeth, John, and Katahdin, my thoughts this morning would be in step with Whittier when he composed this verse:

Keep who will the city's alleys take the smooth-shorn plain;
Give to us the cedarn valleys, rocks and hills of Maine!
In our North-land, wild and woody, let us still have part
Rugged nurse and mother sturdy, hold us to thy heart!

Spur-of-the-moment plans are amazingly synchronized with the loves of my life. First, of course, I'm with Laurie to glory and gloat over our family and good luck. She is content sitting at Burbines picture window, watching on-the-water traffic, and looking across Middle Bay at Big and Little Goose Islands with distant Freeport between them. The Giant Stairs trail on Bailey Island would be too difficult for her to navigate, but Jean and granddaughter Jackie take me where I've never ventured before.

The narrow footpath is an introduction of what's to come. I pay little attention to poison ivy signs never forgetting, however, the consequences of a weeping rash and awful itch. Openings in the brush reveal sights and sounds of white surf pounding over slabs of reef and against strewn blocks of black and brown rock. As a boater, my mind drifts to the crashing and crushing potential of that otherwise striking sight. The Giant Stairs are just that, allowing the young and adventurous to climb among ledge levels. Standing on top, and at my feet, I spy large patches of white and orange-tinted quartz, glacially set in weathered stone that is gray and grooved like an ancient cedar fence-rail.

As broad Atlantic coamers approach shore, I try to estimate when the big rollers will hit pay-dirt and spray explosions of white water upward. I keep trying to catch the right moment with my digital camera. Its deletion capability to erase bad shots makes up for my lack of timing. With each wave retreat, the sea sinks, tide rips swirl, and I await the next lapping or barrage.

I think of friend and artist Arlene Johnson, who adores Harpswell peninsulas. Her perceptive watercolors of Giant Stairs and Mackerel Cove adorn the walls of our Harpswell kin. I gaze out on the clear eastern horizon, and think of Laurie and I standing on a cape in Portugal facing west and thinking of home.

Jean and Jackie take me to Bailey Island Lands End gift shop that sells all things Maine. I grab a pair of bright green-leafed blueberry pattern potholders for Laurie, a plastic Brittany spaniel sign for Barney, and a package of Paine Company dried balsam needles for my pleasure. There are Pam Douglas' summer wreaths made of shells and grass, and I anticipate ordering Christmas wreaths from her in four-and-a-half months. A variety of Whirly-gigs on the railing, display Mainers sawing wood, and lobster boats rotating with the wind. I take a picture. Maybe I can make one? Laurie would laugh at that and remind me of things that I need to fix!

Most impressive and fitting, is the bronze lobsterman sculpture at Lands End. He's positioned down on one knee pegging a lobster claw.

Every cast inch of facial and body profile do justice to the man, his catch, and a plaque dedicated to lobstermen.

We get back in the Jeep, and they drive me to the 88 acre Two Coves Farm at Neils Point on Harpswell Neck. On a knoll facing north, the large white farmhouse, attached barn, and outbuildings are surrounded by clusters shade trees. A green Ford farm tractor rests ready. It is a working farm. I instantly absorb the comfort of walking across grass and along narrow dirt paths among sights and sounds of cattle, geese, dogs, pigs, turkeys, hens and roosters, and sheep. I sense that, once more, I'm back at the Baylis farm in Rossville, New Brunswick. It's like the good old days when folks "Just dropped in" for a visit.

New-cut hayfields slope down to sea coves. The distant cattle herd is called Belted Galloway, each with black on both ends and a white band in the middle. Plots of produce gardens are spread among the pastured acreage. We and another family of toddler-to-elder blend in with the farm folks. Open hay-load-height barn doors light up the wide wood-planked floor, old beams, rafters, and mows filled with hay. My nostrils nostalgically fill with barn smell.

The shed connecting the barn and house has a sign "Farm Store" and is more like a workroom than a retail space. Today, the store is kept by young and wholesome Jennifer and the white barn cat. Fresh eggs, garden vegetables, wild blueberry jam, and a paper with beef, pork, and chicken offerings in the freezer are there for the choosing. My choice is jam, a wrapping of beef, and hamburger patties. Back at Burbines, I tell Laurie about everywhere that we've been and show her my digital photos.

Neighbors from across the road, Phil and Mary Egan, invite us for cocktails and hors d'oeuvres on their open-to-the-bay porch. Cooper, their shih tzu pup, indulges in our food and conversation. The Egans lived in Scituate, and their daughter Mary Alice was a classmate of Joanna McGowan and coincidentally owned the Harpswell house that Jim and Jean bought! Mary bakes and sends over the best-blueberry-cake-ever that we devour from breakfast to bedtime. The Egans are about our age and say that there is no social competition where they winter in Key Largo, Florida. We agree that Harpswell has the same friendly freedom.

Day blends into dusk, and we go three miles down Route 123 to Chip and Joanna's home above Stover's Cove. Their son Charlie is there with four friends. They've had a bit of a start on us, and he greets Laurie and me with a big hug. Though much taller and recently 27 against my 82 today, I share the thought that we both are having problems with balance. Chip has the grille going, and Jo seats Laurie at the kitchen table. She is happy to be in the midst of the gang. Burgers, lobster, beer, sausage, hot dogs, dips, and salad are followed by Charlie's belated birthday cake. Holding a friend's puppy, he blows out all the candles amid cheers and well wishes. We all are a bit into the sauce, and I announce that he, Chip, and I have the same name and are here together. His friends regale when I said that he must be "Baby Charlie!" He is a thoughtful grandson who calls regularly to see how we are doing and keeps us posted on his job, travels, golf, and fishing. Like our Peggy, he is a University of Vermont grad.

After a few beverages and supper, Laurie is beat, and she and Jean leave for home. Jo, Chip, Jackie, me, and Charlie and his friends Liz, Jake, Owen, and Steve, go down on the lawn to sit around a blazing fire-pit.

We gaze thoughtfully into the fire. Under a dark star-lit canopy, there is a masked radiance cast upon each face. Conversation comes easy as we trade tales and opinions. Liz is a good fire-tender. As the flames die and we waft toward stillness, she adds a log or two. Embers dance, shoot upward, and the skies are ours. Two shooting stars zing crossways. Another moves slowly and might be a satellite.

Someone spots the Big Dipper constellation. I tell them that the two end stars are called the pointers because they aim at the North Star (To my Boy Scout satisfaction). Jackie shows us the Milky Way. Steve, the outdoorsman, identifies The Hunter, Orion who carries a sword at his belt. As one by one fall asleep, others observe that I've outlasted Chip and Charlie.

My birthday events and this story end for the present. Laurie and I try to accept each day with independent optimism and thank God for all that we've been given. To stay in touch, we like to revisit places and people of yesteryear as often as possible and keep up with what's happening in today's world.

This twice-lived story has been my inglenook. I hope that it finds a home in many hearths and hearts.

Charles Eugene McGowan, D.M.D.
July 27, 2013

AFTERWORD

This story started with my date of birth and ended with my most recent birthday. The last is among the best…and the next may be better!

My tales are first for those whose families have touched my life. I also hope that my cruiser's axe blazed trails for readers and paths for history seekers.

Though this book is done, I will continue to search through lumber and ashes for clues of pathway and purpose buried beneath family trees. I urge readers to notify me of any particular that I may have missed or of any error in the text.

EMBERS OF ACKNOWLEDGMENT

I have glowing embers of thanks to all who inspired and helped bring to fruition this account of my life (so far). My thanks go out to all who sent letters, black-and-white pictures, and the CD of Nackawic landscapes, homes, and buildings pre- and post-1967 flooding. Their words, facts, and documents fortified my own recollections and bolstered my cross-border tales.

I fortunately found professional genealogist Rose Bradley Staples who surpassed lineage expectations by resourcefully researching my more complicated inquiries.

The book's architect is Elizabeth Peavey. She professionally interpreted, scrutinized, and dedicated hours upon hours to organization and structure. Along the way, I've been blessed to witness her writing, teaching, and friendship.

Patrick Layne, Bangor Public Library reference librarian, and Leigh Hallett, a graduate student in history at UMaine, Orono,

researched my queries and gave me gold. Patrick discovered the first
two accounts of George Rockwell's drowning in Bangor's *Whig and
Courier* newspaper archives, and Leigh located numerous articles in
Fogler Library and Maine State Library files on Morison and Hunting, Georges West Branch logging employers.

Nackawic funeral director, Wendell Flewelling, furnished obituary
data and enabled Laurie and me to design and fund the new George
Rockwell monument in Otis Cemetery. Patty Gunter Trail sent me a
copy of her genealogical manuscript, *The Trail Line*. It confirmed my
findings on Davidson, Rockwell, and Grant links to my Baylis family.

To Patricia M. Lawson, Gail Farnsworth, and M. Anne Hartley
who compiled *the Nackawic Bend, 200 years of history*: My writings
would be less accurate without your resource.

Candy Canders Russell, of the Moosehead Historical Society and
Sharon Maysa Buswell of the Corinth Historical Society & Museum,
gave me material and advice that allowed better insight into the places
and people who were part of George Rockwell's logging life and death
in Maine.

I contacted the New Westminster, British Columbia, Public Library
for information on George Armstrong Grant after he migrated from
Nackawic (c.1912). Wendy Turnbull, in the research sector, retrieved
the Grant family history in New Westminster and Vancouver for me.

When I searched land and title records, the Land Registry staff
at Service New Brunswick (SNB) in Fredericton, and Philip Roper,
SNB district manager in Saint John, were immediately responsive and
helpful.

I'm relieved to have the Rockland-based Indie Author Warehouse
president Jane Karker and staff at my side. Customer service and publicity representative Nikki Giglia clarified the publishing procedure to
get me started. Copyeditor Genie Dailey gave me the encouragement
to press forward with her positive ratings on front matter and random
manuscript passages. I was fortunate to have graphic designer and
author Lindy Gifford to coordinate layout and design.

Our graphic designer daughter Christine Donahue and my artist
wife, Laurie, collaborated on the covers providing the best bookshelf
photocopy that would sustain my tales. Christine's four orientation
illustrations and two vintage Culliton photo collections synchronize
each setting. Harpswell son-in-law Jim Burbine deserves the back

cover photo credit at Dick's Lobsters & Crabs wharf on Potts Point.

My children and extended family have patiently tutored me in deciphering the mysterious workings of my computer. I am now proud to report that I can get around the Microsoft Word basics of navigation, and "save as" and "copy and paste" like a pro.

Dedication at the front of this book to my wife Laurie, says it all. She's been part and parcel of most of what I tell, and puts up with material that's spread over tables and counters. My outright insider, she edits my manuscript for flaws or omissions…to my benefit, credibility, and pride!

Charlie McGowan

BOOKLIST OF TALES AND TRAILS

Adams, Peter. *Early Loggers and the Sawmill.* Toronto, Canada and New York: Crabtree Publishing Company, 1981.

A.M.C. *The A.M.C. White Mountain Guide.* Boston: The Appalachian Mountain Club, 1976.

Baxter, Constance. Excerpts from the writings of Percival Proctor Baxter and a historical essay by Judith A. and John W. Hakola. *Greatest Mountain: Katahdin's Wilderness.* San Francisco: Scrimshaw Press, 1972.

Bean, L. L. *Hunting-Fishing and Camping.* Freeport, Maine: Dingley Press, 1942.

Bean, L. L. *Hunting-Fishing and Camping by Leon Leonwood Bean with Updates by Great-Grandson Bill Gorman, 100th Anniversary Eddition.* Freeport, Maine: L.L.Bean, *Down East*, Rockport, Maine, 2011.

Bean, L. L. *My Story, The Autobiography of a Down East Merchant.* Freeport, Maine: Dingley Press, 1962.

Beavan, Mrs. Frances. *Sketches and Tales Illustrative of Life in the Backwoods of New Brunswick, North America, 1845.* LaVergne, TN and U.K.: Dodo Press, 2010.

Behne, C. Ted, Editor. *The Travel Journals of Tappan Adney 1887-1890.* Fredericton, New Brunswick, Canada: Goose Lane Editions, 2010.

Behne, C. Ted, Editor. *The Travel Journals of Tappan Adney Vol. 2, 1891-1896. Foreword by Andrea Bear Nicholas.* Fredericton, New Brunswick, Canada: Goose Lane Editions, 2014.

Brown, Benj F. *Poems of Life in the Country and By the Sea.* Providence, R.I.: 1920.

By the People of Temperance Vale. *Temperance Vale, The People and Times of a New Brunswick Settlement.* Fredericton, N.B.: New Ireland Press, 1987.

Burpee, Lawrence J. "New Brunswick Down by the Sea." Washington, D.C.: *The National Geographic Magazine*, May, 1941.

Clark, Peter D. *A Treasury of New Brunswick Art and Stories.* Durham Bridge, New Brunswick: Penniac Books, 1997

Clarke, George Frederick. *Six Salmon Rivers and Another.* Fredericton, New Brunswick, Canada: Brunswick Press, 1960.

Clarke, George Frederick. *The Adventures of Jimmy-Why.* Fredericton, New Brunswick, Canada: Brunswick Press, 1954.

Clarke, George Frederick. *The Song of the Reel.* Fredericton, New Brunswick, Canada: Brunswick Press, 1963.

Cody, H. A. *Glazier's Men*, in Stevenson, O. J. *Fifty-Four Narrative Poems.* Toronto, Ontario: The Copp Clark Company, Limited, 1933.

Day, Holman F. *Kin O'Ktaadn.* Boston: Small, Maynard & Company, 1904.

Day, Holman F. *King Spruce.* New York: A. L. Burt Company, 1908.

Day, Holman F. *Pine Tree Ballads.* Boston: Small, Maynard & Company, 1902.

Delano, Carl E., Director of Publicity. *In The Maine Woods*, Bangor, Maine: Bangor and Aroostook Railroad Company, 1952.

DeLorme. *The Maine Atlas and Gazetteer.* Freeport, Maine: DeLorme mapping Company, 1988.

Devine, John Valentine. Logger and composer of "The Badger Drive." Newfoundland: His home at King's Cove, Bonavista Bay, 1912.

Douglas, William O. *My Wilderness: East to Katahdin, 1961.* New York, N.Y.: Pyramid Publications, Inc, 1968.

Duplessis, Shirley. *Hidden in the Woods, The Story of Kokad-jo.* Greenville, Maine: Moosehead Communications, Inc., 1997

Eaton, Louis W. *Pork, Molasses, and Timber.* New York: Exposition Press, Inc., 1954.

Eckstorm, Fannie Hardy. *The Penobscot Man.* A facsimile of the 1924 edition with an introduction by Edward D. Ives. Somersworth: New Hampshire Publishing Company, 1972.

Federal Writers' Project of the Works Progress Administration for the State of Maine. *Maine, A Guide 'Down East'.* Boston: Houghton Mifflin Company, 1937.

Fendler, Donn. *Lost on a Mountain in Maine as told to Joseph B. Egan, 1978.* New York, N.Y.: Beech Tree Books, 1992.

Fendler, Donn. *Lost Trail, Nine Days Alone in the Wilderness*. Camden, maine: Down East Books, 2011.

Gorman, Leon. *L.L.Bean, The Making of an American Icon, Chairman, former President, and Grandson of L. L. Bean*. Boston: Harvard Business School Press, 2006.

Grant, Ruth Winona. *Now and Then*. Southampton, New Brunswick, Canada: 1967

Gray, Roland Palmer. *Songs and Ballads of the* Maine *Lumberjacks*. Cambridge: Harvard University Press, 1924.

Griffin, Carlene. *Spillin' the Beans, Behind The Scenes At L. L. Bean*. Eastport, Maine: Warren Publishing Services, 1992.

Hall, Thomas, and Harmon. *Chimney Pond Tales, Yarns Told by Leroy Dudley*. Cumberland, Maine: Pamola Press, 1991.

Hempstead, Alfred Geer. *The Penobscot Boom*. Rockport, Maine: limited edition 1931 reprint of original, a *Down East* book published by the author, 1975.

Hickman, W. Albert. *Hand Book of New Brunswick (CANADA), exerpts*. Fredericton, New Brunswick, Dominion of Canada: Crown Land Department, 1900.

Hornsby, Stephen J., Konrad, Victor A., and Herlan, James J., Editors. *The Northeastern Borderlands*. Canadian-American Center, University of Maine, Orono: Acadiensis Press, Fredericton, New Brunswick, 1989.

Hornsby, Stephen J. and Reid, John G. *New England and the Maritime Provinces*. Montreal: McGill-Queen's University Press, 2005.

Houghton, George M., General Passenger Agent. *In The Maine Woods*. Bangor, Maine: Bangor and Aroostook Railroad Company, 1930.

Hoyt, Edmund S. *Maine State Year-Book and Legislative Manual, 1886-1887*. Portland: Hoyt, Fogg, & Donham, 1886.

Irving, Jean Elizabeth S. *R.H. Nicholson, Painter and Man of God*. Fredericton, N.B.: Unipress Ltd., 1982.

Ives, Edward D. *Joe Scott, The Woodsman-Songmaker, Music in American Life Series*. Urbana, Illinois: University of Illinois Press, 1978.

Johnson, Kevin. *Early Logging Tools*. Atglen, Pennsylvania: Schiffer Publishing Ltd., 2007.

Kodas, Michael; Condon, Mark; Sherer, Glenn; and Weegar, Andrew. *Exploring the Appalachian Trail, Hikes in Northern New England*. Mechanicsburg, Pennsylvania: Stackpole Books, 1999.

L.L.Bean, Gorman, Jim. *Guaranteed to Last, L.L.Bean's Century of Outfitting America*. Freeport, Maine: L.L.Bean, Melcher Media, 2012.

L.L.Bean, Inc., Barry, William David and Kennett, Bruce. *L.L.Bean Inc., Outdoor Sporting Specialties, A Company Scrapbook*. Portland, Maine: Privately Printed for L.L.Bean, Inc., Anthoensen Press, 1987.

L.L.Bean, Inc., Barry, William David and Kennett, Bruce. *L.L.Bean, Inc., Outdoor Sporting Specialties, A Company Scrapbook, Second Edition*. Freeport, Maine: L.L.Bean, Inc., Thompson-Shore, Inc., Printer, 2002.

L.L.Bean, Inc., Cameron, Angus and Jones, Judith and illustrations by Bill Elliott. *The L.L.Bean Game and Fish Cookbook*. New York: Random House, 1983.

L.L.Bean, Inc., Jones, Judith and Jones, Evan. *The L.L.Bean Book Of New New England Cookery*. New York: Random House, 1987.

L.L.Bean, Inc., Riviere, William. *The L.L.Bean Guide to the Outdoors, With the staff of L.L.Bean*. New York: Random House, Inc., 1981.

L.L.Bean, Inc., Whitlock, Dave, writing and illustration. *L.L.Bean Fly-Fishing Handbook*. New York: Lyons & Burford, 1983.

Lawson, Jessie I. and Sweet, Jean MacCallum. *This is New Brunswick*. Toronto: The Ryerson Press, 1951.

Lawson, Patricia M. and Farnsworth, Gail and Hartley, M. Anne with maps by David Davis. *The Nackawic Bend, 200 years of history*. Nackawic, New Brunswick: Town of Nackawic, Wilson Printing, Fredericton, N.B., 1984.

Liedl, Charles. *Hunting with Rifle and Pencil*. Fredericton, New Brunswick, Canada: Brunswick Press, 1955.

Mallett, David. Singer, Songwriter. Two selected verses from "Fire," two from "Garden Song," and two from "The Haying Song." New York, N.Y.: Cherry Lane Music Pub. Co. Inc., 1977-1979.

Malloch, Douglas. *Tote-Road and Trail, Ballads of the Lumberjack, Illustrated by Oliver Kemp*. Indianapolis: The Bobbs-Merrill Company, 1917.

MacBeath, Dr. George and Taylor, Capt. Donald F. *Steamboat Days on the St. John.* St Stephen, N.B.: Print'n Press Ltd., 1982

McCutcheon, Mary Janet. *2012 Addendum to the Grant Connexion of Ruth Winona Grant 1984.* 140 Candlewood Cres., Waterloo ON N2l-5T4: Nelson P. Grant, 2012.

Montgomery, M. R. *In Search of L. L. Bean.* Boston and Toronto: Little, Brown & Company, 1984.

Nason, David. *Railways of New Brunswick.* Fredericton, N.B.: New Ireland Press, 1992.

Neff, John W. *Katahdin, An Historic Journey.* Boston: Appalachian Mountain Club Books, 2006.

New Brunswick Government Bureau of Information and Travel, *Fish and Hunt in New Brunswick.* Fredericton, N.B., Canada:1937.

Noble, Allen G. and Cleek, Richard K. *The Old Barn Book, A Field Guide to North American Barns & Other Farm Structures.* New Brunswick, New Jersey: Rutgers University Press, 2009.

Parker, Gerry. *Men of The Autumn Woods, The Golden Years 1885-1935.* Sackville, N.B.: Printed and bound in Canada, Gerry Parker, 2004.

Parker, Mike. *Woodchips & Beans, Life in the Early Lumber Woods of Nova Scotia.* Halifax, Nova Scotia: Nimbus Publishing Limited, 1992.

Peck, Mary Biggar. *New Brunswick Album, Glimpses of the Way We Were.* Willowdale, Ontario, Canada: Published by Anthony R. Hawke Limited, 1987.

Pike, Robert E. *Tall Trees, Tough Men.* New York and London: W. W. Norton & Company, Inc., 1967.

Poitras, Jacques. *Imaginary line, Life on an unfinished border.* Fredericton, New Brunswick, Canada: Goose Lane Editions, 2011.

Pride, Fleetwood. Ives, Edward D. and Smith, David C., Editors. *Fleetwood Pride, 1864—1960, The Autobiography of A Maine Woodsman.* Orono, Maine: Northeast Folklore Society, Volume IX 1967, The Northeast Folklore Society, 1968.

Rivard, Paul E. *Maine Sawmills, A History.* Augusta, Maine: Maine State Museum, 1990.

Roberts, Charles G. D. *The Canadian Guide-book, The Maritime Provinces.* New York: D. Appelton and Company, 1891.

Robinson, Daniel. *The Maine Farmers' Almanac, For The Year of*